INFORMATION MANAGEMENT SYSTEMS

VIRTUAL STORAGE

A Practical Guide For Managers

MYLES E. WALSH
Director, Data Base Systems
CBS, Inc.

Reston Publishing Company, Inc.
A Prentice-Hall Company
Reston, Virginia

Library of Congress Cataloging in Publication Data

Walsh, Myles E
  Information management systems

  Includes index.
  1. IMS/VS (Computer system)   I. Title.
QA76.9.D3W34   001.6′424   79-16645

ISBN 0-8359-3075-0

©1979 by
RESTON PUBLISHING COMPANY, INC., Reston, Virginia 22090
A Prentice-Hall Company

10   9   8   7   6   5   4   3   2   1

Printed in the United States of America

Dedicated to the
MIS professionals at CBS
from whom I have
benefited much.

2058662

Preface

In August 1976, I was appointed to the position of Director, Data Base Systems for CBS. I brought into this position about nineteen years experience in the electronic data processing profession, about ten of those years in a managerial capacity. Six years prior to the appointment, I had successfully completed a master's thesis that had included substantial research into what had been, at that time, embryonic versions of today's data base management systems. It is, as of this writing, the summer of 1978. This book, then, is the result of two years experience in directing the activities leading to the successful installation of a data base management system, specifically Information Management Systems/Virtual Storage (IMS/VS); coupled with ten years managerial experience, nearly twenty years electronic data processing experience and proven research capabilities gained via a master's thesis accepted at the Baruch School of Business, City College of New York.

The purpose of this book is to provide, for EDP or MIS managers and other interested individuals, an exposure to what may be the most elaborate data base management system on the market, IMS/VS, a product of IBM. The assumption is made that the reader is familiar enough with electronic data processing concepts so that for example, the difference between computer storage and DASD is understood.

There are two introductory chapters in which the reader is brought up to speed in the "state of the art" in data base systems. Following this, there are

three chapters, two dealing in some depth with Data Base and Data Communications, the two main features of IMS/VS. In between those two there is a
chapter dealing with data access methods and Data Base Administration. Following the chapter on the Data Communications feature, there is one on the
concept of data dictionary including an overview of another IBM product called
Data Dictionary/Directory (DD/D). Conventional data base management system
wisdom, at this point in time, indicates that some kind of data dictionary software
is required for the successful implementation of a data base management system.
This is especially true regarding IMS/VS because of its complexity. There are
chapters on application programming in an IMS/VS environment and on Utilities
and Aids.

The chapter on organizing, staffing and education in an IMS/VS environment provides some guidelines and some specifics regarding curriculum, costs
and job functions. The chapter surveying other data base management systems
gives a brief overview of them and how they compare to IMS/VS. The final
chapter examines other contemporary technology that is related to data base
systems.

As does any author, I must acknowledge my indebtedness to those individuals and institutions who helped me to produce this book. The individuals
include Jim Andrews and Fred Easter, the professionals in the publishing business who advised me. The institutions include CBS, which has provided me a
professional atmosphere in which creativity is encouraged, and the Baruch
School of Business (CCNY) where I was introduced to the subject of Data Base
Systems under the tutelage of Dr. Ivan Flores, my master's thesis advisor. I am
indebted to IBM. This organization granted me permission to use numerous
illustrations from its own tutorials on IMS/VS and its facilities.

In the preparation of any book for publication, a publisher makes use of
reviewers who are totally unknown and unidentified to the author. In the case
of this book, these reviewers were also very helpful. Yet, there were two
observations made by them that I believe were inaccurate. They indicated that
I was biased toward IMS/VS and against minicomputers. If this book leaves that
impression, I wish to disclaim it. No author can claim total objectivity, but I
have tried to report on the facilities and operations of IMS/VS in an unbiased
way. It is a Data Base Management System (DBMS) that requires the support
of a medium or large scale computer. There are other DBMS software packages
that can run on smaller computers. My direct experience has been primarily with
IMS/VS and the objective of this book is to share that experience.

Other individuals who helped include Dianne Bowman and Laurie Buck-
man, who typed much of the manuscript; Bob Syvarth, Stan Barwinski and
Frank Gibbons, who were helpful critics and proofreaders; and Ted Mayerson,
who helped me prepare the Data Dictionary chapter. Other professionals to
whom I am most grateful are John Talley, Barbara Opello, Carol Chaykin,

Sharyn Parr and Ruth Alexeichik—without whose help this book would not have been produced. It was their performance that provided much of the "hands on" experience recorded in this book.

Finally, Diana, my wife; to her I offer my thanks for constraining my ego when necessary and for keeping me honest.

Contents

1
Introduction

WHY A BOOK LIKE THIS?

As the title of this book suggests, there is a need for some clarifying information on IMS/VS. There is an ever-widening gulf between the systems software technician who installs and supports an IMS/VS system and the EDP manager or director who wishes to make use of its capabilities. The technician goes to technical schools, uses technical manuals and learns about "care and feeding" procedures for some very complicated and tempermental software. That software, comprising about 1500 program modules, requires the systems software technician to learn some new concepts and a new language.

In order for IMS/VS to perform efficiently, it has to be given some very precise instructions in "its native language." Complexity is an inherent characteristic of all data base management system software. Some are more complex than others. The complexity of these systems seems to vary directly with their flexibility. Debates continuously rage on the complexity, flexibility and desirability of one product or another. Yet no matter which product is chosen, IMS/VS, IDMS, TOTAL, SYSTEM 2000 or some other, some education and technical training are required. Few would disagree, however, that IMS/VS requires more than the others.

THE GAP BETWEEN THEORY AND PRACTICE

Corporation executives and other interested individuals attend James Martin Seminars,[1] at which they learn about the capabilities and potential of IMS/VS and other data base management systems. They are advised of the advantages offered by data base management systems and how data base management systems are the wave of the future. Many of these executives and the others leave these seminars having been exposed to an overview of data base and networking. They also get some insight into the methodologies and statistical techniques used in such systems. They return to their organizations wondering why the systems software technicians like John Talley are always working so late, and why they can't make it all so simple the way Martin does.

Why the dilemma? Well, it is basically as follows. There is a big step between understanding something conceptually and actually implementing it at the "nuts and bolts" level.

THEORY

Jim Martin has the ability to explain the concepts of a complex technology in simple terms. As a teacher he is magnificent. For example, if he were discussing automobiles, Jim Martin would tell you that automobiles are a means of transportation that have the ability to move people and their baggage from one place to another. He would tell you that an automobile has four wheels on which it rolls along a road. He would also inform you about the passenger compartment and luggage space and how the driver manages the direction, speed and the starting and stopping of the vehicle. He would spend a great deal of time teaching you about the theory of automotive technology. You'd be introduced to terms like "internal combustion engine, carburetor, automatic transmission" and so forth. Coming away, you'd have a general idea of how these things are put together in a specific fashion to produce a vehicle called an automobile. In addition, as a result of Martin's presentation, you would believe that you really should have one.

Martin's seminars provide an essential service. They provide an exposure in one week's time to a host of topics that are of major interest to many individuals. The attractiveness of the seminars is rooted in this fact and in the proven capability of Martin himself. The man is quite impressive in his knowledge, his style of delivery and in the homework he has obviously done in preparing his presentations.

A typical James Martin Seminar may begin with a discussion by Martin about the future evolution of technology. This is often followed by treatment

---

[1]James Martin Seminars. A generic term rather than an exact title, the most current of these, as of this writing, will have been given in the autumn of 1978. Titled *James Martin on Distributed Processing Data Base Networks*, it will have been presented by the Savant Institute of Danvers, Mass. Martin updates his material annually and generally changes the name to reflect current technology.

of the subject of "End User Interface," which deals with the psychological factors in the man/machine dialogs, response times and the effect of intelligent terminals. These two subjects are followed by sessions on Distributed Intelligence, Future Developments in Teleprocessing, Computer Networks, Distributed Processing, Queuing Theory and Network Design. Although not dealing exclusively with data bases, each of these subjects are related to data base systems, especially since most DBMS systems have a data communications feature.

Approximately two days are spent on the above topics and then two additional days are devoted to the topic of data bases. About eight sessions involve discussions of data base subjects. In the first session, architectural concepts are presented. The idea of data independence is introduced. Data base structures and data description languages are discussed in a subsequent session. Two sessions are devoted to the design of a logical data base. The logical data base is designed as a relational data base, which is the theoretical ideal in logical data base design. Final sessions deal with query languages and data base management systems software. The last day of the seminar is spent discussing the available options in distributed processing such as minicomputers and microcomputers, data base administration and other management functions, and the future of technology.

As is readily apparent, an attendee is exposed to an awesome quantity of subject matter in a relatively short time. The exposure is valuable because it gives executives an opportunity to regain a perspective that is often lost in the tense, reactive activities of day-to-day management. Those who find the time to attend are able to get away from the alligators for a while and be reminded that the original objective was to drain the swamp.[2] A major value of the seminar is its "big picture" orientation.

At the same time, there is an additional need of executives that is not met in one of these seminars. Because of its "big picture" orientation and the amount of material covered, treatment, by necessity, must be superficial. As a result, when the executive, exposed to all this information, returns to his office, he is confronted by another difficulty. He finds that all the new things he just learned are on a different plane and he is still unable to communicate effectively with the technician who is to install his data base management system.

---

[2] There was an anecdote that made the rounds a few years ago that gave a reasonably good description of day-to-day management.

"Our mission is to analyze the situation and, through foresight and advanced planning, avoid confusion or circumvent problems before they arise. Should the unexpected occur, then our aim is to swiftly and efficiently arrive at a workable solution. . . . However when you're up to your hips in alligators, it's difficult to remember that your initial objective was to drain the swamp."

PRACTICE

In contrast to James Martin, there is another individual named John Talley. John Talley has the ability (perhaps I should say the perseverance, patience and fortitude) to install, support and fine tune a particular data base management system called IMS/VS. As a system software technician, he is magnificent. Using the automobile example, John would explain in considerable detail the function of valve lifters, differentials and rear main bearings. He would also be able to show you how to diagnose a broken bearing in a rear axle housing. He would be able to show you how to remove and replace it, since he has already done it himself. He has the tools to do it. He would be able to diagnose the cause of engine "pre-ignition" in damp weather. Using a "multi-meter" and a "timing light" from his tool kit, together with some wrenches and a screwdriver, he would be able to remedy the problem. In these cases, however, in order to explain to you what he had done, he would have to presuppose some

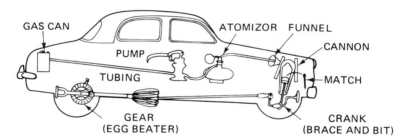

Figure 1–1
THEORETICAL (CONCEPTUAL)

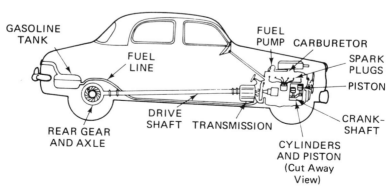

Figure 1–2
INTERFACE (GENERAL—SPECIFIC)

knowledge on your part. The knowledge is something extra, beyond that which you get at a James Martin type of seminar. There is a gap between Martin and Talley. One cannot leave a Jim Martin Seminar, return to the shop and be able to communicate with John Talley in IMS/VSese.

Hence the need for this book. The objective of this book is to provide an interface between James Martin and John Talley. This book bridges the gap between the theoretical and the practical. Relating the theoretical and the practical as illustrated below is the overall goal of this book. The first illustration (Figure 1–1) shows the theoretical (Martin), the second (Figure 1–2), the interface (this book) and the third (Figure 1–3), the practical (Talley). There is ample material on the first and the third; there is next to nothing available on the second.

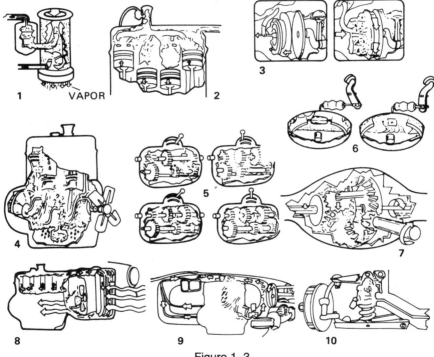

Figure 1–3
PRACTICAL (DETAILED—SPECIFIC)
1) CARBURETOR 2) ENGINE (INTAKE, COMPRESSION, COMBUSTION, EXHAUST) 3) CLUTCH 4) ENGINE LUBRICATION 5) MANUAL TRANSMISSION (FIRST, SECOND, THIRD, NEUTRAL) 6) BRAKE (OFF, ON) 7) DIFFERENTIAL (REAR END) 8) COOLING SYSTEM 9) ELECTRICAL SYSTEM
10) SUSPENSION

(Redrawn from *Under the Hood*, Pantheon Books, N.Y.)

BACKGROUND OF DATA BASE MANAGEMENT SYSTEMS

The remaining pages of this chapter contain a very brief narrative of the evolution of data base management systems, followed by some simple descriptions and illustrations dealing with "chains" and "pointers," which are the basic techniques used in building data bases.

EVOLUTION

Data Base Systems, as they now exist, have been evolving since the 1950s. Originally they were used in non-EDP disciplines like the legal profession. It was in the early and mid-1960s that Data Base theory was put into practice on computers. At that time, the technology was sometimes referred to as Information Retrieval. In the late 1960s the idea of Data Base began to emerge. It was during that time that much of the pioneering work on Data Base Systems was done. Working prototypes of later systems began appearing during that time. However, because of their inherent complexity and high overhead, most computer users dismissed them after a casual examination. These early attempts contained computer programs and storage structures for data that were patterned after the techniques used in the discipline of Information Retrieval. Additional facilities for security and data integrity were added along the way.

These first steps in combining data base, computer and Information Retrieval technology were a theoretical success, but actual working systems were not forthcoming. Development of workable systems was hampered by insufficient computer resources. Electronic Data Processing equipment, at that time, just did not have the computer processing speeds required to support the high instruction execution overhead necessary to store, manipulate and retrieve data elements using sophisticated storage structures.

Furthermore, direct access storage media and equipment, also known as Direct Access Storage Devices (DASD), were insufficient in size and speed to perform the task of storing and retrieving the large volumes of data that were typical of this type of system. More recently, however, the high overhead factor has diminished as the speeds of computer processors have increased appreciably, and the storage media and devices have increased greatly in both size and speed. The inherent technical complexity of Data Base Systems remains.

The gap between the Data Base Systems technology's requirements and the Electronic Data Processing equipment's capabilities was narrowed by the introduction of the "Virtual Storage" (VS) facility. Although not new when announced by IBM, the facility known as Virtual Storage represented a significant step forward in making Data Base Systems technology a reality on Electronic Data Processing equipment. In the trade, when IBM announces something, it then becomes available for mass consumption. The Virtual Storage facility had been around several years before IBM announced it, but that announcement made it available in sufficient quantity and with enough technical support to make its use universal. Virtual Storage is somewhat like a politician's promise. It commits resources that don't really exist in the hope that through superior management it will be possible to make more efficient use of existing resources on a shared basis. This is to be accomplished in such a way that each individual using the resources can be led to believe that he had exclusive use of them. As with politician's promises, the "Virtual Storage" facility was somewhat more costly than originally estimated, but in any event, the advent of Virtual Storage facilitated the use of IMS/VS and other data base management systems.

SOME BASIC EDP/MIS TERMS

Before getting into the discussion of "pointers," let's define some basic terms often used in the EDP/MIS community.

A *Character* is the smallest piece of recognizable data. A, B, C, 1, 2, 3, $, @, ? are characters.

A *Field* is a collection of characters that specifies a unit of data. A social security number and a unit price of an item are examples of fields.

A *Record* is comprised of a collection of fields of data that pertain to the same item. A typical example of a record is an employee payroll master record that contains an employee's name, employee number, department, tax code, base pay, etc.

A *File* is a collection of the same type of records. An example would be the employee payroll master records mentioned above, for all the employees of a company.

Data Base can be a file or group of files from which can be obtained data or information useful to those for which it was designed. (This will be refined later in this book.)

Peripheral Storage Media are storage devices upon which data can be stored and saved for future use by a computer. Among these are magnetic tape, paper tape, disk packs, drums and data cells.

A *Key* is a field or a group of fields that identifies a record. A key serves two functions. An order key is used to enter a record into a file. A search key is used to find the record within a file. The key field is also part of the record; that is, it contains part of the information of the record. To summarize: characters make up fields, fields make up records, records make up files and files make up a data base or data bases. Data thus organized is stored on a number of storage devices.

POINTERS

Records can be structured logically and physically in the same way, or they can be structured logically in a fashion dissimilar to their physical structure. In those records where physical and logical structures are identical, information pertaining to a particular record is entirely included within the physical boundaries of that record. In those records where the logical and physical structures are dissimilar, information handling makes use of concepts such as indexes and lists to store data and make it readily available.

Having established the basis of record structures, let's move on to the organization of data. There are several methods of file organization that serve

LOC	EMP #	EMP NAME	DEP	DIV	JOB	STA	CITY
001	00013	RMNIXON	502	01	7644	NY	NEWYORK
049	00046	LBJOHNSON	604	02	4220	NY	NEWYORK
097	00082	JFKENNEDY	703	01	4586	NJ	NEWARK
145	00114	DDEISENHOWER	502	01	7644	CONN	HARTFORD
193	00362	HSTRUMAN	502	01	4586	NJ	NEWARK
241	01189	FDROOSEVELT	604	02	7644	NY	NEWYORK
289	07416	H HOOVER	703	01	1792	NY	BUFFALO
PHYSICAL SEQUENTIAL FILE ASCENDING SEQUENCE ON EMPLOYEE NUMBER							

Figure 1–4

PHYSICAL SEQUENTIAL FILE ASCENDING SEQUENCE ON EMPLOYEE
NUMBER

LOC	EMP #	EMP NAME	DEP	DV	JOB	STA	CITY
001	00013	RMNIXON	502	01	7644	NY	NEWYORK
049	00046	LBJOHNSON	604	02	4220	NY	NEWYORK
097	00082	JFKENNEDY	703	01	4586	NJ	NEWARK
145	00114	DDEISENHOWER	502	01	7644	CONN	HARTFORD
193	00362	HSTRUMAN	502	01	4586	NJ	NEWARK
241	01189	FDROOSEVELT	604	02	7644	NY	NEWYORK
289	07416	H HOOVER	703	01	1792	NY	BUFFALO
PHYSICAL SEQUENTIAL FILE ASCENDING SEQUENCE ON EMPLOYEE NUMBER							

LOC	EMP #	EMP NAME	DEPT	DIV	JOB	STATE	CITY	POINTER
001	00012	RMNIXON	502	01	7644	NY	NEWYORK	901
901	00046	LBJOHNSON	604	02	4220	NY	NEWYORK	101
101	00082	JFKENNEDY	703	01	4586	NJ	NEWARK	801
801	00114	DDEISENHOWER	502	01	7644	CONN	HARTFORD	201
201	00362	HSTRUMAN	502	01	4586	NJ	NEWARK	701
701	01189	FDROOSEVELT	604	02	7644	NY	NEWYORK	301
301	07416	H HOOVER	703	01	1792	NY	BUFFALO	*
CHAINING OR LINKED LIST								

Figure 1–5

to illustrate some of the basic methods of recorded file handling. The most common method is physical sequential, where records are located within a file in ascending order by a key field, so that record $(n + 1)$ is adjacent to record n, both physically and in logical sequence. An example of a physical sequential file can be seen in Fig. 1–4. A second method is called chaining, where secondary information in a record, a pointer, is used to locate the next record of a file. Chaining neither rules out nor requires sequence on key fields. An example of a linked list or chaining as compared to the physical sequential file can be seen in Fig. 1–5.

The example shows the file to be in ascending sequence by employee number; however, the file is not in physical sequence, nor are the records contiguous. An asterisk in the pointer field of the last record indicates it is the last record of the file. The chained file has advantages and disadvantages relative to the physical sequential file.

One advantage of a chained file is that when a record is to be inserted between two others, or when a record is to be deleted from the file, a simple change to some pointers is all that is necessary. To insert or delete records on a physical sequential file, a complete recopying of the file is necessary.

The disadvantage is that searching of these files must be totally serial. Also, the chained file must be entered at the beginning. To search a physical sequential file, it is possible to judge where the midpoint is and thereby reduce searching time. There is no way to do this with a chained file, since the middle of the list might physically lie anywhere.

File structure can become more complex. Sophistication of file design generally increases to meet demands for faster retrieval.

The file in the next example contains the same information as was contained in the original physical sequential file illustration; however, the fields department, division, job, city and state contained values that were sometimes repeated in different records. In this example (Fig. 1–6) the values in these fields have been replaced by pointers to the values that exist in subfiles. By structuring a file in this manner, values that appear in many records need be physically present only once. The pointers in the main file point to the code values in the tables.

For example, the characteristics for employee H S TRUMAN are readily apparent at first glance in the original physical sequential file illustration. The department is 502, the division is 01, the job code is 4586, the state is NJ and the city is NEWARK. In the illustration the characteristics for H S TRUMAN can be found by locating the record in the main file and then following the pointers to locations 301, 401, 509, 605 and 716. Some of the characteristics are applicable to other employees, yet they are listed only once. Both D D EISENHOWER and R M NIXON work in department 502 as can be seen by examining the pointers in the field PTRA, which points to values in subfile A, which is the department table.

LOC	EMP #	EMP NAME	DEP	DV	JOB	STA	CITY
001	00013	RMNIXON	502	01	7644	NY	NEWYORK
049	00046	LBJOHNSON	604	02	4220	NY	NEWYORK
097	00082	JFKENNEDY	703	01	4586	NJ	NEWARK
145	00114	DDEISENHOWER	502	01	7644	CONN	HARTFORD
193	00362	HSTRUMAN	502	01	4586	NJ	NEWARK
241	01189	FDROOSEVELT	604	02	7644	NY	NEWYORK
289	07416	H·HOOVER	703	01	1792	NY	BUFFALO

PHYSICAL SEQUENTIAL FILE ASCENDING SEQUENCE ON EMPLOYEE NUMBER

MAIN FILE

LOC	EMP #	EMP NAME	PTRA	PTRB	PTRC	PTRD	PTRE
001	00013	RMNIXONbbbbb	301	401	513	607	722
033	00046	LBJOHNSONbbb	304	403	505	607	722
065	00082	JFKENNEDYbbb	307	401	509	605	716
097	00114	DDEISENHOWER	301	401	513	601	708
129	00362	HSTRUMANbbbb	301	401	509	605	716
161	01189	FDROOSEVELTb	304	403	513	607	722
193	07416	H HOOBERbbbb	307	401	501	607	701

SUBFILE A		SUBFILE B		SUBFILE C		SUBFILE D		SUBFILE E	
LOC	DEPT	LOC	DIV	LOC	JOB	LOC	STATE	LOC	CITY
301	502	401	01	501	1792	601	CONN	701	BUFFALO
304	604	403	02	505	4220	605	NJ	708	HARTFORD
307	703			509	4586	607	NY	716	NEWARK
				513	7644			722	NEWYORK

A FILE AND SUBFILES

Figure 1–6

The use of "pointers," shown above in the structuring of files, is a basic building block technique used in building data bases. The crude illustrations provided here were intended to give you a feel for the mechanics of pointers— how they function, where they can be located, their relative size and their cost.

SUMMARY

The present "state of the art" in Data Base Systems incorporates the techniques of Information Systems with the capabilities of contemporary computers. It seems that computers are now fast enough and large enough in terms of internal and peripheral storage to handle the processing and input/output overhead inherent in systems of this sort. In subsequent chapters, there is more contemporary Data Base System terminology and a comprehensive examination of Data Base Management System, IMS/VS.

2
Some Basic Concepts

INTRODUCTION

The theory of data management predates computers. Early attempts at putting the theory into practice with rudimentary equipment were made in the 1940s and early 1950s. Computers were applied to the management of data in late 1950s and early 1960s. These computers were able to process data more quickly and in greater quantities than ever before, but the management of the data (storage, manipulation and retrieval) was still quite unsophisticated. The architecture of computers at that time facilitated sequential processing of large volumes of data or massive computations made on small amounts of data, one job at a time. In the middle 1960s, computer architecture was radically changed. A quantum increase in the size of computer memory and the introduction of operating systems made it possible for computers to do more than one job concurrently. This kind of processing, called multi-programming, has continued right up to the present.

Concurrent with multi-programming came the capacity to do what is called "on-line" or single transaction processing. Rather than process large volumes of data sequentially, it had become economically feasible to access specific information from computer stored files within seconds. In the late 1960s, more sophisticated methods of storing and retrieving data were incorporated into computer software (programs). These programs were the first data base management systems. The idea was just a little ahead of its time. Although computer memories had grown in size from thousands of positions to hundreds of thousands, they were not quite up to the task. However in the early and middle 1970s, computer memories capacities were such that millions of characters could be stored in them, and virtual storage technology had increased the potential size even further. This increase had made possible the implementation of data management software. Since it has become technologically possible (and is at least approaching economic feasibility), the concept of Data Management is now emerging in the business community. Technological advances are making it possible to store data in a way that is radically different from most of the contemporary methods now in use. This new technology is manifesting itself in both hardware and software. Hardware technology is allowing for large amounts of data (billions of characters) to be stored on-line. Software technology is supplying the mechanisms for the storing, updating and retrieving of that data.

The mechanisms for manipulating and retrieving data (converting data to information) are known as Data Base Management Systems (DBMS). There are a number of software packages that provide these mechanisms. One of these packages, IBM's IMS/VS, is examined below in some detail. However, before looking at IMS/VS, it is necessary to prepare a foundation. This foundation is made up of some general concepts of DBMS.

DATA BASE AND DATA BASE MANAGEMENT SYSTEMS—DEFINITIONS

Much of the difficulty in understanding Data Bases and Data Base Management Systems is caused by the numerous definitions of these two terms existing in contemporary literature. Consider the following definitions of data base:

IBM Data Processing Glossary	A collection of data fundamental to an enterprise.
Principles of Data Base Management, James Martin	A collection of interrelated data stored together with controlled redundancy to serve one or more applications in an optimal fashion; the data are stored so that they are independent of programs which use the data; a common and controlled approach is used in adding new data and modifying and retrieving existing data within the data base.
An Introduction to Data Base Systems, C.J. Date	A collection of stored operational data used by the application systems of some particular enterprise.

Introduction to Minicomputer Networks, Edward V. Stelmach	The entire collection of information available to a computer system. Or a structured collection of information as an entity or collection of related files treated as an entity.
Information Management System/Virtual Storage (IMS/VS) General Information Manual, IBM	A nonredundant collection of interrelated data items processable by one or more applications.
Computer Data-Base Organization, James Martin	A collection of the occurrences of multiple record types, containing the relationships between records, data aggregates, and data items.
Techniques for Direct Access, Keith R. London	Consists of all record occurrences, set occurrences, and areas that are controlled by a specific schema. If an installation has multiple data bases, there must be a separate schema for each data base. Furthermore, the content of different data bases is assumed to be disjoint.

These definitions are merely a sample of what exists. There are many more. All these definitions serve to show that the terms "Data Base," "Data Base System" and "Data Base Management System" must be defined by those using them at the time when they are using them. In actuality, as the number of definitions indicate, these terms mean different things to different people at different times in different circumstances.

In this text the terms are used quite often. Each occurrence of each term includes an explanation of its use within its context. The point is that these terms standing alone are quite imprecise. Whenever they are used or heard, they should be defined. Failure to do so may result in poor communication between individuals resulting at least in misunderstanding and confusion or at most in hostility and mistrust.

DATA BASE

To begin with, in this text, a Data Base is defined in broad, general terms. *A Data Base* is a collection or grouping of basic or fundamental elements of data. *A Data Base Management System (DBMS)* provides the facilities for storing, manipulating and preparing data elements for retrieval. When one uses the term *Data Base System,* he is generally referring to the system that includes both data bases and a Data Base Management System.

THE BIBLE AS A DATA BASE

The idea of a data base has evolved. When a broad definition of data base, like "a collection of data fundamental to an enterprise" or "a collection or grouping of basic or fundamental elements of data" is used, then nearly every file or data set qualifies as a data base. What, then, is the difference? What distinguishes a data base from a file or a data set? Is there really a difference, or is the whole thing just some more EDP industry "smoke"? Is a data base any more than a collection of data sets or files?

The answer is: "Yes, Virginia, there is something more to a data base than a mere collection of files or data sets." The basic difference between the idea of a file or data set and that of a data base can be perceived by using an illustration. In the broadest sense of the term, the Bible would qualify as a data base. To some people the Bible is indeed "a collection of all the data necessary to an enterprise." Yet in more precise, or in state-of-the-art terms, an ordinary Bible does not qualify. Although it is a collection of data, the ordinary Bible is nothing more than a collection of sequential data sets or files. An individual who is familiar with the Bible is able to retrieve data directly from it also. Yet these characteristics do not a data base make.

CROSS-REFERENCING ADDED MAKES A DATA BASE

In the late nineteenth century, an individual by the name of Scofield developed a system for cross-referencing related data elements (verses) within the Bible. Through the use of margin notes and footnotes, he was able to link or chain together verses that enhanced or supported one another. He published his work, and it is commonly known as The Scofield Reference Bible.

To illustrate the difference between the two, I have chosen a page from an ordinary Bible, i.e., one without references, and the corresponding page from a Scofield Bible. The section chosen is from the eleventh chapter of the Epistle of the Hebrews, a New Testament book dealing with a number of Old Testament characters and events. The first page is taken from a New American Standard Bible, a version that is virtually devoid of notes. This Bible (Fig. 2–1) is a collection of sequential data sets. It would not be considered a data base.

The other page (Fig. 2–2) is taken from the New Scofield Reference Bible. In the margins of the page can be seen a number of pointers to other places in the Bible to which the elements on this page are related. In a sense, it is the addition of these pointers that transforms a collection of sequential data sets into a data base, while at the same time maintaining the integrity of the sequential data sets.

One can readily see how the pointers work, by examining the text. Periodically throughout the text superscripts appear. In the margins next to the text, these superscripts appear again together with a reference or references that relate to other portions of scripture. In the language of Data Base Management

Systems, specifically IMS/VS as shall be seen later, these relationships are logical, but not necessarily physical. Noah appearing physically in verse 7 of chapter 11 of the Epistle to the Hebrews has a logical relationship to Noah physically appearing in the 14th through 22nd verses of the sixth chapter of the Book of Genesis. The logical relationship is established through the pointer in the margin note.

862 **Hebrews 10, 11**

GEANCE IS MINE, I WILL REPAY." And again, "THE LORD WILL JUDGE HIS PEOPLE."
31 It is a terrifying thing to fall into the hands of the living God.
32 But remember the former days, when, after being enlightened, you endured a great conflict of sufferings,
33 partly, by being made a public spectacle through reproaches and tribulations, and partly by becoming sharers with those who were so treated.
34 For you showed sympathy to the prisoners, and accepted joyfully the seizure of your property, knowing that you have for yourselves a better possession and an abiding one.
35 Therefore, do not throw away your confidence, which has a great reward.
36 For you have need of endurance, so that when you have done the will of God, you may receive what was promised.
37 FOR YET IN A VERY LITTLE WHILE, HE WHO IS COMING WILL COME, AND WILL NOT DELAY.
38 BUT MY RIGHTEOUS ONE SHALL LIVE BY FAITH; AND IF HE SHRINKS BACK, MY SOUL HAS NO PLEASURE IN HIM.
39 But we are not of those who shrink back to destruction, but of those who have faith to the preserving of the soul.

CHAPTER 11

NOW faith is the assurance of *things* hoped for, the conviction of things not seen.
2 For by it the men of old gained approval.
3 By faith we understand that the worlds were prepared by the word of God, so that what is seen was not made out of things which are visible.
4 By faith Abel offered to God a better sacrifice than Cain, through which he obtained the testimony that he was righteous, God testifying about his gifts, and through faith, though he is dead, he still speaks.
5 By faith Enoch was taken up so that he should not see death; and he was not found because God took him up: for he obtained the witness that before his being taken up he was pleasing to God.
6 And without faith it is impossible to please Him, for he who comes to God must believe that He is, and *that* He is a rewarder of those who seek Him.
7 By faith Noah, being warned *by God* about things not yet seen, in reverence prepared an ark for the salvation of his household, by which he condemned the world, and became an heir of the righteousness which is according to faith.
8 By faith Abraham, when he was called, obeyed by going out to a place which he was to receive for an inheritance; and he went out, not knowing where he was going.
9 By faith he lived as an alien in the land of promise, as in a foreign *land*, dwelling in tents with Isaac and Jacob, fellow-heirs of the same promise;
10 for he was looking for the city which has foundations, whose architect and builder is God.
11 By faith even Sarah herself received ability to conceive, even beyond the proper time of life, since she considered Him faithful who had promised;
12 therefore, also, there was born of one man, and him as good as dead at that, *as many descendants* AS THE STARS OF HEAVEN IN NUMBER, AND INNUMERABLE AS THE SAND WHICH IS BY THE SEASHORE.
13 All these died in faith, without receiving the promises, but having seen them and having welcomed them from a distance, and having confessed that they were strangers and exiles on the earth.
14 For those who say such things make it clear that they are seeking a country of their own.
15 And indeed if they had been thinking of that *country* from which they went out, they would have had opportunity to return.
16 But as it is, they desire a better *country*, that is a heavenly one. Therefore God is not ashamed to be called their God; for He has prepared a city for them.
17 By faith Abraham, when he was tested, offered up Isaac; and he who had received the promises was offering up his only begotten *son*;
18 *it was he* to whom it was said, "IN ISAAC YOUR SEED SHALL BE CALLED."
19 He considered that God is able to raise *men* even from the dead; from which he also received him back as a type.
20 By faith Isaac blessed Jacob and Esau, even regarding things to come.
21 By faith Jacob, as he was dying, blessed each of the sons of Joseph, and worshiped, *leaning* on the top of his staff.
22 By faith Joseph, when he was dying, made mention of the exodus of the sons of Israel, and gave orders concerning his bones.
23 By faith Moses, when he was born, was hidden for three months by his parents, because they saw he was a beautiful child; and they were not afraid of the king's edict.
24 By faith Moses, when he had grown up, refused to be called the son of Pharaoh's daughter;
25 choosing rather to endure ill-treatment with the people of God, than to enjoy the passing pleasures of sin;
26 considering the reproach of Christ greater riches than the treasures of Egypt; for he was looking to the reward.
27 By faith he left Egypt, not fearing the wrath of the king; for he endured, as seeing Him who is unseen.
28 By faith he kept the Passover and the sprinkling of the blood, so that he who destroyed the first-born might not touch them.
29 By faith they passed through the Red Sea as though *they were passing* through dry land; and the Egyptians, when they attempted it, were drowned.
30 By faith the walls of Jericho fell down, after they had been encircled for seven days.
31 By faith Rahab the harlot did not perish along with those who were disobedient, after she had welcomed the spies in peace.
32 And what more shall I say? For time will fail me if I tell of Gideon, Barak, Samson, Jephthah, of David and Samuel and the prophets,
33 who by faith conquered kingdoms,

Figure 2–1
BIBLE AS A COLLECTION OF SEQUENTIAL DATA SETS

FACILITIES MAKING UP A BIBLE DBMS

The Data Base Management System that is used by Bible students consists of a number of facilities. The DBMS of the Bible student is totally manual and consists of a number of other books. One of these is a Concordance of which there are several types. Basically a Concordance is a book that contains an alphabetical listing of key words used in the Bible with references, by book

11:6	HEBREWS	11:29

lated that he should not see death, and was not found, because God had translated him; for before his translation he had this testimony, that he pleased God.

6 But without *a*faith *it is* impossible to please *him;* for he that cometh to God must believe that he is, and *that* he is a *b*rewarder of them that diligently seek him.

Noah

7 By faith *c*Noah, being warned of God of things not seen as yet, moved with fear, prepared an ark to the *d*saving of his house, by which he condemned the *e*world, and became heir of the *f*righteousness which is by faith.

Abraham and Sarah

8 By faith *g*Abraham, when he was called to go out into a place which he should after receive for an inheritance, obeyed; and he went out, not knowing where he went.

9 By faith he sojourned in the land of promise, as in a *h*|foreign| country, *i*dwelling in *j*|tents| with Isaac and Jacob, the heirs with him of the same promise;

10 For he *k*looked for a city which hath *l*foundations, whose builder and maker *is* God.

11 Through faith also *m*Sarah herself received strength to conceive seed, and was delivered of a child when she was past age, because she judged him *n*faithful who had promised.

12 Therefore sprang there even of one, and him as good as *o*dead, as many as the *p*stars of the sky in multitude, and as the sand which is by the seashore innumerable.

13 These all died in faith, *q*not having received the *r*promises but having *s*seen them afar off, and were persuaded of *them,* and embraced *them,* and confessed that they were strangers and pilgrims on the earth.

14 For they that say such things declare plainly that they seek a country.

15 And truly, if they had been mindful of *t*that *country* from which they came out, they might have had opportunity to *u*return.

16 But now they desire a better *country,* that is, an heavenly;

wherefore, God is not ashamed to be called their God; for he hath *v*prepared for them a city.

17 By faith Abraham, when he was *x*|tested|, offered up Isaac; and he that had received the promises offered up his only begotten *son, w*Of whom it was said, *z*In Isaac shall thy seed be called;

19 Accounting that God *was* able to *aa*raise *him* up, even from the dead, from which also he received him in a *bb*figure.

Isaac

20 By faith *cc*Isaac blessed Jacob and Esau concerning things to come.

Jacob

21 By faith *dd*Jacob, when he was dying, blessed both the sons of Joseph, and worshiped, *ee*leaning upon the top of his staff.

Joseph

22 By faith *ff*Joseph, when he died, made mention of the departing of the children of Israel, and gave commandment concerning his bones.

The parents of Moses

23 By faith Moses, when he was born, was *gg*hidden three months by his parents, because they saw *he was a hh*|beautiful| child, and they were not afraid of the king's *ii*commandment.

Moses

24 By faith *jj*Moses, when he was come to years, refused to be called the son of Phar′aōh's daughter,

25 Choosing rather to suffer affliction *kk*with the people of God than to enjoy the pleasures of *ll*sin for a season,

26 Esteeming the reproach of Christ greater riches than the treasures in Egypt; for he had respect unto the *mm*recompense of the reward.

27 By faith he forsook Egypt, not fearing the wrath of the king; for he endured, as seeing him who is invisible.

28 Through faith he kept the *nn*passover, and the sprinkling of blood, lest he that destroyed the first-born should touch them.

29 By faith *oo*they passed through the Red Sea as by dry *land,* which

Marginal references (left):
a See Heb. 10:22, *marg.* s
b Rewards: v. 6; Jas. 1:12. (Dan.12:3; 1 Cor. 3:14, *note*)
c Gen.6: 14-22
d See Rom. 1:16, *note*
e Gk. *kosmos.* See Mt.4:8, *note*
f Cp. Rom. 4:13-24
g Gen.12: 1-4
h KJV *strange*
i Gen.13: 3,18
j KJV *tabernacles*
k Heb.13: 14; cp. 12:22
l Cp. Rev. 21:14
m Gen.21: 1-2
n Heb.10: 23
o Rom.4: 19
p Gen.22: 17
q Heb.11: 39; cp. 10:36
r v. 39; Gen.12:7
s Cp. Jn. 8:56
t Gen.11: 31
u Cp. Gen. 24:6-8; Heb.10: 38-39

Marginal references (right):
v Jn.14:2; Rev.21:2
w Gen.22: 1-14; Jas.2:21
x KJV *tried.* Test-Tempt: v. 17; Heb. 11:37. (Gen.3:1; Jas.1:14)
y Or *to*
z Gen.21: 12
aa Resurrection: v. 19; Heb. 11:35. (2 Ki.4:35;1 Cor.15: 52, *note*)
bb Cp. Heb.9:9
cc Gen.27: 26-40
dd Gen.48: 1-22
ee Cp. Gen.47: 31
ff Gen.50: 24-25
gg Ex.2: 1-3
hh KJV *proper*
ii Ex.1:16
jj Ex.2: 11-15
kk Separation: v. 25; Heb. 13:14. (Gen.12: 1; 2 Cor. 6:17, *note*)
ll See Rom.3: 23, *note*
mm Rom. 8:18; 2 Cor.4:17
nn Ex.12: 1-51
oo Ex.14: 13-31; Jude 5

1322

Figure 2–2

BIBLE AS A DATA BASE

chapter and verse, to where these words are used. There are complete and exhaustive Concordances, which contain virtually every word in the Bible and every reference. Other Concordances contain lists that are somewhat less exhaustive. Below (Fig. 2–3) is a page from the New American Standard (NAS) Bible Concordance, which is in the back of the NAS version. It is a collection of the principal common words and their most widely used occurrences.

The New American Standard
CONCORDANCE
to the
Old and New Testaments

A collection of the principal common words with their most widely used examples in text and lesser usages in reference. Related words, or synonyms follow the key word. The key word is abbreviated in the text to its first letter, e.g., "abide" is "a". Variants add suffixes or prefixes, e.g., "abiding" appears as "a-ing".

A

ABANDON—*leave* Judg. 6:13, LORD has a-ed us
 1 Sam. 12:22; Ps. 94:14, LORD ... a His people
 2 Kin. 21:14, I will a the remnant
 Ps. 27:9, Do not a me nor forsake me
 Jer. 23:33, I shall a you
 Acts 2:27, Thou wilt not a my soul to
  27:20, hope of our being saved ... a-ed
 Ps. 16:10; Prov. 17:14; Is. 2:6; Jer. 12:7; Ezek. 29:5
ABASE—*humble* Ezek. 21:26; Mal. 2:9
ABATE—*decrease* Gen. 8:8,11, water was a-d
 Deut. 34:7, his vigor a-d
ABBA Mark 14:36, saying, A! Father
 Rom. 8:15, by which we cry out, A! Father
 Gal. 4:6, crying, A! Father
ABHOR—*despise, detest, loathe*
 Rom. 12:9, a what is evil
 Deut. 7:26; Job 19:19; Ps. 78:59; Prov. 24:24;
 Is. 49:7
ABIDE—*remain, stay* Ps. 9:7, the LORD a-s forever
 Ps. 15:1, who may a in Thy tent
  91:1, will a in the shadow
  102:12, LORD, dost a forever
 John 3:36, wrath of God a-s on him
  5:38, His word a-ing in you
  8:31, you a in My word
  14:25, while a-ing with you
  15:4, A in Me ... it a-s in the vine ... you a in
   Me
  15:6, If anyone does not a in Me
  15:7, a in Me and My words a in you
  15:9, a in My love
  15:10, you will a in My love ... a in His love
 1 Cor. 13:13, But now a faith, hope, love
 Heb. 10:34, a better possession and an a-ing one
 1 Pet. 1:23, living and a-ing word of God
  1:25, BUT THE WORD OF THE LORD A-S FOREVER
 1 John 3:17, how does the love of God a in him
  4:12, God a-s in us
ABILITY—*strength* Ezra 2:69, according to ... a
 Dan. 1:4, who had a for serving
 Matt. 25:15, according to his own a
ABLE—*adequate* 1 Sam. 6:20, Who is a to stand
 Matt. 3:9, God is a from these stones
  9:28, believe that I am a to do this
  10:28, fear Him who is a to destroy
  20:22, Are you a to drink the cup
 John 10:29, no one is a to snatch them
 Acts 6:10, they were un-a to cope with the wisdom
 Rom. 8:39, shall be a to separate us
 1 Cor. 10:13, tempted beyond what you are a
 Eph. 3:18, may be a to comprehend
 2 Tim. 2:2, who will be a to teach
 James 4:12, the One who is a to save
 Jude 24, Now to Him who is a to keep
 1 Kin. 3:9; 2 Chr. 2:6; Rev. 5:3; 6:17

ABOARD Acts 21:2, went a and set sail
ABODE—*habitation* Jer. 31:23; Jude 6
 John 14:23, and make Our a with him
ABOLISH—*destroy* Matt. 5:17, I did not come to a
 Eph. 2:15, by a-ing in His flesh
 2 Tim. 1:10, Christ Jesus, who a-ed death
ABOMINABLE—*detestable, rejected*
 Jer. 44:4, do not do this a thing
 Ezek. 16:25, make your beauty a
 1 Pet. 4:3, drinking parties and a idolatries
 Ps. 14:1; 53:1; Rev. 21:8
ABOMINATION—*detestable thing*
 Ex. 8:26, an a to the Egyptians
 Prov. 3:32, an a to the LORD
  8:7, an a to my lips
 Ezek. 33:29, because of all their a-s
 Dan. 12:11, the a of desolation
 Rev. 17:5, the a-s of the earth
 Lev. 18:26; Deut. 7:26; 29:17
ABOUND—*excel, multiply*
 Ex. 34:6, a-ing in lovingkindness and truth
 Prov. 28:20, a faithful man will a with blessings
 Dan. 4:1, May your peace a
 Rom. 15:13, that you may a in hope
 1 Cor. 15:58, always a-ing in the work of the
 1 Cor. 14:12; 2 Cor. 7:15; 9:8
ABOVE—*over* Ex. 20:4, what is in heaven a or on
 Ps. 8:1, Thy splendor a the heavens
 Matt. 10:24, A disciple is not a his teacher
 John 3:31, He who comes from a is a all
  8:23, I am from a
 Phil. 2:9, the name which is a every name
 Col. 3:1; 2 Thess. 2:4; James 1:17
ABSENT Gen. 31:49, we are a one from the other
 1 Cor. 5:3, though a in body, but present
 2 Cor. 5:6, we are a from the Lord
  5:8, a from the body and to be
  10:1, but bold toward you when a
ABSTAIN—*depart, separate* Num. 6:3
 Acts 15:20, that they a from things
 1 Thess. 5:22, a from every form of evil
 1 Tim. 4:3, a-ing from foods, which
 2 Tim. 2:19, who names ... the Lord a from
  wickedness
 1 Pet. 2:11, strangers a from fleshly lusts
ABUNDANCE—*surplus, plenty, full, plenteous*
 Gen. 41:34, seven years of a
 Ps. 52:7, the a of his riches
  72:7, and a of peace till
 Is. 55:2, delight yourself in a
 Matt. 13:12, and he shall have an a
 Luke 12:15, when one has an a does his life
 Rom. 5:17, receive the a of grace
 Phil. 4:18, everything in full, and have an a
 Gen. 41:29; Deut. 28:47; Neh. 9:25; Ps. 36:8; 72:16;
  73:10; Prov. 24:6; Eccles. 5:10; Phil. 4:12

Figure 2–3

There are other tools in the Bible student's DBMS such as Topical Bibles, Bible Dictionaries and Bible Handbooks. The Topical Bible is a book that is used to explain data elements found in the Bible. It does this by cross reference to other data elements on the same subject. Bible Dictionaries carry the definitions of terms found in the Bible as well as some of the locations (book, chapter and verse) of the term. Bible Handbooks are used to correlate the Biblical characters, places and events to the contemporary cultural and historical characters, places and events that are only alluded to or not mentioned at all in the Bible.

Each of these tools of the Bible student is similar to facilities found in a DBMS. A Concordance is like a secondary index or an inverted file. A Topical Bible is like a Data Directory. A Bible Dictionary has some characteristics of a Data Dictionary, as does a Bible Handbook.

OK, what does all this reveal? First it tells us that a Data Base is data. It is passive. It must be acted upon. By what? It, the data base, is acted upon by the DBMS. The DBMS performs a process. The purpose of the process is to transform the data elements, lying within the data base, into information.[1] In more pragmatic terms, a DBMS is: a system of tools that facilitates the retrieval of information from a Data Base in a timely, accurate and consistent way. The purpose of a DBMS is to transform the data in the Data Base into information. Generally speaking, the data elements as they stand alone by themselves have less meaning than when they are combined with other data elements. A DBMS, then, is a system of tools that facilitates the retrieval of information from a Data Base.

A LIBRARY AS A DATA BASE

A library is another example of a data base. It contains large amounts of interrelated data stored in books, magazines, journals and papers. Interrelationships are established by means of footnotes and bibliographies, which relate data elements of one book, journal, magazine or paper to others. A library is also a dynamic data base as new books, magazines, journals and papers are periodically added to it and deleted from it. The analogy, as do all analogies, breaks

---

[1]Although the terms are often used interchangeably, there is a difference between "data" and "information." A string of numbers and characters is data. An ordered arrangement and classification of those same numbers and characters is information. For example:

136974078302625GODDARDAL

a string—data

EMPLOYEE CLOCK NO.	DATA SOCIAL SEC #	LAST NAME	FI	MI
136974	078-30-2625	GODDARD	A	L

ordered and classified—information

Figure 2–4
A DATA BASE

down. In this case it breaks down when one realizes that footnotes and bibliographies are not adjusted to reflect these additions and deletions. And yet, a
library does provide a reasonable approximation, in concept, to a data base (see
Fig. 2–4).

For this particular data base, one of the tools for retrieving information
is the index files (see Fig. 2–5). In a typical library, the books are stored
according to a numbering system. Most people are neither familiar with that
numbering system nor the number of the book they want. Usually an individual
enters the library, goes to the index, which is arranged alphabetically by title,
and finds the book title card in the index file. That card contains the number of
the book. A quick check of the books on the shelves soon leads the searcher
to the desired book. Retrieval of information related to a particular subject can
be accomplished by retrieving one book and then using the footnotes and bibliographies to enable retrieval of other material. Conceptually speaking, it is this
kind of relationship among data elements that is provided in a DBMS.

DATA BASE SYSTEM

Another term that appears with some regularity in conversations is "Data Base
System." *A Data Base System* is a system that includes both a Data Base and
a Data Base Management System. Taken together these two components have
as their objectives:

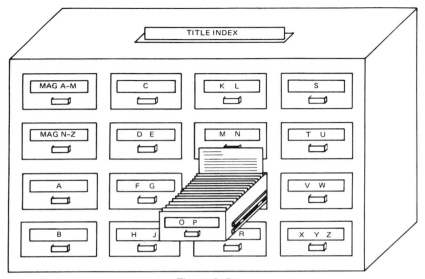

Figure 2–5
DATA BASE MANAGEMENT SYSTEM COMPONENT

1. Providing consistent, timely and accurate information
2. Providing ready access to the information to those who need it
3. Maintaining the integrity of the information

These objectives represent nothing radically new in concept. However, a Data Base System furnishes a technology that facilitates the attainment of these objectives.

Before proceeding further, one additional note of clarification is required. Several pages back, a number of definitions of the term Data Base were presented. There are also a number of definitions of the term "Data Base Management System" as well as for the term "Data Base System." There is a valid reason for this proliferation of definitions, all of which are essentially correct. Data Base Systems technology is evolving. As a result, definitions are modified to reflect changes in technology.

In broadest terms, Data Base Systems include virtually any system that processes data concurrently from two or more files. It is the manner in which this processing is done that changes. As of this writing, Data Base System technology is such that there are integrated relationships among data elements that transcend file boundaries. As progress is made through the material, this current technology will be examined. A simplistic analogy of a Data Base Management System can be seen in the following example, followed by a more orthodox one.

Figure 2–6

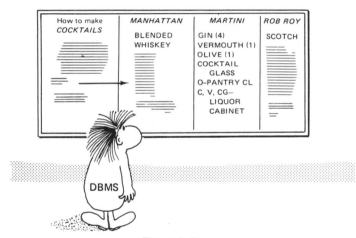

Figure 2–7

TWO ANALOGIES

A SIMPLISTIC ONE

A typical user decides that he wants a martini (Fig. 2–6).

The DBMS, who has been programmed in advance to know both the ingredients of a martini (Fig. 2–7) as well as the locations of those ingredients, reacts by first retrieving the olives from the pantry closet, Data Base #1 (Fig. 2–8). Having retrieved the olives, the DBMS then proceeds to the liquor cabinet to retrieve the remaining ingredients, glass, gin and vermouth. The liquor cabinet can be visualized as Data Base #2 (Fig. 2–9). Upon retrieving the ingredients, the DBMS then combines them according to a predefined algorithm $G(4)$ + $V(1) = .99M$; $.99M + O(1) = M$; where G = gin, V = vermouth, M =

Figure 2–8
DATA BASE #1 (PANTRY) REQUIRED: *OLIVE*

martini and O = olive. The DBMS uses the glass to hold M and delivers it to another satisfied customer (Fig. 2–10).

Completing the analogy in terms of a system that did not make use of Data Base Management System technology: the user would have to either wait longer for his martini or else if he wanted it quickly, he would have to store olives in two locations, the liquor cabinet as well as the pantry. The ability to directly combine data from two separate data bases is a feature of contemporary Data Base Management Systems. Although possible with conventional systems, the feasibility would be questionable due to design complexity and cost.

A BUSINESS ANALOGY

A more orthodox illustration of the justification for using a Data Base and a Data Base Management System is contained in the following.

Consider a typical corporation having a number of files and systems, all independent of one another, as in Fig. 2–11.

Figure 2–9
DATA BASE #2 (LIQUOR CABINET) REQUIRED: *GLASS GIN VERMOUTH*

Figure 2–10

Consider the following scenario; Plant B has an emergency. They need 1200 widgets. The production manager at Plant B calls the production manager at Plant A in order to ask for the widgets. The production manager of Plant A is on vacation. The assistant tells the production manager of Plant B to check with the supervisor of the Inventory Control department. He does, and 900 widgets are available and are sent from Plant A to Plant B. The Inventory Control supervisor makes an entry to delete the 900 widgets from the Inventory file. He calls the production manager's assistant and tells him that he was able to help Plant B, neglecting to specify an amount.

The Assistant, assuming 1200 sent, makes an entry to produce 1200 widgets to replace those sent to Plant B. Also within this time frame, it seems that the Accounting Department is cooperating with the Engineering Department to develop a standard cost for producing widgets. The Engineering Department uses the production file for quantity on hand and the Accounting Department

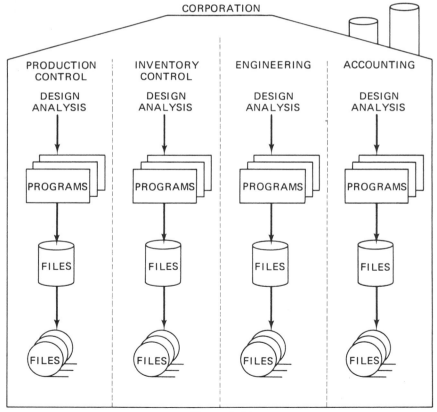

Figure 2–11

uses their own file, which is updated each night on a batch basis by each day's activity against the Inventory file.

All reports are produced from the computer center located near Plant A. Because of special processing requirements at the computer center, Plant B transactions are processed a day late.

Transactions like the transfer of widgets described above, together with hundreds of other transactions necessary to record the standard activities of a multi-plant, multi-warehouse manufacturing and shipping organization, are taking place each day. Supported by a multi-file, multi-system data processing environment, there are occasions where the department managers are beside themselves in confusion because the reports produced by these systems contain conflicting information. The widget example alone could produce two or possibly three different on-hand figures for widgets (as seen in Fig. 2–12).

The technology of data bases is such that it tends toward the reduction of redundant data. Rather than carry "on hand" and other similar data in multiple files, the Data Base tends to have "on hand" data stored in one place from which it can be accessed by all systems. The same data or information is available

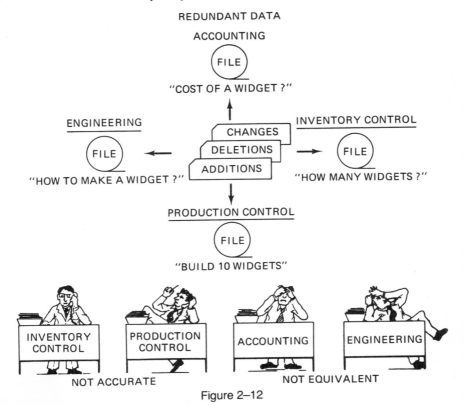

Figure 2–12

to all those who have a need for it. The potential exists to reduce one source of confusion by using a Data Base, which has a central location for all the data elements (Fig. 2–13).

NEW METHODOLOGY OF STORING DATA AND RETRIEVING INFORMATION

In support of contemporary Data Base Systems, new technology is emerging in the methodology of storing data and retrieving information. To explain this, a contrast between a conventional record and a data base record provides a starting point. A conventional record, whether stored on a five-by-seven card or on magnetic tape or disk, has certain characteristics. On the next page is an example (Fig. 2–14) of a conventional record. Notice that the basic elements of the data, called fields, are physically contiguous. In many cases the records themselves are also physically contiguous.

The transition from conventional record processing to Data Base technology has been a gradual one. The transition began taking place outside of the electronic data processing field. Computer driven Data Base Management Systems are a relatively recent phenomenon.

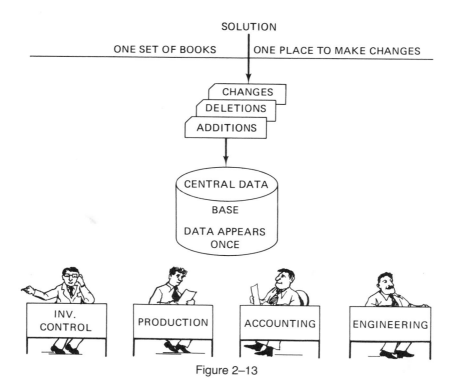

Figure 2–13

CONVENTIONAL RECORD

CAR SERIAL #	CAR MAKE	CAR MODEL	CAR YEAR	ENGINE TYPE	ENGINE CYLINDERS	ENGINE DISPLACEMENT	TRANSMSN TYPE	TRANSMSN CONTROL
746553297	DODGE	DART	1974	STRAIGHT	SIX	225 CU IN	MANUAL	FLOOR MOUNT

TRANSMSN SPEEDS	CARBURETOR MFCTR	CARBURETOR FEEDS	CARBURETOR CHOKE	TIRE SIZE	TIRE TYPE
FIVE	CARTER	SINGLE	MANUAL	D78–14	WHITEWALL

END OF ONE RECORD

EXTERIOR COLOR	INTERIOR COLOR	CAR SERIAL #	CAR MAKE	CAR MODEL
GREEN	GREEN	749864529	DODGE	DART

BEGINNING OF NEXT RECORD

Figure 2–14

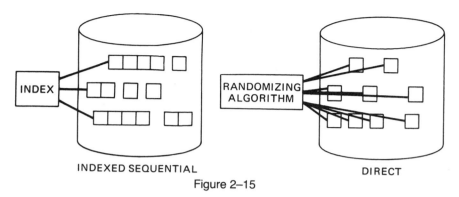

INDEXED SEQUENTIAL   DIRECT

Figure 2–15

Initially, techniques of working with non-contiguous records included methods such as direct access processing and indexed sequential processing. In these methods the fields are physically contiguous, but the records quite often are not physically contiguous. Records are retrieved through a randomizing algorithm in direct access processing and with the use of an index in indexed sequential processing. Figure 2–15 illustrates this.

TRADITIONAL BASIC PROCESSING METHODS

A more graphic distinction of the three basic processing methodologies, sequential, direct and indexed, can be illustrated by using the Bible as an example.

SEQUENTIAL PROCESSING takes place when one starts at the beginning of a list or a file or a book and processes all the elements in that list, file or book until the end is reached. For example, in processing the Bible sequentially, (reading is considered processing), one would start with Genesis, Chapter 1, Verse 1, and continue reading until Revelation, Chapter 22, Verse 21. The table of contents[2] below (Fig. 2–16), copied from *The Way,* The Living Bible, shows the sequence of the books of the Bible.

DIRECT PROCESSING takes place when one wishes to retrieve one or more specific data element(s) from a list, file or book. In order to accomplish this task one must be able to identify the unique data element(s). Direct processing, using the Bible, is accomplished through the use of the unique identifier of Book, Chapter and Verse. For example, if an individual wished to retrieve verse 16 of the third chapter of the Gospel according to John, he would turn directly to that place in the Bible and the data in those verses would be available to him (Fig. 2–17).

---

[2]Table of Contents from *The Way,* an edition of the Living Bible. Copyright © 1972 by Youth for Christ International and published by Tyndale House Publishers, Wheaton, Illinois. Used by permission.

THE OLD TESTAMENT

Book	Page	Book	Page	Book	Page
Genesis	1	2 Chronicles	383	Daniel	717
Exodus	30	Ezra	415	Hosea	734
Leviticus	90	Nehemiah	425	Joel	744
Numbers	120	Esther	439	Amos	748
Deuteronomy	158	Job	449	Obadiah	754
Joshua	190	Psalms	473	Jonah	756
Judges	213	Proverbs	532	Micah	759
Ruth	238	Ecclesiastes	554	Nahum	763
1 Samuel	243	Song of Solomon	563	Habakkuk	766
2 Samuel	271	Isaiah	570	Zephaniah	768
1 Kings	297	Jeremiah	617	Haggai	772
2 Kings	325	Lamentations	666	Zechariah	774
1 Chronicles	354	Ezekiel	672	Malachi	784

THE NEW TESTAMENT

Book	Page	Book	Page	Book	Page
Matthew	799	Ephesians	1019	Hebrews	1062
Mark	833	Philippians	1028	James	1076
Luke	857	Colossians	1034	1 Peter	1082
John	897	1 Thessalonians	1039	2 Peter	1056
Acts	926	2 Thessalonians	1042	1 John	1091
Romans	962	1 Timothy	1046	2 John	1095
1 Corinthians	982	2 Timothy	1050	3 John	1096
2 Corinthians	999	Titus	1055	Jude	1097
Galatians	1011	Philemon	1059	The Revelation	1100

Figure 2–16

INDEXED PROCESSING is one by which data elements of a list, file or book can be processed through the use of an index. The index allows for the processing of the list, file or book according to the order of the index rather than the order of the data elements. Again turning to the Bible for an illustration: It is commonly known that the data elements of the Bible are not in chronological order. Yet some Biblical scholars have made attempts at rearranging the material into chronological order. One method for doing this is to establish an index which contains the data elements in chronological order. The Bible is left in its existing order. One reads the Bible according to the index rather than according to the way in which the data actually appear in the Bible (Fig. 2–18).

A NEW CONCEPT OF DATA GROUPING

These examples illustrate the basic ways in which records are processed using contemporary techniques. In Data Base Systems, a new concept of data

8:20, note	down from heaven, *even* the ᵐSon of man who is in heaven.	23 ¶ And John also was baptizing in Ænon, near to Salim, because there was much water there; and they ᶠᶠcame, and were ᵉᵉbaptized.	cc See 1 Jn.1:7, note
n *Inspiration*: v. 14; Jn.4: 37. (Ex. 4:15; 2 Tim.3: 16); Num.21: 9)	14 ¶ And, ⁿas Moses ᵒlifted up the serpent in the wilderness, even so must the ᵐSon of man be lifted up,	24 For John was not yet cast into ᵉᵉprison.	dd Jn.15: 4–5; 1 Cor.15: 10
o *Sacrifice* (of Christ):	15 That whosoever ᵖbelieveth in him should not perish, but have eternal �𐞥life.	25 ¶ Then there arose a question between *some* of John's disciples and the Jews about purifying.	ee Cp.Jn. 4:2; see Acts 8: 12, note
vv. 14, 16; Jn.6: 33. (Gen. 3:15; Heb.10: 18, *note*)	16 ¶ ʳFor God so ˢloved the ᵗworld, that he ᵒgave his only begotten ᵘSon, that whosoever ¹ᵖbelieveth in him should not ²perish, but ᵛhave everlasting ᑫlife.	26 And they came unto John, and said unto him, Rabbi, he that was with thee beyond *the* Jordan, to whom thou barest ʰʰwitness,	ff Mt.3: 5–6
			gg Mt.4: 12; cp. Mt.14:3
			hh Jn.1:7

of God (Gal.3:26; 1 Pet.1:23) and a partaker of the divine nature, the life of Christ Himself (Gal. 2:20; Eph.2:10; 4:24; Col.1:27; 2 Pet.1:4; 1 Jn.5:10–12). And (5) in view of Ezek.36:24–26, Nicodemus should have known about the new birth. Observe the correspondence between the "clean water," the "new spirit," and the "new heart" of the Ezekiel passage and the "water," "Spirit," and new birth ("born again") of Jn.3:3,7.

¹(3:16) Belief in the N.T. denotes more than intellectual assent to a fact. The word (Gk. *pistis*, noun; *pisteuō*, verb) means *adherence to, committal to, faith in, reliance upon, trust in* a person or an object, and this involves not only the consent of the mind, but an act of the heart and will of the subject. "Whosoever believeth in him" is equivalent to "whosoever trusts in or commits himself to him [Christ]." Belief, then, is synonymous with faith, which in the N.T. consists of believing and receiving what God has revealed. See Faith, Heb.11:39, *note*.

Figure 2–17

grouping emerges. The term *segment* is used by IMS, a DBMS marketed by IBM, but it also serves well in a generic sense in all Data Base Systems. A *segment* is a group of one or more fields of data. Suffice it to say at this point that a segment is smaller than a record. Using the record from an earlier example, segmenting might take place as shown in Fig. 2–19.

Examples of segments are shown in Fig. 2–20.

As will become apparent as more of the data base technology is examined, segments and data bases will begin to emerge as new components of data elements to be dealt with, while the components now known as records and files become more nebulous. This takes place as segments are related to one another within files as well as across file boundaries, and records are made up of segments from various files. It is complex and it is radical, but it represents the future in data management technology.

To illustrate this, picture for a moment three files, each containing three segments (Fig. 2–21). Suppose that segment D2, C2 and P2 contained the same information in all three files. By using pointers, which often require less space than the data, a net saving of space results. Segments D1, C1 and P1 all point to C2. C2 contains pointers linking it back to the appropriate file. The relationship among the segments is pictured in Fig. 2–22.

The examples used in the preceeding pages are admittedly simplistic. In reality, the relationships among segments are far more numerous. The files or data bases are much larger and contain many more segments. As the size and quantity grows, so grows the complexity. It is to this complexity that the Data Base System addresses itself.

★ Genesis 1-22	Song of Solomon	Ezekiel
Job	1 Kings 5-11	2 Chronicles 36: 22,23
Genesis 23-50	Ecclesiastes	Ezra 1-5:1
Exodus	1 Kings 12-22	Haggai
Psalm 90	2 Kings 1-14:25	Zechariah
Leviticus	Jonah	Psalms 107,126
Numbers	2 Kings 14:26-29	Ezra 5:2-6:22
Deuteronomy	Amos	Esther
Psalm 91	2 Kings 15-25	Ezra 7-10
Joshua	Psalms 1,2,10,33,43,	Nehemiah
Judges	66,67,71,80,92-100	Malachi
Ruth	102,104-106,111-125,	Matthew
1 Samuel 1-16:13	127-136, 146-150	Mark
Psalm 23	1 Chronicles 1-16	Luke
Psalm 59	85,87,88	John
1 Samuel 19:12-21:15	1 Chronicles 17-29	Acts 1-14
Psalms 34,36	2 Chronicles 1-21	James
1 Samuel 22:1,2	Obadiah	Acts 15
Psalms 57,142	2 Chronicles 22	Galatians
1 Samuel 22:3-23	Joel	Acts 16
Psalm 52	2 Chronicles 23-26:8	Philippians
1 Samuel 23	Isiah 1-5	Acts 17:1-10
Psalms 54,63	2 Chronicles 26:9-23	1 Thessalonians
1 Samuel 24-31	Isaiah 6	2 Thessalonians
2 Samuel 1-7	2 Chronicles 27-32	Acts 7:11-18:11
Psalm 30	Isaiah 7-66	1 Corinthians
2 Samuel 8:1-14	Hosea	2 Corinthians
Psalm 60	Micah	Acts 13:12-20:1
2 Samuel 8:15-12:14	Nahum	Ephesians
Psalms 31,32	2 Chronicles 33,34	Romans
2 Samuel 12:15-15:37	Zephaniah	Acts 20:2-28:30
Psalms 3,69	2 Chronicles 35	Colossians
2 Samuel 16-20	Habakkuk	Hebrews
Psalms 61,70	Jeremiah 1-6,11,12	Titus
2 Samuel 21,22	26,7-10,11-20,35,36	Philemon
Psalm 18	45,25,46-49,13,22-24,	1 Timothy
2 Samuel 23,24	27-29,50,51,30-33	2 Timothy
Psalms 4-9,11-17,19	21,31,37-39,52,40-44	1 Peter
-22,24-29,31,35-41	Lamentations	2 Peter
53,55,58,61,62,65,68	2 Chronicles 36:1-8	1 John
68,72,86,101,103,108	Daniel	2 John
-110,133-141,143-145	2 Chronicles 36:9-21	3 John
1 Kings 1-4	Psalm 137	Jude
		Revelation

---

³This particular chronological arrangement is that of Dr. Stanley Horton.

Figure 2–18

IMPORTANT TERMS IN DESCRIPTIONS OF DATA BASES

The world of Data Bases and Data Base Management Systems has introduced a whole new lexicon of "buzz words." This new vocabulary contains terms that express concepts of Data Base organization and structure. Three terms that are often seen in descriptions of Data Bases are:

1. Hierarchical or Tree Structures

2. Networks

3. Relational (Normalization and flat files)

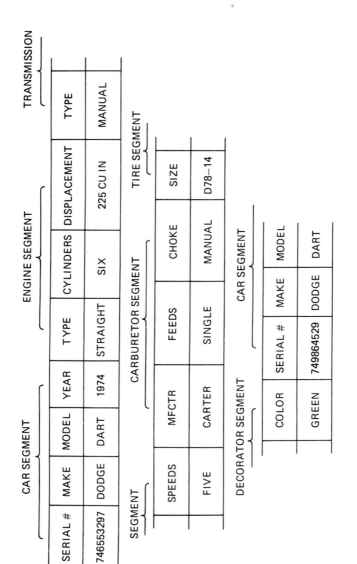

Figure 2-19

CAR SEGMENT

MCFCTR	MAKE	MODEL	YEAR
CHRYSLER	DODGE	DART	1974

CARBURETOR SEGMENT

MFCTR	FEED	CHOKE	GIZINTA[*]
CARTER	2 BARREL	AUTOMATIC	POINTER

Figure 2–20

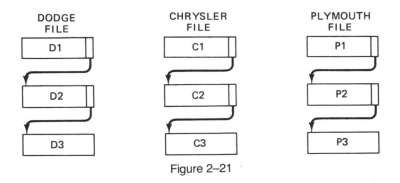

Figure 2–21

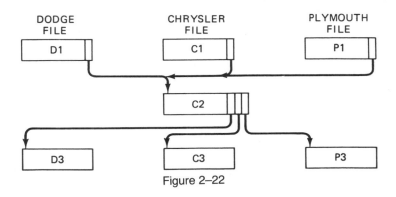

Figure 2–22

33

HIERARCHICAL AND NETWORK

The illustrations shown in Fig. 2–23 display the concepts of a hierarchical or tree structure and a network.

In a hierarchical or tree structure there exists a relationship between nodes (segments) such that the highest level has only one node (segment) called the root. All nodes (segments) except the root are related to only one node (segment) in a level above themselves. As can be seen in Fig. 2–23, the structure is pictured like an upsidedown tree.

A network exists when a subordinate node (segment) can relate to more than one node (segment) in a level above itself. Figure 2–23 also shows a network structure.

A hierarchical structure can be thought of as a form of a network. It merely has some rules imposed upon it so as to make it a particular type of a network. On the other hand, a network can be separated into a number of hierarchical structures containing some redundant data. For instance the network in Fig. 2–23, if labelled, could be made up of the hierarchical structures shown in Fig. 2–24.

The consequence of separating a network into hierarchical structures is the redundancy of some nodes (segments). The combining of hierarchical structures into networks, eliminating redundant data, is one of the objectives of a data base system. The trade-off between the simplicity of design of a hierarchical structure and the efficiency of storing a network is an important consideration in data base system implementation. (Figure 2–25)

RELATIONAL (NORMALIZATION) DATA BASES

Relational Data Bases, or "flat files," are actually conventional files. They are two-dimensional files that are related to one another. Unfortunately for mere mortals, the process of creating them consists of a rather elaborate procedure called "normalization." Developed by a Data Base theoretician named E. F. Codd, the procedure comes complete with its own terminology. The schematic shown in Fig. 2–26 is provided to present a glimpse at the concept of Relational Data Bases.

In the normalization process, the three-dimensional "Purchase Order" file is replaced with two-dimensional "Purchase Order" and "Purchase Item" files, which are "flat files." Figure 2–26 shows why they are called flat. The purpose of using "flat files" is to reduce complexity in the long run. A relational data base comes about as the result of a lot of analyses of a particular enterprise's data. If the assumptions made are correct and the normalization process is done properly, the ultimate data base will result. Physically the redundancy will be reduced to a minimum and logically, all the appropriate relationships among the segments will be established. Logically the data base will consist of a number of hierarchical relationships, while physically the data base will be a network. Normalization is a three-step process. The result of the process is a reduction

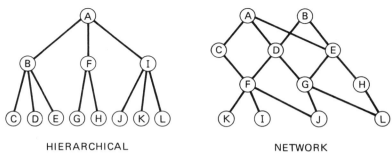

HIERARCHICAL   NETWORK

Figure 2–23

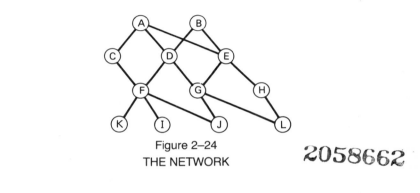

Figure 2–24
THE NETWORK

2058662

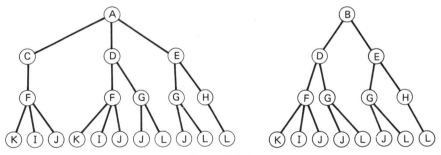

Figure 2–25
HIERARCHICAL STRUCTURES

of all relationships among data elements to two-dimensional tabular form. The data elements when reduced to a relational data base are said to be in a structure called third normal form.

The foregoing survey of Data Base System fundamentals has laid the groundwork for that which follows. For a more detailed description of the fundamentals, the author recommends *Principles of Data Base Management* by James Martin.

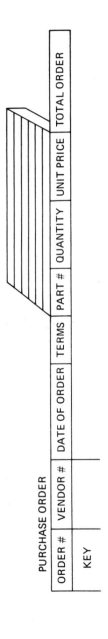

PURCHASE ORDER

ORDER #	VENDOR #	DATE OF ORDER	TERMS	PART #	QUANTITY	UNIT PRICE	TOTAL ORDER
KEY							

PURCHASE ORDER

ORDER #	VENDOR #	DATE OF ORDER	TERMS	TOTAL ORDER
KEY				

PURCHASE ITEM

ORDER #	PART #	QUANTITY	UNIT PRICE
KEY			

Figure 2–26
RELATIONAL DATA BASE

A FUNCTIONAL DESCRIPTION OF A DATA BASE SYSTEM

An additional source for another perspective on Data Base Systems is an article written by Daniel S. Appleton in the January 1977 issue of DATAMATION. In a piece titled "What A Data Base Isn't," Appleton distinguishes three basic control systems in a DBMS. The following, a paraphrase of a section of the article dealing with those control systems, provides a functional description of a Data Base System. This functional description is included so as to complement the fundamentals. Appleton postulates the following:

Three basic control systems in a data base management system:

data base input control system

data base output control system

data base storage and processing control system

The input control system: is

that part of the system that collects and manages input to a data base. It has as its primary purpose the maintenance of data quality and integrity. It also provides input techniques, edits, audits, security and diagnostic controls. Once established, this portion of the system should be quite static. Most management information can be fabricated from less than a thousand basic data items.

The output control system:

must have a dynamic quality. Changes in the information requirements of a corporation can be triggered by numerous factors, such as management styles, personalities, economics, politics, organizational structures and so on.

The storage and processing control system:

manages the data base itself, receiving data from the input control system and passing it, on demand, to the output control system. The storage and processing control system is an independent data base management system with built-in capabilities for controlling backup, recovery, data availability, security and computer efficiency. It also controls the data base's physical structure. This structure is not static; it has to respond to needs for optimizing resource efficiency and cost effectiveness. It is this system that is used to effect a balance in the trade-off between data redundancy and processing time.

WHAT A DATA BASE SYSTEM DOES

So much for definitions and concepts. Having described what a Data Base System is, the next step is to describe what a Data Base System does. This can be done by stating objectives. Some textbooks list as many as twenty-eight objectives of Data Base Systems. This becomes self-defeating. A more manageable number would be five. The objectives of a Data Base System are as follows:

1. Provide consistent, timely and accurate information.

2. Provide ready access to the information to those who need it.

3. Maintain the integrity of the data base.

4. Provide security for both the information and the data.

5. Contain within itself the facilities to bring about changes in the structure of the data base so it can evolve (take new form) over time.

These objectives are quite basic to the implementation of a successful Data Base System.

SUMMARY OF DATA BASE SYSTEMS

Having presented the fundamentals, it is now time to examine a specific Data Base Management System. Before doing that, a quick review of the preliminary material is presented. To recap up to this point:

1. The definitions of the terms Data Base and Data Base Management Systems are imprecise.

2. There are as many definitions of these terms as there are books that carry them.

3. Before using the terms in communications with others, whether written or verbal, spend some time making sure that all parties to the communications have the same understanding of the terms.

4. Segments and data bases are going to replace records and files in the Data Base Management Systems of the future.

5. Three concepts of Data Base organization and structure—hierarchical, network and relational—were discussed.

6. Three distinguishable parts serve to describe the three functions of storing, manipulating/processing and retrieval that make up a Data Base Management System.

7. Five basic objectives suffice to recommend a Data Base System.

IMS/VS

There is some similarity among Data Base Management Systems. In the contemporary marketplace there are many systems. A partial list appears at the top of the following page.

Although there are architectural differences among these various systems, a detailed examination of one of the most elaborate provides a good general knowledge on how they all work. IMS/VS has been chosen since it is the most complex. To some individuals, IMS/VS is the "Cadillac" of the Data Base Management Systems; to others, it is the "Edsel." Regardless of one's point of view, it is an elaborate and sophisticated system. A detailed examination of the IMS/VS Data Base Management System serves in that it leaves little doubt as to the magnitude of the complexities and expense associated with Data Base technology.

IMS/VS is a Data Base Management System. The initials IMS/VS represent Information Management System/Virtual Storage. Known as IMS/VS, it is an

DBMS	Vendor
ADABAS	Software AG
DATACOM	Insyte Datacomm Corp.
DBMS-20	DEC (Digital Equipment)
DBMS-11	Burroughs
IDMS	Cullinane
IDS	Honeywell
IMAGE	Hewlett-Packard
IMS	IBM
SYSTEM 2000	MRI Systems
TOTAL	Cincom Systems

IBM developed software package. As IBM bills it: "The package was designed to facilitate user implementation of a Data Base System in a batch and/or on-line environment supporting a wide variety of applications." IMS/VS could also be defined in another way: IMS/VS is a software package that enables a user to install a data base system in a telecommunications environment. The package contains two features: the Data Base feature, known as DB or DL/1; and the Data Communications feature, known as DC. The DB feature provides the facilities that are necessary to (a) establish a "Data Base" and (b) to process batch applications using that "Data Base." The DC feature provides the facilities that are necessary for message or transaction processing and telecommunications using the "Data Base."

The broadest overview of IMS/VS shows it as a configuration involving four major components (see also Fig. 2–27):

1. a Terminal Network
2. a Computer
3. a Collection of Application Programs
4. a Data Base

In slightly different form, the two features of IMS/VS are actually two separate systems. They can be pictured as shown in Fig. 2–28.

Three facets of IMS/VS are looked at in the next three chapters. The Data Base (DB) feature is examined first, the Data Communication (DC) feature is described last. In between the two, the file storage structures (access methods) of IMS/VS are examined within the context of a discussion of the Data Base Administration in an IMS/VS environment using the Data Dictionary/Directory package.

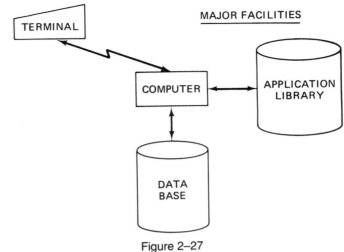

Figure 2–27
MAJOR FACILITIES

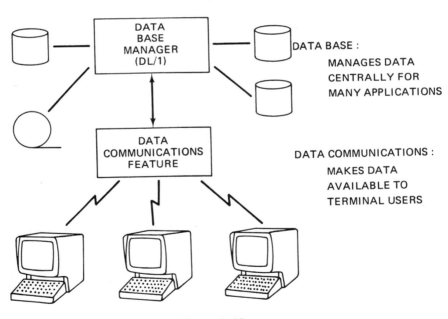

Figure 2–28

40

3
IMS/VS—The DB Feature

IMS/VS LANGUAGE—DL/1

IMS/VS has two features, the Data Base feature, known alternately as DB or DL/1 and the Data Communications feature, known as DC. The DL/1 designation comes from the input/output language of IMS/VS, which is called Data Language/1 or DL/1. This particular designation dates back to the time when IMS/VS was just plain IMS. There was no DC feature at that time. The system was a batch Data Base Management System known as IMS. There is a more thorough explanation of the actual use Data Language/1 later in the book. At this point it is briefly discussed as one of the parts of the DB feature.

DL/1 statements are source coded (written by programmers) into application programs. The function of these statements is the transfer of data to and from IMS/VS data bases. Under IMS/VS-DB application programs written in COBOL, Assembler Language or PL/1 can be interfaced with IMS/VS Data Bases through the DL/1 facility. There is a separate interface for each of the three programming languages that can be used between DL/1 and the application programs. For example, when COBOL is used, there is a precompiled set of instructions that is incorporated into the program when it is compiled. That set of instructions constitutes the interface between the COBOL program and the

DL/1. When the retrieval instructions of DL/1 are encountered during the execution of the COBOL program, it is instructions of the precompiled interface that are used to effect the actual transfer of data between the computer and auxiliary storage. The precompiled interface includes whatever OS/VS access method is required (Fig. 3–1).

As a retrieval language, DL/1 is not a programming language in the sense that COBOL and PL/1 are programming languages. Data Language/1 is used as a Data Management tool. It is an input/output language. The DL/1 macro instructions replace the normal input/output instructions of the application programming language. The DL/1 input/output instructions invoke precompiled subroutines that "GET, INSERT, DELETE and REPLACE" segments in IMS/VS Data Bases.

Below is a list of the DL/1 function codes:

FUNCTION	CODE
RETRIEVING	
GET UNIQUE	GUbb
GET NEXT	GNbb
GET NEXT WITHIN PARENT	GNPb
GET HOLD UNIQUE	GHUb
GET HOLD NEXT	GHNp
WITHIN PARENT	GHNp
ADDING	
INSERT	ISRT
DELETING	
DELETE	DLET
UPDATING	
REPLACE	REPL

Each of these function codes (as invoked) retrieve, add, delete or update a segment, not a record. More about these later.

DATA STRUCTURES

Data structures in IMS/VS are quite different than data structures in conventional files. It is a new technology and there is a new terminology to go with it. In subsequent pages this new technology and the terminology will be examined. The terms that will be explained are:

1. Hierarchical Structure
    Segment
    Root

      Parent

      Child

      Twin

2. DBD & PSB & PCB

3. IMS Storage Structures

      HSAM

      HISAM

      HDAM

      HIDAM

4. Physical Data Base

5. Logical Data Base

6. Secondary Index

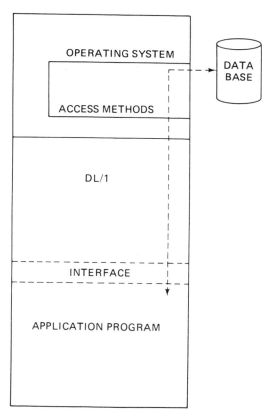

Figure 3–1

The most radical change that is encountered in IMS/VS is the way in which data elements are stored. The terms "logical" and "physical" are used to describe the way in which data is stored. In order to understand the "Logical Data Bases" and "Physical Data Bases," it is first necessary to understand the hierarchical structure of data within a single Data Base record.

HIERARCHICAL STRUCTURE OF DATA

The schematic in Fig. 3–2 shows the concept of a hierarchical structure and the terminology associated with it. Each block represents a segment. A root segment is a segment that is not subordinate to any other segment. In the illustration, A is a root segment. A parent is a segment that has subordinate segments. A and B are parents. A child is a segment that is subordinate to another segment: B, F, C, D and the occurrences of E are children. Twins are multiple occurrences of the same segment type. The occurrences of E are twins.

    The hierarchical structure is a logical relationship among segments. Physical storage of segments can be of two basic types, sequential and direct. The schematic (Fig. 3–3) shows the logical view and the physical storage organizations. Reading of a hierarchical structure proceeds "top to bottom, left to right." This is reflected in the physical organization of the segments.

DBD

In order to understand IMS/VS data organization in more detail, it is advisable to have a basic understanding of how IMS/VS handles the data. Figure 3–4 illustrates data handling in a conventional environment. In this traditional case, each programmer had to include in his program file description information for each file that he used.

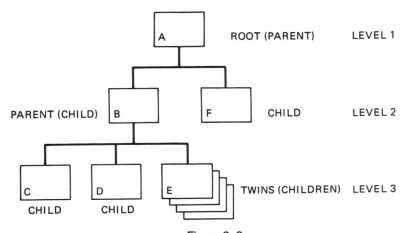

Figure 3–2

THE TERMINOLOGY OF HIERARCHICAL STRUCTURES IN IMS/VS

In a Data Base environment, the programmer merely defines the segment(s) that he needs. The job of file description is given to the "Data Base Administrator" (DBA), a job that is examined in more detail later on. The illustration in Fig. 3–5 shows this.

Two new terms are introduced in the above illustration, the Data Base Description (DBD) and the Program Specification Block (PSB). The DBD describes the global view of a Data Base, that is, it maps an entire data base. The PSB describes a program's view of a group of segments from one or more data bases. In a Data Communication environment, the PSB also includes a view of a terminal or group of terminals. This will become clearer when Program Communication Blocks (PCBs) are explained. That explanation follows immediately

DATA BASE ORGANIZATION

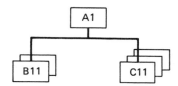

- TWO PHYSICAL ORGANIZATIONS

    - SEQUENTIAL

        - THE HIERARCHICAL SEQUENCE OF EACH DATA BASE RECORD IS MAINTAINED BY USING PHYSICALLY ADJACENT STORAGE LOCATIONS

A1	B11	B12	C11	C12	C13	A2	B21

- DIRECT

    - THE HIERARCHICAL SEQUENCE OF EACH DATA BASE RECORD IS MAINTAINED BY USING DIRECT ADDRESS POINTERS.

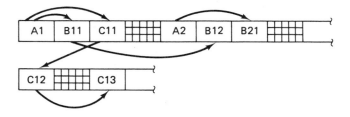

Figure 3–3

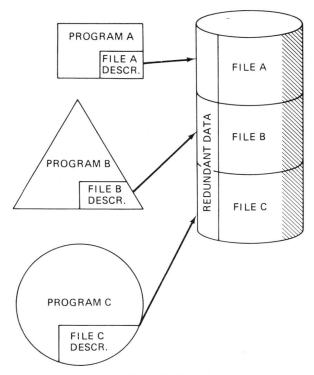

Figure 3–4

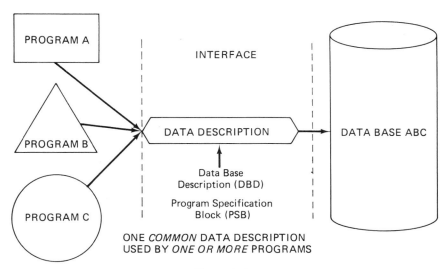

Figure 3–5

after this discussion of PSBs and DBDs. The schematic in Fig. 3–6 shows the distinction between the views of the PSB and the DBD.

Notice that the "address" segment is in the DBD while not in the PSB. The program that contains this PSB has no need for the "address" segment. It is this separation of global data descriptions from specific descriptions that provides a degree of data independence (see Fig. 3–7).

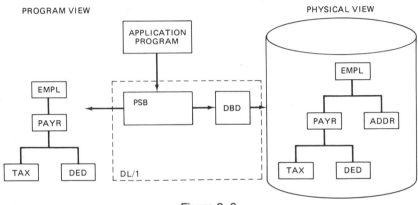

Figure 3–6

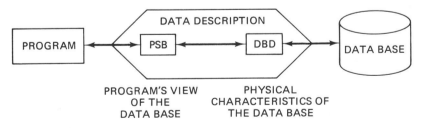

Figure 3–7

At this point in the discussion, there are three views of data structures: the Application Programmer's view, the Data Base Administrator's view and the Systems Programmer's view. These views overlap to some extent. The Data Base Administrator, a many faceted individual, in one of his functions, acts as an interface between Applications Programmers and Systems Programmers. The schematic in Fig. 3–8 illustrates this.

One more technique in data definition requires explanation. The Program Communication Block (PCB) is an application program's view of a specific group of segments. In a Data Communications (DC) environment, it provides a view of a specific terminal. A PSB is made up of one or more PCBs. Each application program has one PSB, which is made up of a number of PCBs. There is one PCB for each view of a Data Base and for each "logical terminal" used by the program. The term "logical terminal" is explained under the discussion of the Data Communications feature later on. The schematic in Fig. 3–9 illustrates the PSB-PCB-DBD relationship.

These methods of describing data will be examined in greater detail later in the discussion of the Data Base Administration function.

A QUICK REVIEW

Before going into more detail on Data Base organizations, a quick review of the material thus far follows. To recap up to this point:

1. IMS/VS is a Data Base Management System containing two features: Data Base (DB) and Data Communication (DC).

2. The IMS/VS-DB, sometimes called DL/1, feature is radical in that its data organization techniques are different than the traditional.

3. IMS/VS-DB uses the hierarchical structure type of Data Base organization.

4. Data Language 1 (DL/1) is the interface between the Data Base and the application program.

5. Data Base descriptions are made up, not by application programmers, but rather by Data Base Administrators.

PHYSICAL STORAGE ORGANIZATION METHODS

The next area to be discussed is that of the physical storage organization methods of DL/1. There are four major organizing methods and a few minor ones. The major ones are shown in Fig. 3–10.

Having established this, let's have a closer look at the Data Base organization of IMS/VS. There are four major data organizations in IMS/VS: Hierarchical Sequential Access Method (HSAM), Hierarchical Indexed Sequential Access Method (HISAM), Hierarchical Direct Access Method (HDAM) and Hierarchical Indexed Direct Access Method (HIDAM). Figure 3–11 shows these four data organizations.

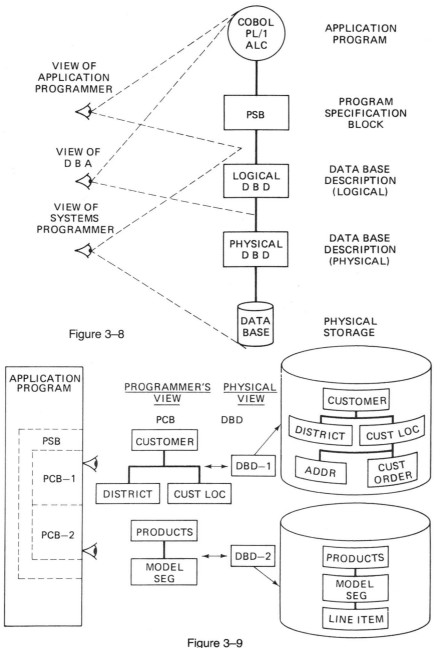

Figure 3–8

Figure 3–9
PSB-PCB-DBD RELATIONSHIP

Looking at Figure 3–11, we see two sequential (HSAM and HISAM) and two direct (HDAM and HIDAM) data organizations. HSAM is the most simple with data base segments stored in physical sequence, contiguously, one following another. A short cut method for remembering HSAM is: ''Think tape.'' HISAM

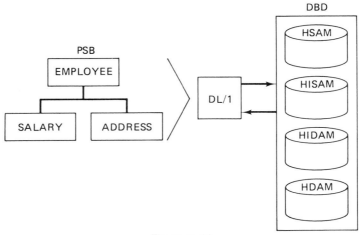

Figure 3–10

DATA BASE ORGANIZATIONS

SEQUENTIAL

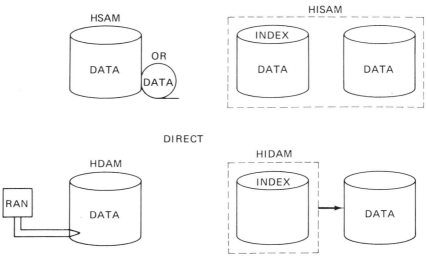

Figure 3–11

data bases have their records stored in logical sequence, with segments stored in physical sequence, contiguously within basic record subdivisions of index portion and data portion. Access to HISAM records is achieved through the index, which holds a unique identifier of each record. This identifier is known as a key. HDAM data bases have their segments related by direct address pointers. The segments do not have to be contiguous, but rather can be located all over a storage device. Access to HDAM records is achieved through a randomizing algorithm (arithmetic performed on the key) which turns the key into a direct storage device address of the root segment. HIDAM data bases have their segments related by direct address pointers, also. However, access to the root segment is through an index rather than through the use of a randomizing module. The index segments of HIDAM data bases contain the key and a pointer to the data portion of the data base.

In our discussion of the IMS/VS data organizations, one important observation should be made. HSAM, HISAM, HDAM and HIDAM are not access methods in the commonly understood sense of the term. Access methods like BSAM, QSAM, ISAM, VSAM, BDAM, etc.[1] are software mechanisms that actually cause the transfer of data between peripheral storage devices and computer memory. The letters "AM" at the end of these acronyms have traditionally signified "*Access Method.*" The "AM" letters on the end of the IMS/VS storage organizations methods also signify the term "*Access Method,*" but they are not access methods in the traditional sense. They describe data organizations, but they do not themselves transfer data. Rather they interface with the actual access methods like BSAM, VSAM, and ISAM. The actual access method transfers blocks of data between peripheral devices and computer storage. The IMS access methods transfer segments of data between sections of computer storage (buffers) and work areas in application programs. The schematics (Fig. 3–12 and 3–13) show the relationship between the "access methods" of IMS/VS and the access methods of the operating system which actually transfer data from peripheral devices to computer storage.

Figure 3–12 shows the interface of DL/1 with non-VSAM/data sets and

---

[1]BSAM, QSAM, ISAM, VSAM, BDAM, etc. BSAM signifies "Basic Sequential Access Method," where one physical record is one logical record and one access retrieves one logical record. Records are stored contiguously. QSAM signifies "Queued Sequential Access Method," where one physical record contains several logical records. One access retrieves several logical records. This access method is used to reduce the number of actual input/output operations, which can consume a relatively great amount of time when processing large amounts of data. ISAM signifies "Indexed Sequential Access Method," where records are stored in logical sequence by means of an index. The records do not have to be stored in actual physical sequence, though some of them may be. VSAM signifies "Virtual Storage Access Method." It is impossible to do justice to it in a footnote. Suffice to say, VSAM is a more elaborate ISAM that makes more use of virtual storage machines and their operating systems. BDAM signifies "Basic Direct Access Method" where records are stored and retrieved according to a randomizing module which creates storage device address from a key.

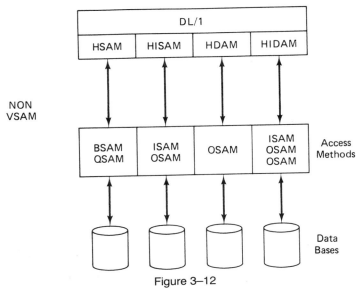

Figure 3–12

access methods. With the exception of OSAM, a direct access type of access method and data set structure developed specifically for the support of IMS/VS, the other access methods are carryovers from non-virtual storage computers. Figure 3–13 shows the interface with VSAM. Although not part of IMS/VS, VSAM is an access method and a data set structuring methodology developed for virtual storage computers. A discussion of VSAM would be out of place here. Suffice it to say that two of the data set types in VSAM are: entry sequence data sets (ESDS), in which data are stored in the sequence in which they are entered, and key sequence data sets (KSDS) in which data are stored in logical sequence according to a key field.

Access methods as a subject could easily fill a book. The treatment offered here serves merely to make the distinction between what is referred to as "access methods" in IMS/VS literature and access methods as they really are.

PHYSICAL DATA BASE

An IMS/VS physical data base is nothing more than a file that is structured in hierarchical form. The hierarchical form is only a logical view of the data. The words needed to describe these concepts can be the source of some confusion. To avoid this confusion, remember that logical view is not the same as logical data base, which is described below. As shown in an illustration earlier in this chapter (Figure 3–3), the logical view of the data and the way in which the data are stored are dissimilar. A computer stores data linearly or in a string, not in an inverted tree structure as it looks in hierarchical form.

Physical storing of data differs depending upon the "access method" used.

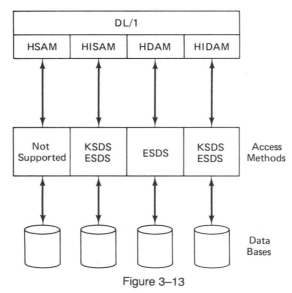

Figure 3–13

For example, in a HISAM data base, the segments of a record are related by their physical adjacency. In HDAM and HIDAM data bases, the segments of records are related by pointers. These ideas are shown in Figure 3–3. The dissimilarity between physical storage and logical view is increased even more by the access method itself. VSAM, for example, has its own data storage conventions as well as its own catalog. It is totally transparent to VSAM whether or not the collection of data elements it transfers is an IMS/VS segment, a conventional record or something else.

An IMS/VS physical data base is described by a DBD statement, which lists in parameter form the characteristics and attributes of the data base. In this sense, the data base can be thought of as a file in hierarchical form. Logical data bases, on the other hand, are those which unite some segments of one or more physical data bases in hierarchical form.

LOGICAL DATA BASE

Using the HISAM, HDAM and HIDAM storage structures provides the user with an additional capability. Since the segments in these two structures require pointers anyway, there is an additional capability that can be added by simply using a few more pointers. This additional capability is known as a logical relationship.

HISAM logical relationships are somewhat different than HDAM and HIDAM in that symbolic pointers are used. The direct access methods make use of relative byte address pointers since the segments once stored are never moved. In the explanations that follow there are a host of new terms used. It is not the

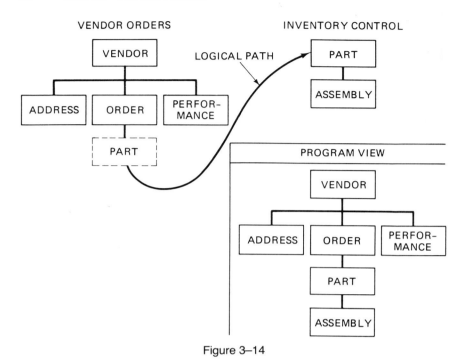

Figure 3–14

purpose of this discussion to plumb the depths of logical relationships, but merely to provide a conceptual understanding of what they are. There are numerous works already available describing logical relationships in considerable detail.[2,3] Some terms will be introduced, but not explained. The purpose here is to introduce the concept and those wishing to pursue more detail on the subject may do so in the abundant literature available on the subject.[4] The simplest way to introduce the functions of logical relationship is by way of illustration.

Using block diagrams and hierarchical structures, consider the following example: two separate physical data bases exist, one for vendor orders, the other for parts (Inventory Control). Assume there is a need for the part segment in the vendor order data base. Rather than store the part information twice, it can be stored once, and a logical relationship can be established between the data bases. Schematically it can be shown as in Fig. 3–14.

[2]Kapp, Dan and Joseph F. Leben, *IMS Programming Techniques, A Guide to Using DL/1*, Van Nostrand Reinhold Company, New York, 1978.

[3]Date, C. J., *An Introduction to Data Base Systems*, 2nd Edition, Addison-Wesley Publishing Company, Inc., Philippines, 1977.

[4]The IBM World Trade Systems Center IMS/VS Primer, #S320-5767, pp 1.7—1.12 and 2.11—2.31.

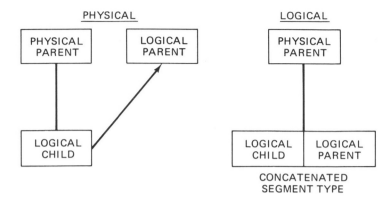

Figure 3–15
UNIDIRECTIONAL LOGICAL RELATIONSHIP

The terminology of logical relationships includes LOGICAL RELATION-SHIPs among segments establish LOGICAL DATA BASE RECORDs. A collection of LOGICAL DATA BASE RECORDs form a LOGICAL DATA BASE. In signifying logical as opposed to physical structures, one can use the adjective "logical" to modify all the terminology associated with hierarchical structures. There now exists LOGICAL PARENTS, LOGICAL CHILDREN and LOGICAL TWINS. There are three ways of establishing a logical relationship: UNIDIRECTIONAL, PHYSICALLY PAIRED BIDIRECTIONAL and VIRTUALLY PAIRED BIDIRECTIONAL. Now, if you think that's bad; when you get done with all that—you get a CONCATENATED SEGMENT TYPE. Last but not least, no overview of logical relationships would be complete without a list of the various types of pointers that are employed in the implementation of all of the above. There are LOGICAL PARENT pointers, LOGICAL CHILD FIRST pointers, LOGICAL CHILD LAST pointers, LOGICAL TWIN FORWARD pointers, LOGICAL TWIN BACKWARD pointers and PHYSICAL PARENT pointers. These pointers when used reside in a part of a segment called the "Prefix" and they do constitute overhead.

Let's take a brief look at the types of logical relationships.

UNIDIRECTIONAL LOGICAL RELATIONSHIP

Of the three methods of establishing a logical relationship, the Unidirectional Logical Relationship (Fig. 3–15) is the most simple. It simply establishes an additional hierarchical relationship where a subordinate segment becomes a logical child as well as a physical child. The concatenated segment type results in a joining of the data from both the logical child and logical parent.

BIDIRECTIONAL LOGICAL RELATIONSHIP

In a bidirectional logical relationship, the relationship is two-way. The resultant structures include two concatenated segment types. The schematics shown in Fig. 3–16 illustrate a bidirectional logical relationship.

Suppose the existence of two physical structures is as follows: There is a "parts" (No. 1) data base with a root segment containing "part" information and subordinate segments containing "stock status" information in multiple locations and "purchase order" information about vendors from whom the "parts" are purchased. There also exists a "customer orders" (No. 2) data base with a root segment containing information needed for customer orders and subordinate segments containing order line information for the line items on the order as well as shipping information. Suppose that a two-way relationship between the "order line" segment in the "customer order" data base and the "part" segment in the "parts" data base is established. This makes possible the retrieval of all "part" information for each order line of a customer order as well as relating each part to the customers who had ordered it.

The relationship between the physical data bases could be shown as in Fig. 3–17. Logically the relationships result in the structures shown in Fig. 3–18.

Logical relationship pointers also reside in segment "prefixes." The pointers in the prefixes are maintained and controlled by the IMS/VS-DB software. The establishment of pointers is specified by parameter entries made in the Data Base Definition (DBD) statements. As will be seen a little later on, the DBD

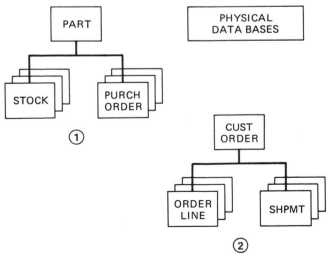

Figure 3–16
PHYSICAL DATA BASES

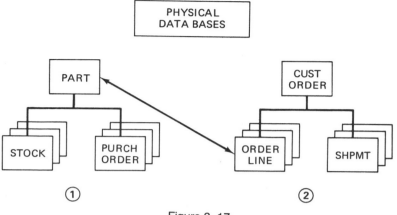

Figure 3–17
PHYSICAL DATA BASES

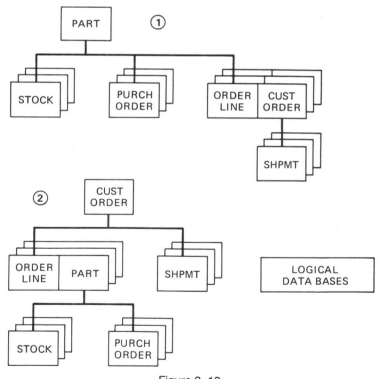

Figure 3–18
LOGICAL DATA BASES

statements specify information of structures (HSAM, etc.), logical relationships, physical relationships and secondary index relationships. It is to this last relationship that our attention is now focused.

SECONDARY INDEX

There is another way of relating data in one data base to that in another, namely, Secondary Indexing. It is quite a bit simpler to use and understand than a logical relationship.

The best way to define an IMS/VS Secondary Index is by using some new

Figure 3–19

terminology. Before doing that, a tool of Bible students can be used to illustrate the principle. There is another book called a Concordance, which lists every key word in the Bible in alphabetical order. Each occurrence of the word is carried within its immediate context and there is a reference (pointer) to book, chapter and verse on the same line. In Fig. 3–19, the word "world" as found in the Concordance, has as one of its occurrences, the verse in John's gospel that was used earlier. In this illustration, the Bible itself is the Data Base and the Concordance is the Secondary Index.

Another example of secondary indexing might be one which has an automobile data base and a secondary index by type of tire. In the illustration (Fig. 3–20), the tire data base is the secondary index. As can be seen, the segments of that data base contain the tire type and pointers to the specific automobiles (in the other data base) which use that type of tire.

One last set of schematics is presented to illustrate a secondary index as opposed to a primary index. The primary index could be set up in order to establish a HIDAM Data Base. Consider an employee data base as in Fig. 3–21.

Consider the same data base as a HIDAM data base where the order of the data base is employee number. The sequence of the data base and its index, in this example (Fig. 3–22), are in identical sequence. The primary index provides the user with direct access capabilities.

LOC	MAKE & MODEL	TIRE
040	Dodge Dart	C78-14
060	Dodge Sport	C78-14
060	Dodge Sport	C78-14
080	Dodge Aspen	C78-14
100	Dodge Colt	B78-13
120	Dodge Coronet	F78-14
140	Dodge Monaco	G78-14
160	Chrysler New Yorker	G78-14
180	Chrysler Brogham	G78-14
200	Chrysler Newport	G78-14
220	Plymouth Belvedere	D78-14
240	Plymouth Scamp	C78-14
260	Plymouth Fury I	E78-14
280	Plymouth Fury II	E78-14
320	Ford Fairlane	D78-14
340	Ford Galaxie	E78-14
360	Ford Custom	D78-14
380	Ford Mustang	C78-14
400	Ford Pinto	B78-13
420	Ford Maverick	C78-13
440	Mercury Monterey	D78-14
460	Mercury Montclair	F78-14
480	Mercury Meteor	D78-14
500	Mercury Comet	C78-14
520	Lincoln Continental	G78-14
540	Lincoln Mark IV	G78-14
560	Thunderbird	G78-14

LOC	MAKE & MODEL	TIRE
600	Chevrolet Caprice	F78-14
620	Chevrolet Impala	F78-14
640	Chevrolet Belair	E78-14
660	Chevrolet Nova	C78-14
680	Oldsmobile 98	G78-14
700	Oldsmobile 88	F78-14
720	Oldsmobile Cutlass	E78-14
740	Oldsmobile Omega	D78-14
760	Pontiac Gran Prix	E78-14
780	Pontiac Firebird	E78-14
800	Pontiac LeMans	D78-14
820	Pontiac Granville	E78-14
840	Pontiac Catalina	F78-14
860	Buick Skylark	D78-14
880	Buick Riviera	F78-14
900	Buick Wildcat	F78-14
920	Cadillac Fleetwood	G78-14
940	Cadillac Eldorado	G78-14

Tire	Pointers
B78-13	100, 400
C78-13	420
C78-14	040, 060, 080, 240, 380, 500, 660
D78-14	220, 320, 360, 440, 480, 740, 800, 860
E78-14	260, 280, 340, 640, 720, 760, 780, 820
F78-14	120, 460, 600, 620, 700, 840, 880, 900
G78-14	140, 160, 180, 200, 520, 540, 560, 680, 920, 940

Figure 3–20

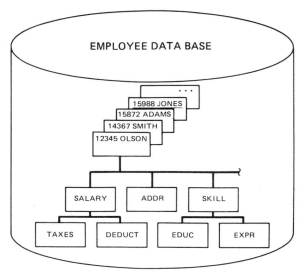

Figure 3–21

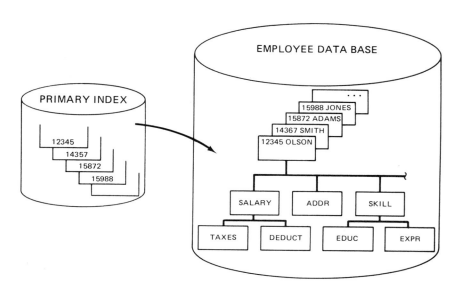

Figure 3–22
EMPLOYEE DATA BASE SEQUENCED ON EMPL. NO. INQUIRIES ARE BY
EMPL. NO.

ALTERNATE SEQUENCE VIA SECONDARY INDEXING

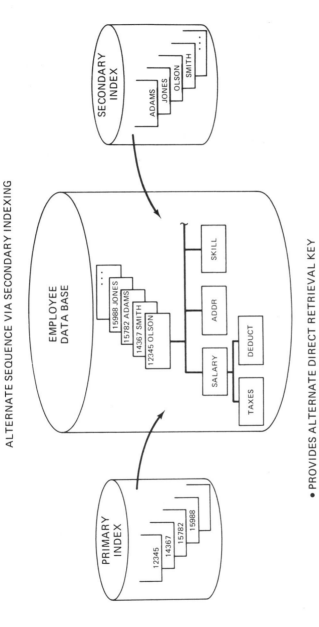

- PROVIDES ALTERNATE DIRECT RETRIEVAL KEY
- PROVIDES ABILITY TO PROCESS IN OTHER THAN ROOT KEY SEQUENCE

Figure 3–23

Suppose that the user needs to retrieve information by "employee name." The creation of a secondary index (Fig. 3–23) ordered on "employee name" makes that possible.

REVIEW

Before going on to the Data Base Administration (DBA) function, the material first discussed is recapped as follows:

1. There are four major access methods, or more properly called storage structures in an IMS/VS data base environment: HSAM, HISAM, HDAM and HIDAM.

2. Implementation of physical storage structures in IMS/VS is done in such a fashion as to create hierarchical structures.

3. Logical storage structures can be specified in addition to or "on top of" the physical storage structure. Logical storage structures are called logical relationships.

4. Secondary indexing provides processing of a data base by using an argument other than the primary key of the data base.

4
Data Base Administration in an IMS/VS Environment

DEFINITIONS OF DATA BASE ADMINISTRATOR

The "Data Base Administrator—(DBA)" is a brand new title for a brand new position that has come into existence as a result of the interest in data base processing. Like the terms "Data Base" and "Data Base Management Systems," there are as many definitions of the DBA as there are books on the subject. Samples appear below:

The Data Base Administrator (DBA)

C.J. Date

The Data Base Administrator (DBA) . . . is the person (or group of persons) responsible for overall control of the data base system. The DBA's responsibilities include the following:

● Deciding the information content of the data base

● Deciding the storage structure and the access strategy

● Liaising with users

63

● Defining authorization checks and validation procedures
● Monitoring performance and responding to changes in requirements

James Martin, *Principles of Data Base Management*

An individual with an overview of one or more data bases, who controls the design and use of these data bases.

Leo Cohen, in a speech at an AMA seminar

An experienced kamakazie pilot.

James Martin, *Computer Data Base Organization*

To oversee and maintain the global view of the data a new job title was introduced: data base administrator. The data base administrator is the custodian of the corporation's data—or that part of it which his system relates to. He controls the overall structure of the data.

Daniel S. Appleton "What a Data Base Isn't," *Datamation,* January 1977

. . . a data base will be supported by a storage and processing control system. This system manages the data base itself, receiving data from the input control system and passing it, on demand, to the output system. The processing and control system is an independent data base management system with built-in capabilities for controlling backup, recovery, data availability, security, computer efficiency, and so on. It is generally controlled by an individual called a Data Base Administrator.

IBM *IMS/VS DB Primer*

Because the actual implementation of the DBA function is largely dependent on a company's organization, we limit ourselves to a discussion of the characteristics of a DBA . . .

● The DBA provides standards for and controls the administration of the data bases and their use.

● The DBA provides guidance, review and approval of data base design.

● The DBA determines the rules of access to the data bases and monitors their security.

● The DBA controls the data base integrity and availability, . . .

● Etc.

For the following two basic reasons, I am not going to attempt a thorough discussion of the DBA function:

1. It is still quite fluid; many people are writing about it and the dust has not settled yet.

2. The scope of this book encompasses an installation and use of IMS/VS and Data Dictionary/Directory DD/D. A "full blown" discussion of the DBA function would exceed that scope.

I do believe that the description of the Data Base Administrator function found in this context is quite sound. It represents the experience of practitioners, and it fits in with all the definitions cited on the opening page of this chapter.

ACCESS METHODS

In an IMS/VS environment, a DBA has to be thoroughly familiar with the "access methods" of the system. These "access methods" or storage structures represent the ways in which segments of data are physically stored on the storage media, usually DASD devices, in an IMS/VS environment. Mentioned briefly in the preceding chapter, they are now examined in greater detail here.

HSAM: HIERARCHICAL SEQUENTIAL ACCESS METHOD

First, HSAM: Hierarchical Sequential Access Method is a sequential processing type of structure. Sequential processing is the most familiar type of processing. One starts at the beginning and processes each succeeding record until the end is reached.

Looking at HSAM in some detail, the following characteristics can be observed:

1. Segments of a data base record are related by physical adjacency

2. Data is stored and processed as a sequential data set although some random processing is possible

3. Only access method that uses tape

4. Only access method not supported by VSAM

5. No logging, recovery or reorganization

6. No capability for update, inserts or deletes

7. *Uses:* Historic files

A good description of HSAM would be "tapelike." It is supported by the sequential access methods (SAM, BSAM and QSAM) (see Fig. 4–1).

The next schematic (Fig. 4–2) shows the actual logical structure and the physical storage of a HSAM data base record. Notice especially the "top to bottom, left to right'' storage of the segments as dictated by the hierarchical structure.

In IMS/VS, a HSAM Data Base is structured hierarchically and the sequence is such that one segment follows another contiguously. Block size is established when the Data Base is defined (Data Base Definition—DBD). The schematic shows the logical structure and the physical organization. In a HSAM data base, the segments and the records are contiguous within the constraints of the block size.

HISAM: HIERARCHICAL INDEXED SEQUENTIAL ACCESS METHOD

The Hierarchical Indexed Sequential Access Method (HISAM) is an indexed sequential type of processing. The actual data to be retrieved need not necessarily be in absolute physical sequence, but an index to the data is arranged in sequence.

The HISAM organization has the following characteristics:

1. Segments of a data base record are related by physical adjacency

2. Access to a data base record is through a root segment key via an index

3. Space of deleted segments is seldom reusable until reorganization

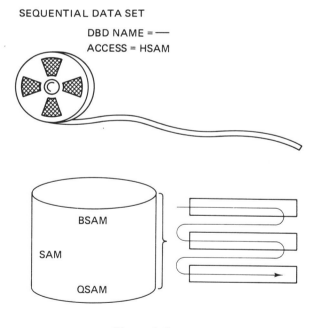

SEQUENTIAL DATA SET

DBD NAME = —

ACCESS = HSAM

Figure 4–1

HSAM

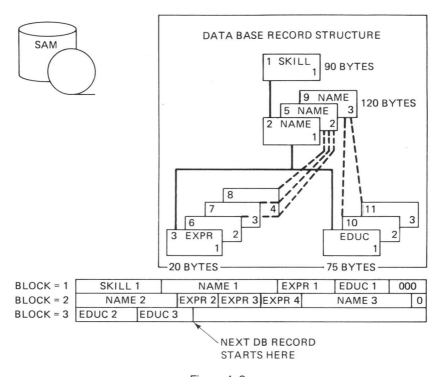

Figure 4–2

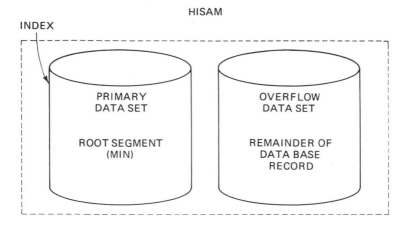

Figure 4–3
HISAM: THE TWO DATA SETS

4.   Large volume of inserts and deletes can degrade *performance*

5.   Capability for recovery and reorganization

6.   *Uses:* Applications that process data sequentially

    A HISAM Data Base consists of at least two data sets, a primary data set and an overflow data set. The primary data set must contain the root segment. It may contain other segments. The overflow data set contains those segments that do not fit in the primary data set. The data in the primary data set is accessed via an index. The data in the overflow data set is accessed via pointers.

    The following illustrations convey the idea of the HISAM organization. The first (Fig. 4–3) shows the two data sets, the second (Fig. 4–4) shows the logical structure and the physical organization on the storage device.

HDAM: HIERARCHICAL DIRECT ACCESS METHOD

The Hierarchical Direct Access Method (HDAM) is one in which segments are retrievable by location or address. The characteristics of a HDAM data base are:

1.   Segments of a data base record are related by direct address pointers

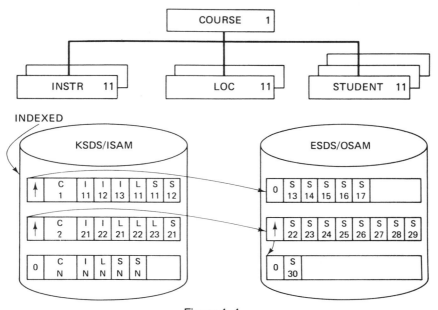

Figure 4–4

HISAM: LOGICAL STRUCTURE AND PHYSICAL ORGANIZATION ON THE
STORAGE DEVICE

2. Access to a data base record is through a root segment via a randomizing module

3. Segments once stored never move

4. Space of deleted segments is immediately reusable

5. Capability for recovery and reorganization

6. *Uses:* Applications processing data primarily randomly and on-line.

The schematic (Fig. 4–5) illustrates the HDAM methodology. The HDAM Data Base is one in which root segments are retrievable by location or address. The application program must contain a randomizing algorithm that calculates the address from the search key of the data segment to be retrieved. As with HISAM, some additional segments can cohabitate in the same physical block as the root segment (that segment containing the key). Those segments that do not physically fit in that block are stored in an overflow block.

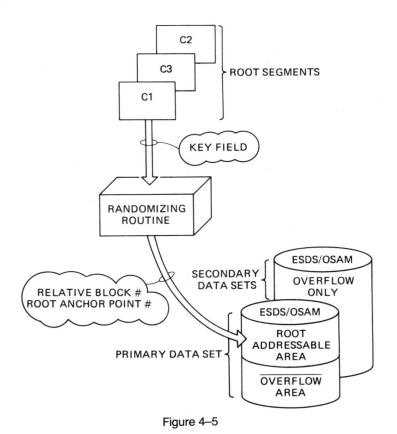

Figure 4–5

This next schematic (Fig. 4–6) shows the logical structure and the physical storage organization of the data in a HDAM data base. Notice the pointers even in those instances where the data segments are physically contiguous. Pointers are necessary since (even though segments may be contiguous) they quite often are not contiguous and must be retrieved through the use of the direct address pointer mechanism.

Since the root segments of a HDAM data base reside in a root addressable area of an OSAM or ESDS data set, two pieces of information are used to constitute the physical location of that segment: the relative block number and the root anchor point. The relative block number identifies the block within the

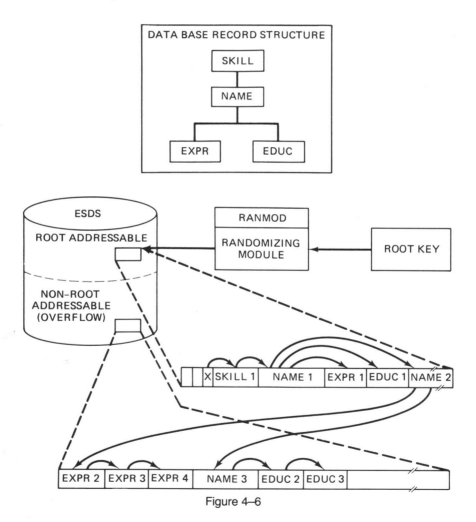

Figure 4–6

physical data base, the root anchor point (RAP) identifies the root segment within the block. Figure 4–7 illustrates the RAP.

HIDAM: HIERARCHICAL INDEXED DIRECT ACCESS METHOD

The Hierarchical Indexed Direct Access Method is one in which access to a data base record is through an index rather than through a randomizing algorithm. This structure represents an attempt to structure data in such a way that it can be processed both directly and sequentially. The characteristics of a HIDAM data base are listed below:

1. Segments of a data base record are related by direct address pointers

2. Random access to a data base record is through a root segment via an index

3. Segments once stored never move

4. Space of deleted segments is immediately reusable

5. Capability for recovery and reorganization

6. *Uses:* Applications processing mixture of sequential and random
    Large number of segments within the data base record
    Large volume of insert/delete activity

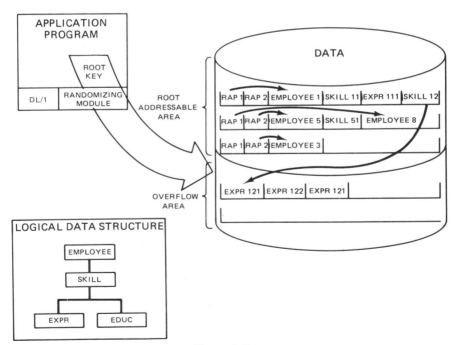

Figure 4–7

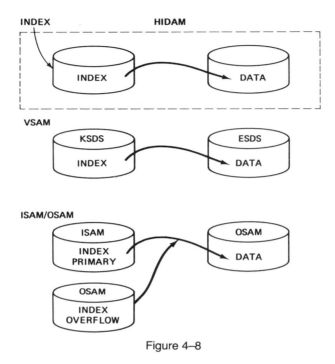

Figure 4–8

When using HIDAM, there is a subtle difference between using it with VSAM data sets and using it with non-VSAM data sets. With VSAM, the index is always kept in physical sequence, even when inserts are made. With non-VSAM, that is ISAM/OSAM, index inserts are put into an overflow data set. Although logical sequence is maintained, physical sequence is not. The obvious trade-off is that VSAM inserts take longer, but the retrieval overhead is kept to a minimum. Figure 4–8 shows the different kinds of data sets used in the alternative methods.

The next illustration (Fig. 4–9) shows the relationships as they appear with a HIDAM data base.

GSAM AND SHISAM

There are two other IMS/VS access methods worth mentioning since they have specific uses. The Generalized Sequential Access Method (GSAM) provides accessing support for simple sequential data sets, such as tape files, SYSIN and SYSOUT data sets and the like, which are not hierarchical. The Simple Hierarchical Indexed Sequential Access Method (SHISAM) supports root segments only. It is used to process non-DL/1 data sets as DL/1 data sets. It is used as a migration tool during conversions. It is not recommended for new data bases.

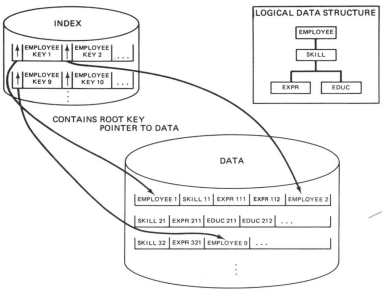

Figure 4–9

REVIEW OF ACCESS METHODS

One final look at the IMS/VS structures, by way of a comparison, is shown in the following chart:

ACCESS METHOD COMPARISON

Characteristics	HSAM	HISAM	HDAM	HIDAM
Reorganization requirements	no	high	low	low
Recovery capability	no	yes	yes	yes
Number of data sets	1	2 or more	1	2 or more
Ability to reuse space	no	some	good	good
Application Requirements				
Sequential processing of root	yes	yes	no	yes
Random processing of root	no	yes	best	yes
High insert/delete activity	no	fair ·	good	good

DBA FUNCTION

Basically, the DBA is responsible for what was once file design, but is now significantly more complex. The DBA in an IMS/VS environment defines Data Bases from both a global perspective (DBD) and from an individual program's perspective (PCB and PSB). It is the function of the DBA to establish an interface between the program and the Data Base, maintaining a separation between the program and the physical characteristics of the Data Base.

WHO IS THE DBA?

Many of the definitions and much of the contemporary literature on the subject of Data Base Administration seems to indicate that the "DBA" is an individual. This is quite often not the case. Data Base Administration is a function that consists of many jobs or tasks that have to be done. As a function, depending on the size and complexity of a specific organization, the DBA function often consists of several individuals, all technically skilled. In the near future this skill will become as necessary and critical as the current "Systems Software" skill, which is so integral a part of every large scale computer installation.

NORMAL OS APPLICATION PROGRAM

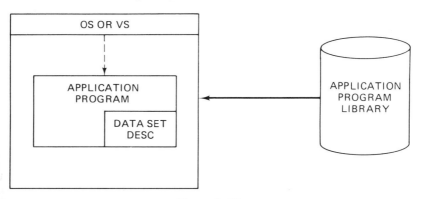

Figure 4–10

SEPARATE THE PROGRAM FROM THE
PHYSICAL CHARACTERISTICS OF THE
DATA FILES

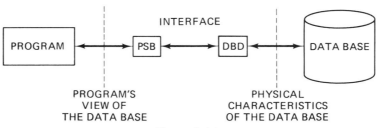

Figure 4–11

FILE RESPONSIBILITIES

To put the function of the DBA in perspective, recall the file definitions or data set descriptions of conventional data processing or computer programming. Each application program that is written must contain a file definition or data set description for each file or data set that it uses (Fig. 4–10).

The function of defining an entire file (data base) is being removed from the application programmer and being given to the DBA. This does not, contrary to popular belief, remove all responsibility for file (data base) specification from the programmer. The programmer still must specify in his program that portion of the file (data base) which he is to use. However, the DBA is responsible for the design and specification of the global file (data base) and responsible also for the subsetting of the data base by segments to specific application areas. In broad terms, the DBA is responsible for keeping application programs from being dependent on the physical characteristics of data bases. Schematically, an overview of the DBA function is shown in Fig. 4–11.

DATA PARAMETERS: DBD AND PSB

In order to perform the function in an IMS/VS Data Base environment, the DBA must supply some parameters to the system. These parameters take the form of two basic types, the Data Base Description (DBD), which describes both physical and logical Data Bases, and the Program Specification Block (PSB), which describes individual programs' views of Data Bases and Terminal Networks. The DBD is designed to perform two functions:

1. DEFINE THE PHYSICAL STORAGE OF THE DATA
    DATA SET GROUPS
    ACCESS METHODS

2. DEFINE THE LOGICAL STRUCTURE OF THE DATA
    DATA BASE NAME
    SEGMENT NAMES AND RELATIONSHIPS (PHYSICAL RELATION-SHIPS, LOGICAL RELATIONSHIPS, SECONDARY INDEX RELATIONSHIPS)
    FIELD NAMES AND ATTRIBUTES
        KEY FIELDS
        SEARCH FIELDS
        INDEXED FIELDS

The DBA enters parameters in a source level form. The information is generally keypunched into cards for entry into the computer. It then goes through a compiler and in "load module" format it is stored in a library as a control block. The control block is retrieved by IMS/VS at the times required, that is, when application programs needing that control block information are ready to execute. The following series of schematics illustrate:

1. The "DBDGEN" data flow (Fig. 4–12)
2. A sample of DBD statements (Fig. 4–13)
3. A DBD structure as defined by the sample DBD statements (Fig. 4–14)

DATA BASE DESCRIPTION (DBD)

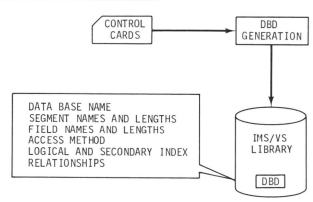

Figure 4–12
DATA BASE DESCRIPTION (DBD)

DBD	NAME = BUDGET, ACCESS = HISAM
DATASET	DD1 = BUDGHISM, DEVICE = 3330, OVFLW = BUDGOVF
SEGM	NAME = DIVSUMM, PARENT = 0, BYTES = 30, FREQ = 50
FIELD	NAME = (DIVID, SEQ, U), BYTES = 2, START = 1, TYPE = C
FIELD	NAME = ACCTTYPE, BYTES = 1, START = 3, TYPE = C
SEGM	NAME = DEPTSUMM, PARENT = DIVSUMM, BYTES = 40, FREQ = 10
FIELD	NAME = (DEPTID, SEQ, U), BYTES = 2, START = 1, TYPE = C
FIELD	NAME = MGRID, BYTES = 3, START = 3, TYPE = C
FIELD	NAME = BUDGAMT, BYTES = 5, START = 6, TYPE = C
SEGM	NAME = ITEMSUMM, PARENT = DEPTSUMM, BYTES = 36, FREQ = 10
FIELD	NAME = (ITEMID, SEQ, U), BYTES = 2, START = 1, TYPE = C
FIELD	NAME = ITEMTYPE, BYTES = 2, START = 3, TYPE = C
SEGM	NAME = BUDGTSEG, PARENT = ITEMSUMM, BYTES = 10, FREQ = 10
FIELD	NAME = (BUDGTYR, SEQ, U), BYTES = 4, START = 1, TYPE = C
SEGM	NAME = DEBTDAI, PARENT = ITEMSUMM, BYTES = 12, FREQ = 10, RULES = FIRST
FIELD	NAME = (DEBTDATE, SEQ, M), BYTES = 6, START = 1, TYPE = C
SEGM	NAME = CRDTDAI, PARENT = ITEMSUMM, BYTES = 12, FREQ = 10, RULES = FIRST
FIELD	NAME = (CRDTDATE, SEQ, M), BYTES = 6, START = 1, TYPE = C
DBDGEN	
FINISH	
END	

Figure 4–13
SAMPLE DBD

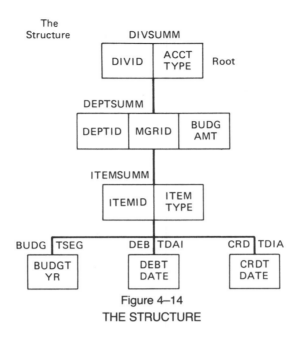

Figure 4–14
THE STRUCTURE

Below are the characteristics of a PSB. The PSB is designed to:

1. DEFINE TO IMS WHICH LOGICAL TERMINALS (LTERM'S) THE APPLI-CATION PROGRAM WISHES TO USE

2. DEFINE TO IMS WHICH DATA BASES (DBD'S) THE APPLICATION PRO-GRAM WISHES TO USE

3. DEFINE TO IMS WHICH SEGMENTS OF THE SELECTED DATA BASE(S) THE APPLICATION PROGRAM WISHES TO USE

4. DEFINE TO IMS HOW THE APPLICATION PROGRAM WISHES TO USE THE SELECTED SEGMENTS (GET, INSERT, REPLACE, DELETE)

5. DEFINE ADDITIONAL INFORMATION SUCH AS CONCATENATED KEY LENGTHS, MULTIPLE OR SINGLE POSITIONING AND SECONDARY INDEX DATA BASE USED TO PROCESS THE NAMED DATA BASE

There is one PSB per application program running in the system at any given time.

The process of putting together a PSB is similar operationally to the putting together of the DBD. Entering parameters, compiling, creating of control blocks and storing in a library are the operational steps taken. A couple of additional observations should be made at this point. First, the PSB is made up of individual PCBs. A PCB is a Program Communications Block. For each data base view and logical terminal used by the program, there is one PCB. All PCBs taken

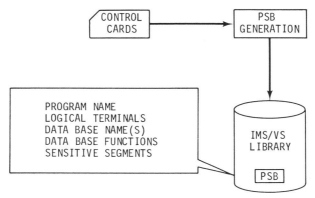

Figure 4–15
PROGRAM SPECIFICATION BLOCK (PSB)

```
PCB        TYPE = DB, DBDNAME = LEDGER, PROCOPT = A, KEYLEN = 12
SENSEG     NAME = ACCTSUMM, PARENT = Ø, PROCOPT = GR
SENSEG     NAME = DEBTDTL, PARENT = ACCTSUMM
SENSEG     NAME = CRDTDTL, PARENT = ACCTSUMM
PCB        TYPE = DB, DBDNAME = BUDGET, PROCOPT = A, KEYLEN = 12
SENSEG     NAME = DIVSUMM, PARENT = Ø
SENSEG     NAME = DEPTSUMM, PARENT = DIVSUMM, PROCOPT = G
SENSEG     NAME = ITEMSUMM, PARENT = DEPTSUMM
SENSEG     NAME = BUDGTSEG, PARENT = ITEMSUMM, PROCTOPT = GRD
SENSEG     NAME = DEBTDAI, PARENT = ITEMSUMM
PSBGEN     LANG = ASSEM, PSBNAME = YOURPROG
END
```

Figure 4–16
SAMPLE PSB

The Structures

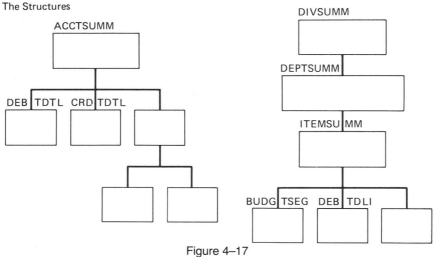

Figure 4–17
THE STRUCTURES

together for one application program comprise a PSB. The second observation regards the DBD and PSB control blocks. At the time that a program is to execute, information from the DBD control block and the PSB control block are combined into another control block called an Application Control Block (ACB). When a batch program is run, the ACB is put together just before the program executes. When on-line, transaction programs are run, the ACB is put together ahead of time and kept in an ACB library. This "precompiled" ACB is retrieved "ready for execution" when a transaction program is called, so as to minimize run time for that program.

The following schematics illustrate:

1. A "PSBGEN" data flow (Fig. 4–15)
2. A sample of PSB statements (Fig. 4–16)
3. PSB structures as defined by the sample PSB statements (Fig. 4–17)

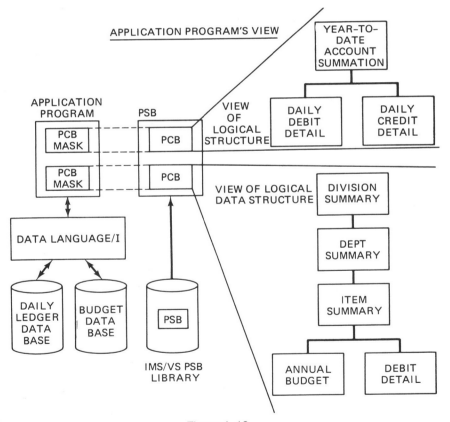

Figure 4–18
APPLICATION PROGRAM'S VIEW

DATA BASE PROCESSING

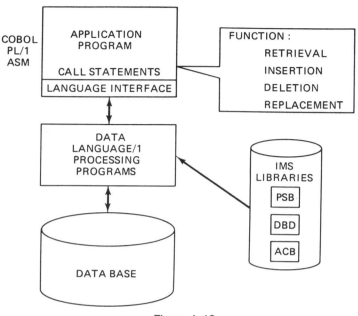

Figure 4–19
DATA BASE PROCESSING

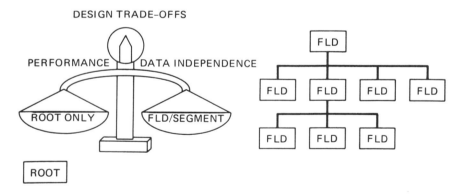

- FASTEST ACCESS
- SIMPLEST DESIGN
- LESS IMS DASD OVERHEAD
- LESS CPU OVERHEAD

- SECURITY BY SEGMENT TYPE
- DATA INDEPENDENCE
- ELIMINATION OF REDUNDANT
  DATA (LOGICAL RELATIONSHIPS)

Figure 4–20
A BALANCE BETWEEN EXTREMES

This next schematic (Fig. 4–18) provides a conceptual overview of the procedures just discussed, the PCB, the PSB and their interface through DL/1 to the Data Bases.

SUMMARY OF DATA BASE

Before beginning an examination of the Data Communications (DC) feature of IMS/VS, a summary of the Data Base (DB) feature is in order. The DB feature provides the facilities to define physical and logical data bases (DBD). Specific views of subsets of data bases can also be defined (PSB). There is an interface routine for each of the programming languages of PL/1, COBOL and ALC, which facilitates application programming using DL/1 access methods and structures (HSAM, HISAM, HDAM and HIDAM). A pictorial summary, Fig. 4–19, indicates these facilities.

This next illustration (Fig. 4–20) shows in broadest terms the Data Base design trade-offs. For example, a root only data base (actually the same thing as a conventional record) provides fast access, but at the cost of potentially providing for and transferring extraneous data when it is not being used. The trade-offs are obvious from the illustration. There is a strong indication here for the DBA to consider carefully the usage of the data in designing the Data Base.

One final note. Creating a data base structure is quite complex and requires careful study, but that does not complete the effort. The actual creation of the Data Base with the data in it is also quite a task. Creating a data base structure is like building the frame of a house. Creating a data base is like making that frame into a home, with windows, a furnace, furniture, plumbing, curtains and carpets. The creator must be able to get "the data," and then get it into the data base structure. This second half of the job is often more difficult than the first and is often overlooked in the planning stages.

5
IMS/VS—the DC Feature

The two preceding chapters had a lot of explanation regarding the DB feature of IMS/VS. To many of you, the type of processing described in those pages represented something of a departure from the kind of processing with which you were already familiar. To many, the idea of structuring data segments and relating those segments to one another in a fashion transcending file and record boundaries represents something new. It is that kind of data structuring that makes IMS/VS and other Data Base Management Systems different from more conventional processing.

The DC feature, on the other hand, does not represent anything quite so radical—at least from a conceptual point of view. The Data Communication feature is a teleprocessing network management system that is used exclusively with IMS/VS-DB. Those of you who have worked with "on-line" teleprocessing systems will find nothing conceptually different in IMS/VS-DC. Consequently, the treatment of the DC feature of IMS/VS is shorter than the treatment of the DB feature.

IMPORTANCE OF DC FEATURE

And yet, even though treatment is less, the real power of IMS/VS is realized only when the DC feature is installed together with the DB feature. It is the implementation of the DC feature that requires the most significant amount of effort from systems software personnel. It is the installation of the DC feature that permits the "on-line" access to IMS/VS data bases. It is the DC feature that requires a Master Terminal Operator to monitor the activity in the system to make operational adjustments to the system and to react to unusual conditions that arise. Subsequent pages contain a description of the DC feature and its components.

THE DC FEATURE AND ITS COMPONENTS

The Data Communication feature of IMS/VS is a facility for processing single transactions in an "on-line" environment, using Data Bases. Figure 5–1 illustrates the difference between a "batch" and an "on-line" environment.

The next two schematics (Figs. 5–2 and 5–3) present different overviews of the IMS/VS-DC feature. The first (Fig. 5–2) is a conceptual overview of an IMS/VS-Data Base/Data Communications system. Included in the environment under the operating system, IMS/VS includes a terminal manager, a processing manager and a data manager. Collectively these three managers are known as the IMS Control Region, as can be seen in the second schematic. This second schematic (Fig. 5–3) is an architectural overview.

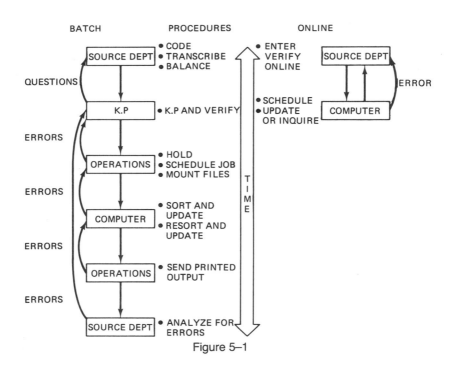

Figure 5–1

IMS CONTROL REGION

The entire system runs under the operating system. IMS/VS has the capability of initiating and running multiple jobs on a concurrent basis. These jobs can be a mix of on-line and batch programs. The IMS control system, which resides in the IMS Control Region, oversees and manages the activities of the various programs running under IMS/VS.The control system interfaces between the operating system and the programs and provides other services as shown in Fig. 5–4.

The next schematic (Fig. 5–5) shows a number of the specific functions performed by the IMS/VS Control Region. It handles messages from remote terminals, schedules application programs, performs system logging functions, manages message queues, etc.

A typical IMS/VS-DC setup contains a number of processing regions, which can be a mixture of on-line processing type regions, known as message processing regions (MPRs) and batch processing type regions, known as batch message processing regions (BMPs). In addition, a separate Data Base (DB) region can also process transactions apart from the IMS/VS-DC Control Region. This separate DB region does not have access to the Data Bases that are under the control of the IMS/VS-DC Control Region. This DB region also has its own log file for each job that executes. The IMS/VS-DC region, on the other hand, shares Data Bases among all jobs running under its control, both batch and on-line. It also has a common log.

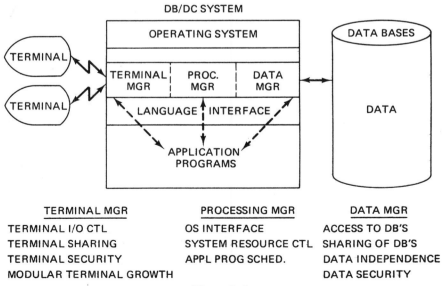

Figure 5–2
A CONCEPTUAL OVERVIEW

Figure 5–6 shows a number of Message Regions and a Batch Message Region. These regions are all under the control of the IMS Control Region. Any program running in these regions can access IMS data bases also under the control of the IMS Control Region. The system log records all transactions, "before" and "after" versions of the modified data base segments, checkpoint inquiries, commands and other system data.

STAND ALONE REGIONS

In addition, Fig. 5–6 shows a separate region, a batch region, not under the control of the IMS Control Region. This represents a "stand alone" DB or DL/1 region that can process concurrently with the IMS Control Region. However, this region has its own log facility, which closes a log tape at the conclusion of every batch job run in that region. Only batch jobs can run in this separate region, and they cannot access either data bases or log files that are under the

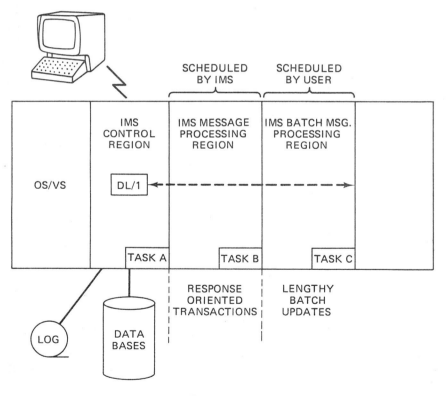

Figure 5–3
AN ARCHITECTURAL OVERVIEW

control of the IMS Control Region. This stand alone batch DL/1 region could be thought of as a completely separate OS/VS job, completely unrelated to the IMS/VS Control Region.

THE DC FEATURE SUPPORTS PHYSICAL AND LOGICAL TERMINALS

The Data Communications (DC) feature of IMS/VS does for terminal networks what the Data Base (DB) feature does for Data Bases. Whereas the DB feature supports physical and logical data bases, the DC feature supports physical and logical terminals. The application programmer does not have to be concerned with writing the programming instructions for a particular physical device.

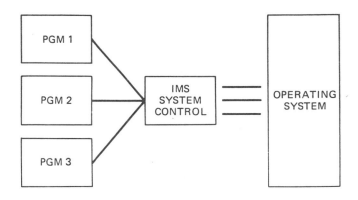

* PROGRAM SCHEDULING – CLASS/PRIORITY
                  – DEMAND
* PROGRAM ISOLATION
* TERMINAL MANAGEMENT
* CHECKPOINT/RESTART
* SECURITY
* MASTER TERMINAL FUNCTIONS
* CONCURRENT DATA BASE USE BY BATCH AND ON-LINE PROGRAMS
* STATISTICS AND UTILITIES
* RESOURCE MANAGEMENT – MSG QUEUE
                  – POOLS

Figure 5–4

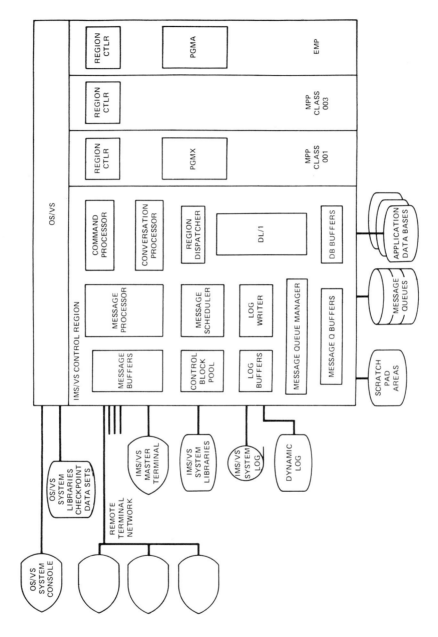

Figure 5–5

88

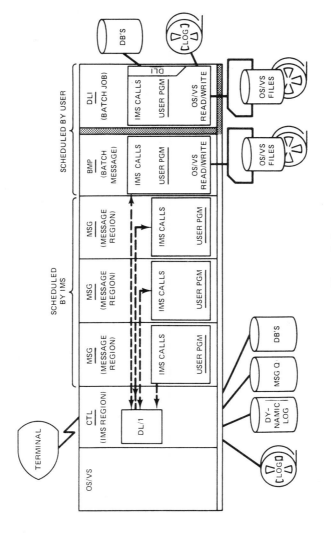

Figure 5-6

89

There is another individual called the Data Communications Administrator (DCA) who handles the communications network descriptions in much the same way as the DBA handles the data base descriptions. The skill this individual possesses is one of the jobs that falls within the jurisdiction of the Data Base Administration function. In actuality, there may be a need for several individuals to perform the DCA tasks, depending upon the size and complexity of the communications network in the organization being served. Figure 5–7 portrays the Logical Terminal concept.

This next illustration makes a pictorial comparison of what DB does for a data base and what DC does for a terminal through the statements of a PCB (see Fig. 5–8).

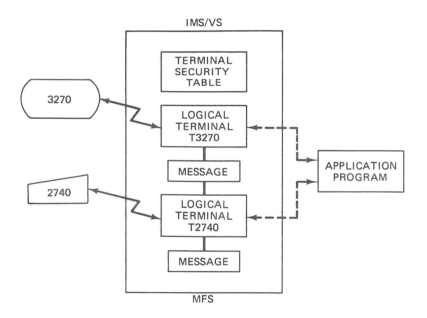

- ALL PHYSICAL TERMINALS ARE ASSIGNED A LOGICAL TERMINAL NAME (T3270, T2740)

- APPLICATION PROGRAMS ACCESS TERMINALS BY LTERM NAME, INDEPENDENT OF:
  - TERMINAL ADDRESS
  - LINE DISCIPLINE
  - DEVICE CHARACTERISTICS

- INTEGRAL WITH TERMINAL SECURITY

Figure 5–7

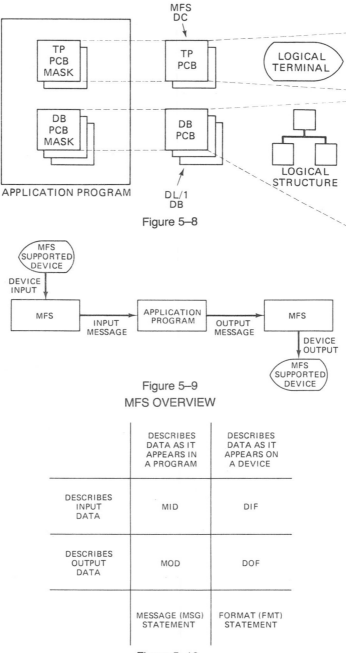

Figure 5–8

Figure 5–9

MFS OVERVIEW

	DESCRIBES DATA AS IT APPEARS IN A PROGRAM	DESCRIBES DATA AS IT APPEARS ON A DEVICE
DESCRIBES INPUT DATA	MID	DIF
DESCRIBES OUTPUT DATA	MOD	DOF
	MESSAGE (MSG) STATEMENT	FORMAT (FMT) STATEMENT

Figure 5–10

MESSAGE FORMAT SERVICES

The specific facility of the Data Communications feature that allows the user to deal with simple logical messages without having to concern himself with device characteristics is called Message Format Services (MFS). MFS statements are prepared by a Data Communications Administrator. They are compiled, in a fashion similar to the DBDGEN and PSBGEN (described earlier) and stored in a library. When needed, they are retrieved from the library. Figure 5–9 provides an MFS overview.

The MFS facility contains four kinds of descriptions or formats:

1. Message Input Description (MID)
2. Message Output Description (MOD)
3. Device Input Format (DIF)
4. Device Output Format (DOF)

The grid in Fig. 5–10 indicates the function of MIDs, MODs, DIFs and DOFs.

The compilation and storage of MFS control blocks is an off-line operation, but once in place, the on-line Message Format Service flow could be pictured as in Fig. 5–11.

A final MFS schematic (Fig. 5–12) is used to illustrate a formatting scheme as it might be done for a group of different terminal device types.

DC FEATURE IN ACTION

One final look at the DC feature is seen in Fig. 5–13 showing the flow of a transaction through the IMS/VS-DB/DC system.

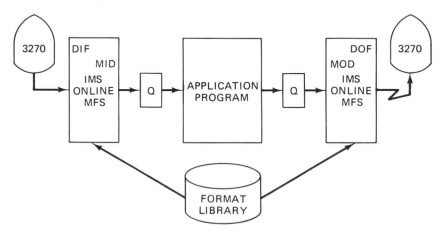

Figure 5–11

1. The Communications Control subsystem invites input and reads it from the terminal.

2. MFS edits the input message, restructuring it to get it out of device format and into a form suitable for the program processing it.

3. The logging subsystem logs the input.

4. The queue managing routines enter the message onto the input queue.

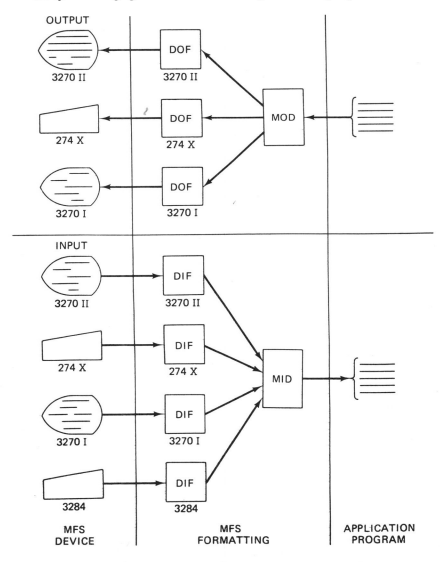

Figure 5–12

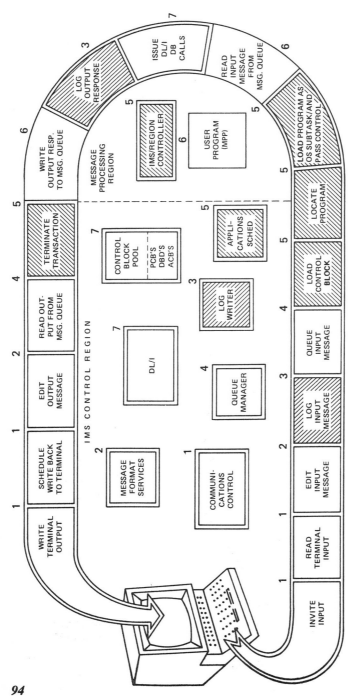

Figure 5-13

5. The region controller and application scheduler then retrieve the necessary control blocks (DBD-PSB or ACB), locate the program and load it into a message processing region (MPR) or a batch message processing region (BMP).

6. The user program reads the input message from the queue and processes it.

7. While processing is going on, DL/1 calls are issued against data bases.

3. A response is formed, and the log writer puts out the response to the log.

6. The user program writes the response to the output queue

5. The application scheduler terminates the processing of the transaction.

4. The queue manager gets the response from the queue and passes it to MFS.

2. MFS puts the response into a format suitable to the device to which it is being sent.

1. Finally, the communications control subsystem schedules the message to be written to the device and then sends it back to the terminal.

MASTER TERMINAL OPERATION

Another area of IMS/VS worthy of mention is the Master Terminal Operation (MTO) function. Control of the system belongs to a function called Master Terminal Operations. This function interacts directly with the system. The Master Terminal Operations function is directly or indirectly responsible for starting up communications lines, reassigning terminals, starting message processing regions (for processing transactions), invoking certain checkpoints, displaying system status, etc. The Master Terminal function is a system resource controller. The illustration (Fig. 5–14) shows the activities of the MTO. Appendix B contains a more detailed treatment of this function.

SUMMARY

To summarize, IMS/VS is a versatile Data Base Management System. It may be the largest DBMS on the market today. It is a powerful tool, but it is also expensive. In order to use the facilities it offers, a significant cost will be paid in overhead, both processing and storage. However, it must be pointed out that DBMS themselves are inherently expensive in terms of overhead. On balance, IMS/VS is a DBMS that gives you what you pay for. It may be more expensive than some systems, but the facilities offered justify the expense. If you don't need the facilities, then don't get the system; but if you need or want the facilities, then be forewarned, they ain't free. Figure 5–15 is simply a way of showing graphically that in IMS/VS (or in any other DBMS), "There's a lot of software between you and your data bases."

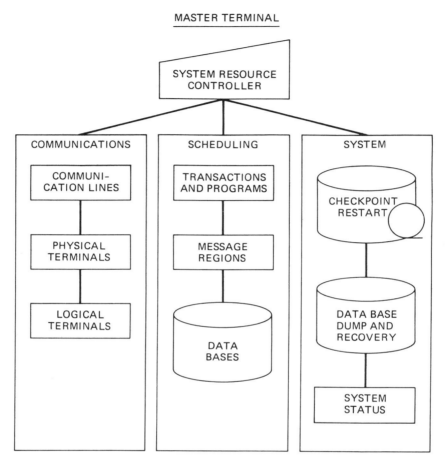

Figure 5–14

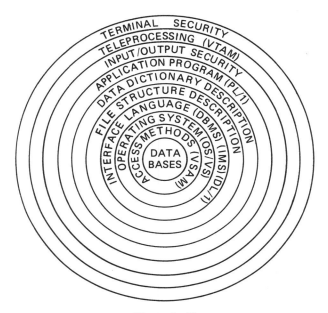

Figure 5–15

6
Data Dictionary

Currently there is a great deal of attention being given to Data Base Management Systems (DBMS). Yet it is not Data Base Management Systems that provide the essential facilities for data base administration and data administration. Although technically complex, a DBMS is merely an operating system for data. As a matter of fact, when IBM's operating system was first announced, its main features were known as job management, task management and data management. Data management in that context involved the access to and retrieval of data from files or data sets. Data base management adds a degree of sophistication to data management in that it permits the access to and the retrieval of data from data bases. The degree of sophistication is added since data bases are composed of files and data sets whose parts are interrelated with one another in associations that transcend file and data set boundaries. At the present time everyone is talking about them because they represent a significant technological step forward. The techniques employed by Data Base Systems are technically sophisticated and therefore, many bright, technically inclined individuals are attracted by them.

WHAT A DATA DICTIONARY DOES

The subject of Data Dictionary, on the other hand, is quite dull. From a historical perspective, Data Dictionaries have been essentially automated documentation

•	
•	
•	
A R K	1328, 1799, 1436
CALIF	6473, 9214
•	
•	
•	
WISC	7217, 7366, 4211, 8467, 3244
WYO	5211, 4835, 9476

Figure 6–1

tools, and many bright, technically inclined individuals have not been attracted by them. However, contemporary Data Dictionary packages and facilities have evolved to the point where they are more than documentation tools. Data Dictionaries provide the essential facilities for data base administration and data administration.

An awareness of this situation has led to the development of Data Dictionary software packages that contain facilities beyond those of mere documentation. For example, IBM's package Data Dictionary/Directory (DD/D) has the ability to generate definition statements that are used as input into the IMS/VS Data Base Management System. It is also capable of producing computer programming language data definitions. These data structures (PL/1 INCLUDES, Assembler and COBOL COPYs) are stored in computer libraries. They can subsequently be retrieved and used together with procedural statements in the compilation of application programs. The DD/D package also includes a facility called a "Directory," which contains information about relationships among data bases, data segments and data elements. These features are offered in addition to the documentation capabilities, which are also part of the package.

THE CONCEPT OF DATA DIRECTORY

At this point, a digression is necessary, so that the concept of a Directory can be discussed. This term, like several others found in the vocabulary of DBMS practitioners, has more than one meaning. Facilities called Directories or Data Directories are found in some Data Base Management Systems packages. They are also found in some Data Dictionary packages. The precise definition of a Data Directory is a function of the type of software package in which it is found.

In most DBMSs containing a Data Directory, the feature is a table or index facility. The tables or indices contain two types of elements. One type of element is a data value, like "CALIF." for state. The other type of element is addresses. The addresses specify the actual location of the values. Figure 6–1 is a crude example used to illustrate a "Directory" in this context. The values ARK, CALIF, . . . WISC and WYO are state names that appear in various places within files, data sets or data bases. The values 1328, 1799 . . . 9476 are addresses of storage locations where the values can be found within the files, data sets or data bases.

Data Directory features are also quite often included in Data Dictionary packages. In the Data Dictionary/Directory (DD/D) System, for example, the directory feature is that by which relationships among data elements are established and maintained. It is these relationships that facilitate searching of dictionary data bases for specific types or classes of information. Contemporary Data Dictionary packages generally do not contain a Data Directory facility in which there are tables or indices having actual data element addresses. There are, however, some Inquiry packages[1] that contain both Data Directory and Data Dictionary features and carry both under the single name Data Dictionary. What exists here is another example of semantic confusion. Two different facilities are being called by the same name. This is not terribly uncommon. An examination of a number of contemporary Data Base Management Systems would reveal several other examples of this very thing. In the future, as DBMS and Data Dictionary software are combined, the semantic difficulty surrounding the term "Data Directory" may or may not be resolved. If it is, confusion can be minimized; if it is not, confusion can be expected to increase.

CURRENT THINKING ON DATA DICTIONARIES

At this time, current literature "in the trade" is heavily weighted toward treating the intricacies of Data Base Management Systems. The amount of material on Data Dictionaries is microscopic by comparison. Yet there is some. Let's use some of the current literature to get a feel for the current thinking on Data Dictionary. In two of his books, James Martin defines a Data Dictionary as: "A catalogue of all data types giving their names and structures."[2] Martin goes on to state:

> The data dictionary can be used in two types of ways. It can be used by people, and it can be used by the data base software . . . .
> The data dictionary is used in different ways by different types of people. The data base administrator needs a dictionary to help ensure consistency among the data items, to educate users about the data base content, and to help ensure that different departments define the same data in the same way. The systems analysts may use it to see what data are available when they are designing applications. The programmers may use it to ensure that they have the name and coding of data items or segments correct in their programs. Terminal users may employ it to

---

[1]An Inquiry package is one through which a user is given easy access to data bases. These packages are designed so that a user with a minimum of training can extract information, in the form of reports or CRT displays, by using either high level language statements or by entering some parameters into a predefined retrieval language.

guide their interrogation of the data base. Management may use it as a guide to what data could be made available to them.[2]

Martin's conceptual description of Data Dictionaries includes the idea of both documentation tool and data directory. What has happened, is that the concept of a "Data Dictionary" seems to have changed over time. Not too long ago, the idea of a data repository was adequate. More recently however, especially with the advent of Data Base systems, it has changed. This is reflected in a recent piece written by another recognized professional in the field of DBMS. The following appeared in Leo Cohen's *Newsletter*. Mr. Cohen's ideas include Martin's and even transcend them.

> Three functional areas are likely to be addressed by a data dictionary system. The first of these has to do with the design of data base systems; a data dictionary which assists in this area may be called a design aid. In this interpretation of the data dictionary problem, the data dictionary serves as a repository of information collected during the analysis that leads to the creation of the data base. Such information typically includes the definition of data elements, estimates of usage frequencies, delineation of security requirements and so forth. Subsequent to implementation of the data base, this information serves both as documentation for the system, and a base line for monitoring changes in usage patterns and data requirements. If these changes are extensive, then the data dictionary may serve as a redesign aid.
>
> A second functional area is in the actual implementation of data base systems. A data dictionary can provide a number of services, which collectively improve the productivity of data base administration and programming. Such services might typically include data base description, sub-schema generation, data description for application programs and so forth. . . . We can call this type of data dictionary capability administrative aids.
>
> The last functional area is "in-line" operational aids. In this interpretation, the data dictionary becomes part of an executing data base manager, and contains information that assists in scheduling jobs, verifying security, validating transactions and so forth. At the same time, statistics may be gathered on actual data base usage. . . . A data dictionary is a repository of information about the data base system; a data dictionary system uses this information to perform one or more of the functions discussed above.[3]

DATA DICTIONARY SYSTEM

The three functional areas, addressed by Mr. Cohen in that piece, reflect some of the most current thinking in the area of Data Dictionaries. It can be pointed out that the idea of Data Dictionaries has been expanded to encompass more

---

[2]James Martin, *Principles of Data Base Management*, Prentice-Hall, Englewood Cliffs, N.J., 1976, p. 329; and *Computer Data Base Organizations*, 2nd ed., Prentice-Hall, 1977, p. 222.
[3]Leo J. Cohen, "Data Dictionary Systems, What Are They?" Data Base Newsletter, Performance Development Corp., September 1977, pp. 2–3.

than just a repository of data. The idea of a Data Dictionary now includes a system as well as a repository. The term Data Dictionary System can now be added to the lexicon of terms used to describe the functions of data base systems.

In the final paragraphs of his article, Mr. Cohen makes some observations that are quite interesting. He observes that in addition to the axiomatic need for a Data Dictionary System, it also serves ideally as "first" application for a newly acquired DBMS. The Data Dictionary acts as a good basic training ground in DBMS technology. Since Data Dictionaries, like DBMSs, are themselves packages, the developmental risk is reduced.

Finally, Mr. Cohen discusses "an undercurrent of feeling in some quarters that the facilities we have identified with the data dictionary problem should, in fact, be integral to the DBMS."[4] There is little doubt, that Data Dictionaries will soon become components or features of Data Base Management Systems. Whether they do or not, however, is of little significance. It matters little, if at all, to the users of the facilities whether the Data Dictionary is part of a DBMS, runs under the control of a DBMS or is a stand alone system. What is of importance are the facilities themselves and how they are used.

FUNCTIONS/PURPOSES OF A DATA DICTIONARY

To list the functions of a Dictionary would be incredibly dull, and nobody would read it. Rather, a better idea is to describe the purposes of a Data Dictionary and how it is used. To an MIS manager, a Data Dictionary System can be thought of as a "front end" of a Data Base Management System. To a non-MIS manager, it can be thought of as an inventory of data types that are used by an enterprise. The idea of an inventory of data types can best be explained by way of example.

In any corporation there are products produced, there are plant and office locations, there are employees and there are tax rates to be applied on incomes, sales, purchases, real estate and profits. These categories of data are data types; the value assigned to a specific data element constitutes actual data. In a number of cases, the data itself is in the form of a numeric code, like social security number, product number or location code. The table on page 104 shows the difference between data types and actual data.

A corporation may produce a number of products, one of which is typewriters. Other products such as computer main frames, peripheral devices, typewriter ribbons and software packages may also be produced by the firm. Records must be kept for all these products. Each product usually has a unique name and number. The unique values are actual data and it is this data resource that is managed (stored, manipulated and retrieved) by a Data Base Management System. The types of data, that is, the categories of data, are managed by the

---

[4]Ibid. p. 3.

Data Types	Data
Product Name	TYPEWRITER
Product Number	TYP432E
Plant Location	503
Office Location	426
Employee Name	CALABRESE
Social Security Number	078-30-2677
Sales Tax Rate	.025
Realty Tax Rate—Plant	.003475
Income Tax Rate—N.Y.	.22

Data Dictionary System. In most cases, the types or categories themselves are seen as data as far as the Data Dictionary System is concerned, and the Data Dictionary System may use the facilities of the DBMS to assist in managing its data. In tabular form, it looks like this.

Data to a DBMS
TYPEWRITER
TAPE CARTRIDGE
DISKETTE
DISK PACK 3330
•
•
•
•
•
•
PROCESSOR 370
PROCESSOR 360

Data to a Data Dictionary System
PRODUCT NAME
PRODUCT NUMBER
QUANTITY ON HAND
•
•
•
•
REORDER LEVEL
PRICE PER UNIT

DATA DICTIONARY SYSTEMS THAT ARE AVAILABLE

There are a number of Data Dictionary Systems in the marketplace. Some, like the Arthur D. Anderson & Co. product, LEXICON, have been available for several years. Others, like Cullinane's Integrated Data Dictionary (IDD), are relatively recent arrivals on the scene. No doubt, as more data base managers and DBAs become aware of their importance, there will be a proliferation of Data Dictionary Systems. Below is a list of some of the contemporary Data Dictionary systems.

Dictionary System	*Vendor*
Cincom Data Dictionary	Cincom Systems
CONTROL-2000	MRI Systems Corp.
Data Base Directory	Eastern Air Lines, Inc.
Data Catalogue	Synergetics Corp.
DATAMANAGER	Management Systems and Programming
DB/DC Data Dictionary/Directory (DD/D)	IBM
Integrated Data Dictionary (IDD)	Cullinane Corp.
LEXICON	Arthur Andersen & Co.
UCC TEN	University Computing Co.

IBM'S DATA DIRECTORY SYSTEM—DATA DICTIONARY/DIRECTORY

A survey of the characteristics of a particular Data Dictionary System may contribute to a fuller understanding of Data Dictionary Systems and their usefulness. IBM's Data Directory System, called Data Dictionary/Directory (DD/D) is a reasonable choice. This particular system must be installed as an application in IMS/VS environment. It should be stated that not all Data Dictionary Systems require a DBMS environment in which to function. DATAMANAGER and LEXICON, for example, do not require a DBMS. DD/D however, does require a DBMS environment, specifically IMS/VS. Data Dictionary/ Directory uses the resources of IMS/VS to control and manage its data.

The DD/D system rents for $655 a month (price as of 4/78). The DD/D system is used later on as an example to illustrate the mechanics involved in using a Data Dictionary System. This will give the reader greater insight into the complexities involved in using both Data Dictionary Systems in general and DD/D in particular.

AN OVERVIEW

The sketch in Fig. 6–2 shows the DD/D system in schematic form. It shows DD/D as a system containing data bases. Within those data bases is kept basic descriptive information about files, data bases, records, segments, fields, etc. By means of commands, the DD/D system is able to produce CRT displays and printed reports containing information about the data in the data bases. It is also able to produce several types of structure statements about files, data bases, records, segments, fields, etc. Each type of these structure statements has a specific use. For example, among the outputs of the DD/D system are DBD and PSB source statements, which are used as input to IMS/VS; also produced as output of DD/D are COBOL, Assembler Language and PL/1 data structures, which are stored in operating system libraries so that they can subsequently be used in the compilation of application programs requiring them.

Since it uses the facilities of IMS/VS, the Data Dictionary/Directory System itself contains several IMS/VS data bases. These data bases contained within the DD/D system can be used for two basic purposes. They can be used to document conventional systems (non-IMS systems) and they can be used to document IMS-data base systems. The DD/D package contains five major data bases.

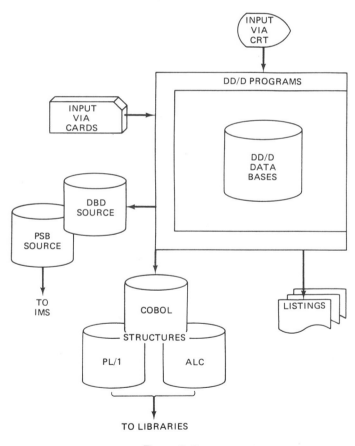

Figure 6–2

FIVE DATA BASES OF THE DD/D SYSTEM

These five data bases of the Data Dictionary/Directory System shown in Fig. 6–3 are referred to as

1. The DATA BASE or FILE data base
2. The SEGMENT or RECORD data base
3. The ELEMENT or FIELD data base
4. The PCB data base
5. The SYSTEM data base

In the DATA BASE or FILE data base are stored the definitions of IMS/VS data bases or non-IMS data sets. The definitions include the data base or data set name, and attributes and characteristics such as block size, access method, relationships with segments, with PCBs, with elements as well as user descriptive information.

In the SEGMENT or RECORD data base one finds definitions of IMS/VS segment or non-IMS records. The definitions include attributes such as segment or record length, user descriptive information about segments, relationships with other segments, with PCBs, with data bases as well as the name of the segment.

The ELEMENT or FIELD data base contains the element or field name. Relationship data relating to subordinate elements, data bases, segments and PCBs can also be found here. User descriptive information is also included.

In a PCB data base, there are descriptions of data relating to a program. The PCB data base also includes the name of the PCB in its definition as well as the type of PCB, data base or terminal. User descriptive information can be included in the PCB data base.

The SYSTEM data base contains information on jobs within systems, programs, modules, transactions and PSBs.

IMPLEMENTING A DATA DICTIONARY SYSTEM

The next several pages contain something of a narrative in that they describe the process employed by an IMS/VS Project Team at CBS to implement a Data Dictionary System. The project team was made up of a group of individuals combining both managerial and technical talent. There were individuals from the Systems Software area, Corporate Data Base Administrators, Divisional Data Base Administrators, Project Managers and a couple of MIS Directors. Among a number of other things, the CBS Corporation operates a centralized data center and an MIS technical services function, which serve many of its divisions. Several of the larger divisions maintain their own Systems and Programming departments although their applications are implemented on the computers at the Corporate Data Center. The members of the project team represented both

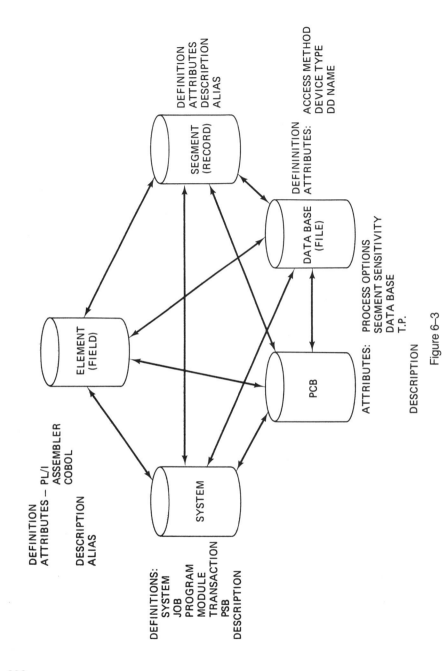

DEFINITION
ATTRIBUTES

DESCRIPTION
ALIAS

SEGMENT
(RECORD)

DEFININITION
ATTRIBUTES:

ACCESS METHOD
DEVICE TYPE
DD NAME

DATA BASE
(FILE)

DEFINITION
ATTRIBUTES – PL/I
ASSEMBLER
COBOL

DESCRIPTION
ALIAS

ELEMENT
(FIELD)

PCB

ATTRIBUTES: PROCESS OPTIONS
SEGMENT SENSITIVITY
DATA BASE
T.P.

DESCRIPTION

SYSTEM

DEFINITIONS:
SYSTEM
JOB
PROGRAM
MODULE
TRANSACTION
PSB
DESCRIPTION

Figure 6–3

divisional and corporate functions. Systems Software is a Data Center function; the Corporate DBAs were from the MIS Technical Services department. Project Managers and Divisional DBAs were from a division. One MIS Director was from a division, the other was a corporate representative.

DECIDING TO GET A DATA DICTIONARY SYSTEM

At one of its early meetings as a group, immediately following the decision to use IMS/VS, it became apparent that a Data Dictionary System was a "must." The magnitude of the data base administration job indicated this. For the first few months, the divisional data base administrator had performed the dictionary function by documenting data types in a notebook. However, it soon became obvious to all involved that this method was inadequate. A centralized source of data types was needed by individuals who were located in different locations. The notebook could only be in one place at a time. The idea of making copies was dismissed because it represented a logistical "nightmare." Since changes were frequently being made, the difficulty in maintaining several notebooks in synchronization with one another was judged to be impossible. Those involved decided that an on-line Data Dictionary should be used. The system chosen was the IBM Data Dictionary/Directory (DD/D). This choice was made more for pragmatic reasons than technical. It was felt that in so complex and new (to CBS) a project as IMS/VS that a multi-vendor situation was something that was not advisable. Also it was felt that the DD/D would probably be integrated into IMS/VS at some future date.

FORMULATING STANDARDS AND POLICIES

Concurrent with the placement of the order for DD/D was the formation of a subcommittee to formulate standards for IMS/VS and DD/D. Within ten months, a complete set of standards was developed. Although somewhat restrictive on individual creativity and ingenuity, the establishment of standards was considered by all members of the project team as necessary and important.

In addition to setting standards, three policies were set. First, as far as updating, the CBS corporate DBAs were given exclusive access to the Data Dictionary/Directory for updating, changing, adding and deleting. In this way specific individuals were assigned responsibility for the data integrity and documentation of the Data Dictionary/Directory's data bases.

Secondly, as far as access to the Data Dictionary/Directory data bases was concerned, the corporate DBAs were given exclusive control. The corporate DBAs were the only individuals who were allowed on-line access to the DD/D data bases. Using DD/D command language statements, they were able to produce reports that they subsequently sent to the divisional DBA. The divisional DBA was then able to disseminate the information from the reports at his discretion. In this way, the corporate DBAs were able to maintain procedural control over the data in the Data Dictionary/Directory's data bases. As more divisions began to use the DD/D resources, divisional DBAs were given on-line inquiry access to their division's data. The divisional DBA is allowed to see and examine his division's data, but is not permitted to change, delete or add to it. This function remains under the control of the corporate DBAs.

Finally, since the Data Dictionary/Directory System had the capability of producing source input such as Data Base Definitions (DBDs) and Program Specification Blocks (PSBs) to the IMS/VS system, it was established that all input to the IMS/VS system would be produced by the DD/D system. In this fashion, all IMS/VS data base creations, additions, changes and deletions had to be entered first into the Data Dictionary/Directory. The basic motivation that prompted setting these policies was partially dictated by the organization of CBS's MIS function, described earlier. CBS has a centralized Data Center, Operations and Systems Software, which support a number of divisional applications. The divisions contain their own Systems, Programming and Data Base Administration functions. In addition to the centralized Data Center, there is a Corporate MIS Staff, which, among other things, contains the Corporate Data Base Administration function. Within the CBS environment, these policies were instituted for the purpose of establishing central control of and responsibility for data integrity as well as assurance that the best possible use would be made of Data Center resources.

DEVELOPING FORMS

Concurrent with the establishment of the policy designating the corporate DBAs as "guardians of the Dictionary," was the development of forms to be used by divisional system application analysts, project leaders and DBAs in specifying data base, data element and index definitions. The forms are issued together with a set of instructions on their use so that the divisional personnel can use them. The forms can be filled out, in a cooperative effort, by divisional systems applications analysts, project leaders and divisional DBAs. If questions arise during this process, the corporate DBAs can be contacted. This is often the case, and as a result, a cooperative interaction is established in the early stages of data base definition. When completed, the forms are sent to the corporate DBA department. The value of having interaction between the corporate DBAs and the divisional personnel in the early stages of data base definition becomes quite apparent at this point because it is the corporate DBAs who have the responsibility for the contents of the Data Dictionary/Directory data bases. These individuals, by assisting in the design of the Data Bases, become thoroughly familiar with the data bases and the application. The early interaction generally obviates the need for any major discussion when the forms are submitted. In the event that some minor questions do arise, the divisional DBA keeps a copy of the forms so that these final questions are often resolved by means of a telephone conversation between the corporate and divisional DBAs.

ENTERING DEFINITIONS INTO THE DATA DICTIONARY

Upon receipt of the forms and following clarification of any questions that may have arisen, the corporate DBAs then enter the definitions from the forms into the Data Dictionary through a CRT terminal device. Once the data has been entered into the Dictionary, it is subsequently possible to produce DBD and PSB source statements. These statements become input to the IMS/VS system so that they can become part of the IMS/VS configuration as control blocks. To convert them from source to control block form requires an IMS/VS process called a "GEN." After a successful DBD "GEN" or PSB "GEN" has taken place, and the control blocks have become part of the IMS/VS system, the forms are marked with the completion date and are then filed in alphabetical order in loose-leaf binders. Figure 6–4 illustrates this process.

The original data definitions coded by the DBAs that have been entered are stored in their appropriate data bases within the Data Dictionary/Directory System. A series of reports can be produced that portray in printed form the contents of the Data Dictionary's data bases. The reports are also filed sequentially by DBD and PSB names. They are kept in large binders and are used by corporate and divisional DBAs and software support technicians for reference purposes. Figures 6–5 through 6–9 contain samples of a few of the types of the reports generated by the Data Dictionary System.

PRODUCING REPORTS

The reports are produced by the Data Dictionary System when the DBAs invoke the REPORT command. This command, together with parameters specifying the desired information, is entered into the system through the use of a CRT Keyboard terminal. The reports contain a profile of data bases, segments, elements, PCBs, PSBs and other IMS/VS related information. For example, the report labelled "DBS = SEG = DTE REPORT" (Fig. 6–5) provides the first page of a detailed description of a data base named DDSPDBS. Three segments, named DBS, DBSDTE and DBSSEG, are listed as well as elements with names such as DBSNAME, DBSPFX1 and so on. A copy of this report appears in Fig. 6–5. Figure 6–6, a PSB-OUT report, contains the information contained in the segments of a PSB named EMPINQUR. Figures 6–7 and 6–8 contain a two-page report about a DBD named EMPLOYEE. Figure 6–9 is a printed form of output from a DD/D feature called Structures Out. This report contains the structures as they are specified in the Assembler, PL/1 and COBOL programming languages.

STATUS CODES

There is one additional facility of DD/D that deserves mention, namely: status codes. It is this facility of DD/D that permits several levels of a data base to exist at the same time. There are eleven status codes, 0–9, T and P. "P"

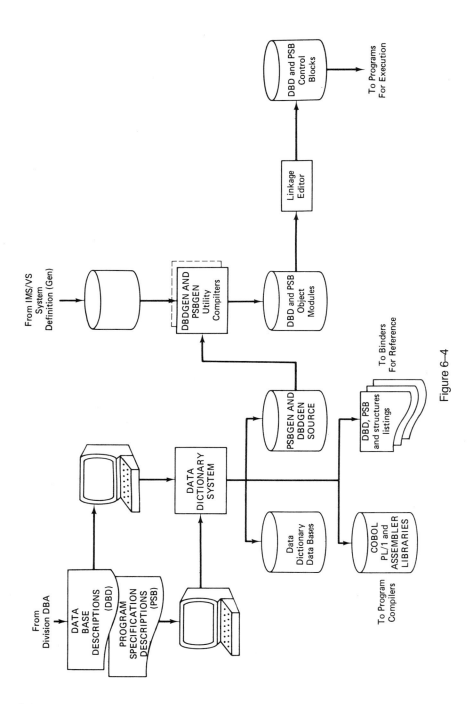

From Division DBA

From IMS/VS
System
Definition (Gen)

DATA
BASE
DESCRIPTIONS
(DBD)

PROGRAM
SPECIFICATION
DESCRIPTIONS
(PSB)

DATA
DICTIONARY
SYSTEM

DBDGEN AND
PSBGEN
Utility
Compilers

PSBGEN AND
DBDGEN
SOURCE

DBD and PSB
Object
Modules

Linkage
Editor

DBD and PSB
Control
Blocks

To Programs
For Execution

DBD, PSB
and structures
listings

To Binders
For Reference

Data
Dictionary
Data Bases

COBOL
PL/1 and
ASSEMBLER
LIBRARIES

To Program
Compilers

Figure 6-4

112

```
* * * * * * * *       DB/DC DATA DICTIONARY REPORT          10/09/76   14:50:56
* * * DBS = > SEG = > DTE REPORT * * * *                          PAGE:0001

DBSNAME: DP DDSPDBS 0
   SEGMENTS:   DA DBS 0
                  LEVEL: 1          PARENT:
                                 ELEMENTS: DA DBSNAME      0
                                                           START: 1    SEQ: U
                                           DA DBSPFX1      0
                                                           START:  1   SEQ: G
                                           DA DBSPFX2      0
                                                           START: 2    SEQ: G
                                           DA DBSNMFL      0
                                                           START: 3    SEQ: G
                                           DA DBSSFX       0
                                                           START: 34   SEQ: G

               DA DBSDTE 0
                  LEVEL: 2          PARENT: DA DBS         0
                                 ELEMENTS: DA DTENAME      0
                                                           START: 1    SEQ: U
                                           DA DTEPFX1      0
                                                           START: 1    SEQ: G
                                           DA DTEPFX2      0
                                                           START: 2    SEQ: G
                                           DA DTENMFL      0
                                                           START: 3    SEQ: G
                                           DA DTESFX       0
                                                           START: 34   SEQ: G
               DA DBSSEG 0
                  LEVEL: 2          PARENT: DA DBS         0
                                 ELEMENTS: DA SEGNAME      0
                                                           START: 1    SEQ: G
                                           DA SEGPFX1      0
                                                           START: 1    SEQ: G
                                           DA SEGPFX2      0
                                                           START: 2    SEQ: G
                                           DA SEGNMFL      0
                                                           START: 3    SEQ: G
                                           DA SEGSFX       0
                                                           START: 34   SEQ: G
                                           DA PPNAME       0
                                                           START: 35   SEQ: G
                                           DA PPPFX1       0
                                                           START: 35   SEQ: G
                                           DA PPPFX2       0
                                                           START: 36   SEQ: G
                                           DA PPNMFL       0
                                                           START: 37   SEQ: G
                                           DA PPSFX        0
                                                           START: 45   SEQ: G
```

Figure 6–5.

represents Production status, for data bases that are being used in day-to-day operations. "T" represents Test status as do digits 0–9. The 0–9 levels can be used to store data base structures in various parts or versions as they are developed. Using this facility, it is possible to test parts or versions of data bases that can subsequently be integrated and tested before going into production. The "T" status can be used for that testing just prior to giving a "P" status to a data base.

```
INPUT RECORD  /SETLANG = A  SETSTAT = 0  SETDBTP = P
DBD0026 I OK**

INPUT RECORD  /PSB_OUT  EMPINQUR  DEST = L
*  *  *  *  *  *  *  *  *  *  *  *  *  *  *  *  *  *  *  *  *  *  *  *  *  *  *  *  *  *
*
*   DB/DC DATA DICTIONARY PSB_OUT FUNCTION  10/09/76
*
*   PSB DICTIONARY KEY = OPEMPINQUR            000
*
*  *  *  *  *  *  *  *  *  *  *  *  *  *  *  *  *  *  *  *  *  *  *  *  *  *  *  *  *  *
        PCB          TYPE = TP, MODIFY = YES
        PCB          TYPE = DB,                        X
                     DBDNAME = EMPLOYEE,               X
                     PROCOPT = G,                      X
                     KEYLEN = 20
        SENSEG        NAME = EMPLOYEE,                 X
                      PARENT = 0
        SENSEG        NAME = ADDRESS,                  X
                      PARENT = EMPLOYEE
        SENSEG        NAME = MEDICAL,                  X
                      PARENT = EMPLOYEE
        SENSEG        NAME = DISAB,                    X
                      PARENT = MEDICAL
        SENSEG        NAME = DISACOMM,                 X
                      PARENT = DISAB
        PSBGEN        LANG = COBOL,                    X
                      PSBNAME = EMPINQUR
                      END
DBD0503 I END OF PSB_OUT PROCESSING FOR OP EMPINQUR 0
```

Figure 6–6

INPUT RECORD /SETLANG=A SETSTAT=0 SETDBTP=P
DBD0026 I OK**

INPUT RECORD /DBD_OUT EMPLOYEE DEST=L
* *
*
*   DB/DC DATA DICTIONARY DBD_OUT FUNCTION 10/09/76
*
*   DBD DICTIONARY KEY = OPEMPLOYEE   000
*
* *
    DBD   NAME = EMPLOYEE,   X
                ACCESS = HDAM,   X
                RMNAME = (MOD, 10, 100, 300)
    DATASET   DD1 = EMPLDD,   X
                DEVICE = 3330,   X
                BLOCK = (2048)
    SEGM   NAME = EMPLOYEE,   X
                PARENT = 0,   X
                BYTES = 114
    FIELD   NAME = (EMPNO, SEQ, U),   X
                BYTES = 6,   X
                START = 41,   X
                TYPE = C
    SEGM   NAME = ADDRESS,   X
                PARENT = EMPLOYEE,   X
                BYTES = 50
    SEGM   NAME = AWARDS,   X
                PARENT = EMPLOYEE,   X
                BYTES = 51
    SEGM   NAME = TERM,   X
                PARENT = EMPLOYEE,   X
                BYTES = 8
    SEGM   NAME = PAY,   X
                PARENT = EMPLOYEE,   X
                BYTES = 30
    SEGM   NAME = BANK,   X
                PARENT = PAY,   X
                BYTES = 20
    SEGM   NAME = HISTSAL,   X
                PARENT = PAY,   X
                BYTES = 22
    SEGM   NAME = THRIFT,   X
                PARENT = PAY,   X
                BYTES = 15
    SEGM   NAME = OT,   X
                PARENT = PAY,   X
                BYTES = 9
    SEGM   NAME = MISCDED,   X
                PARENT = PAY,   X
                BYTES = 30
    SEGM   NAME = MISCADD,   X
                PARENT = PAY,   X
                BYTES = 25

Figure 6-7

```
SEGM        NAME = TAXES,                        X
            PARENT = PAY,                        X
            BYTES = 14
SEGM        NAME = EDUCOUT,                      X
            PARENT = EMPLOYEE,                   X
            BYTES = 12
SEGM        NAME = EDUCDDS,                      X
            PARENT = EMPLOYEE,                   X
            BYTES = 20
SEGM        NAME = MEDICAL,                      X
            PARENT = EMPLOYEE,                   X
            BYTES = 12
FIELD       NAME = (EMPMEDCD, SEQ, U),           X
            BYTES = 3,                           X
            START = 10,                          X
            TYPE = C
SEGM        NAME = DISAB,                        X
            PARENT = MEDICAL,                    X
            BYTES = 12
SEGM        NAME = DISACOMM,                     X
            PARENT = DISAB,                      X
            BYTES = 47
SEGM        NAME = EMPOSIT,                      X
            PARENT = EMPLOYEE,                   X
            BYTES = 20
SEGM        NAME = EVAL,                         X
            PARENT = EMPLOYEE,                   X
            BYTES = 28
SEGM        NAME = EVALCOMM,                     X
            PARENT = EVAL,                       X
            BYTES = 40
DBDGEN
FINISH
END
DBD0307 I END OF DBD_OUT PROCESSING FOR OP EMPLOYEE 0
```

Figure 6-8

INPUT RECORD   /SETLANG = A   SETSTAT = 0   SETDBTP = P
DBD0026 I OK**

INPUT RECORD /SO SEG MEDICAL DEST = L MEMBER = DDSTRUC
LANGUAGE = A
./ ADD NAME = DDSTRUC
./ NUMBER NEW1 = 100,INCR = 100
```
    MEDICAL         DS      CL12
                    ORG     MEDICAL
    EMPSTDTE        DS      CL6
                    ORG     EMPSTDTE
    MONTH           DS      CL2
    DAY             DS      CL2
    YEAR            DS      CL2
    EMPDURAQ        DS      PL3
    EMPMEDCD        DS      CL3
```
DBD0726 I STRUCTURES OUT COMPLETE

INPUT RECORD /SO SEG MEDICAL DEST = L MEMBER =
DDSTRUC LANGUAGE = B
./ ADD NAME = DDSTRUC
./ NUMBER NEW1 = 100, INCR = 100
```
  DCL
      1 EMP_MED_DATA,
        3 EMP_MED_START—DTE,
          5 MONTH CHAR (2),
          5 DAY CHAR (2),
          5 YEAR CHAR (2),
        3 EMP_MED_DUR—QTY FIXED DECIMAL (3),
        3 EMP_MED_CDE CHAR (3),
   /* END OF STRUCTURE */;
```
DBD0726 I STRUCTURES OUT COMPLETE

INPUT RECORD /SO SEG MEDICAL DEST = L MEMBER =
DDSTRUC LANGUAGE = C
./ ADD NAME = DDSTRUC
./ NUMBER NEW1 = 100, INCR = 100
```
        01   EMP—MED—DATA.
             03 EMP—MED—START—DTE.
              05 MONTH PIC XX.
              05 DAY PIC XX.
              05 YEAR PIC XX.
             03 EMP—MED—DUR—QTY USAGE COMP—3 PIC S999.


             03 EMP—MED—CDE PIC X (3).
```
DBD0726 I STRUCTURES OUT COMPLETE

Figure 6–9

7
Using IMS/VS

As an organization contemplates using a sophisticated Data Base Management System like IMS/VS, there are several factors that ought to be taken into consideration before a commitment is made. There are benefits to using IMS/VS, such as: a degree of data independence, an increase in the speed of data retrieval and reduction of data redundancy. Many words have been spoken and written extolling these benefits. There is nothing to be gained by reviewing them again. Suffice it to say, these benefits are potential, and it is possible to realize them with the proper use of the IMS/VS system. On the other hand, there are other factors that are somewhat vague when IMS/VS is being initially evaluated. As the MIS professionals within an organization get intimately involved with IMS/VS, the vagueness tends to dissipate and ideas become crystalized. In our case, a number of factors that once were vague ideas, have crystalized into specific functions. It is these that I wish to share with you. Specifically, the following subjects will be examined:

1. Setting up IMS/VS

2. Application Programming

3. Data Base Administration (IMS/VS style)

SETTING UP IMS/VS

In a manner similar to "GENing" an operating system, a system definition of IMS/VS must be performed. As is commonly known, a "SYSGEN" of an operating system requires the services of a skilled systems software technician. The same situation exists with IMS/VS. The IMS/VS "GENs" are a process whereby parameters are specified so as to establish the particular IMS/VS system for one's own installation. The IMS/VS system definitions or GENs specify items such as IMS/VS libraries, data sets, buffer pool sizes, passwords, data base definitions, program control blocks, screen formats and terminal device and network characteristics.

In an ideal setting, a complete IMS/VS GEN would take place each time that IBM issued a new release or new version of the system. Partial GENs, such as those required when new data bases or program control blocks are needed, must be scheduled to meet the demand of a particular installation. It is not unusual for these to be required on a monthly basis. In addition to the GENing of the system, it is suggested that it be thoroughly tested before it is put into use. It is possible to develop a comprehensive job stream with which to do this. As with the GEN itself, this development of a test vehicle also requires skilled IMS/VS systems software expertise.

While all this is going on, it is also quite possible that some other software products, either IBM's or other vendors' designed to work in support or in conjunction with IMS/VS, will also be installed. These products, like Batch Terminal Simulator (BTS), Data Base Prototype (DB Prototype), Data Dictionary/Directory (DD/D) from IBM and Control IMS/VS Realtime from Boole and Babbage, also require systems software technical expertise to install, maintain, test and use.

As applications are developed that use the facilities of IMS/VS and the associated software, further demands are made on systems software technicians to answer technical questions and to assist in the trouble-shooting of the inevitable problems that occur. "Bugs," which have made computer programming an interesting occupation since its inception, have become more exasperating as the technology has become more sophisticated. In a typical IMS/VS environment, when a problem does occur, it may take a substantial amount of time and talent to track it down. Since there is so much software involved, i.e., IMS/VS itself, MVS (the operating system), VSAM, VTAM or other access methods, application programs, as well as hardware, i.e., TCUs, modems, lines and terminals, a great deal of coordination of individuals with differing kinds of technical expertise is required to pursue and isolate a problem.

In summary, my experience has shown that it is possible to begin the IMS/VS systems software staff with two experienced systems software technicians. Within a year an additional one is required. After two years, depending upon the number of applications using the facility, it is necessary to add an additional systems software technician at the rate of one per major application.

APPLICATION PROGRAMMING IN AN IMS/VS ENVIRONMENT

Application programming in an IMS/VS environment, using the conventional programming languages COBOL, PL/1 and Assembler, is only slightly different than application programming in a non-IMS/VS environment. Only the input/ output (I/O) operations are different. The procedural portion of an application program, that is, that part of an application program than analyzes, processes and changes data, is no different in an IMS/VS environment than it would be in a non-IMS/VS environment.

INPUT/OUTPUT OPERATIONS

The I/O operations are different, since transferring data between computer storage and peripheral devices is a more sophisticated process in an IMS/VS environment than it is in a non-IMS/VS environment. The I/O operations are more sophisticated since the data transferred is in the form of segments, which are parts of records within hierarchical structures, rather than in the simpler form of records within files as in the case in the more conventional non-IMS/VS situation. Yet, from an application programming perspective, even the I/O operations are basically no more complex in the IMS/VS environment because the IMS/VS system itself handles the increased complexities of I/O common to the hierarchical structures through its access methods, HSAM, HISAM, HDAM and HIDAM. Theoretically, all the complexity and sophistication is transparent to the application programmer. The only additional information required by the program is the data base structure information that is contained in a PCB.[1] The PCB is originally prepared by the Data Base Administrator,[2] in source form.[3] It is subsequently compiled into control block form and stored in an IMS/VS library (on DASD storage). As a member of this library it is accessible to an application program, prior to the execution.

I/O OPERATION CODES ARE FUNCTION CODES

There are nineteen I/O operation codes, commonly known as function codes, in the repertoire of IMS/VS. Nine of them comprise what are known as system service calls. Although they are potentially quite significant in an IMS/VS en-

---

[1]PCB. Program Communication Block. An IMS/VS control block that contains information about a specific data structure. The information is required so that an application program, during its execution, can retrieve data from that structure. There is one PCB for each data base and terminal accessed by a program.

[2]Data Base Administrator (DBA). Currently there are a host of definitions of this function. For the purposes of this piece, let's just say that, among other things, the DBA designs and defines data base structures.

[3]Source form. In this case, source describes the PCB as it is coded by the DBA in mnemonics. PCB information includes information such as data base name, length of key, number of segments and other control information.

vironment, a description of the system service calls would tend to cloud rather than clarify the general overview of application programming being presented here. Of the remaining ten function codes, an examination of nine of them is sufficient to provide a reasonable feel for IMS/VS application programming.

The basic input/output operations (function) codes of IMS/VS are GET (six variations), REPLACE, INSERT and DELETE. Six variations of the GET operation code are needed. There is a direct access GET, a sequential GET, a limited sequential GET, and HOLD versions of each GET, which permit updating and file maintenance. Since retrieval of data in IMS/VS is accomplished by segment, rather than by record, the six GETs specify retrieval of segments. The mnemonic operation codes and their functions are listed below.

Operation Code	*Function*
GU	GET UNIQUE: this is a direct access GET, which makes possible the retrieval of a specific segment from a data base or terminal.
GN	GET NEXT: this is a sequential access GET, which makes possible the retrieval of the next sequential segment in data base or from a terminal.
GNP	GET NEXT WITHIN PARENT: this is also a sequential access GET, but with a limited range.
GHU GHN GHNP	Corresponding to the GU, GN and GNP operations, the H signifying HOLD, these three special operations are used in conjunction with the REPLACE and DELETE operations.
ISRT	INSERT: this is a PUT operation used to initially load or to add segments to a data base or to a terminal.
REPL DLET	REPLACE and DELETE: these two operations work in conjunction with the three GET HOLD operations. After retrieval, segments can be written back (REPL) or deleted (DLET). The REPL operation facilitates updating, while DLET accomplishes purging.

The nine function codes just described can be used in transferring segments of data between data bases on DASD and computer storage. In addition, three function codes, GU, GN, ISRT can be used to transfer data segments between terminals and computer storage, as well as between data bases and computer storage.

PARAMETER LIST AND INTERFACE LANGUAGE

When used in an application program, these function codes are combined in an I/O statement with other information. All of this information taken together makes up what is known as a parameter list. When an I/O operation is to transfer data between data bases and computer storage, the parameters in the statement include the function code, a description of the data structure in which the desired data segment resides, the name of an area in which the data is to reside while it is in computer storage and occasionally qualifies the data to be retrieved. When transferring data between terminals and computer storage, the parameters vary depending upon the specific function code being used.

INTERFACE LANGUAGE FOR I/O OPERATIONS

In order to handle input/output operations, IMS/VS is equipped with an interface language. It is this interface language that requires the parameters of the I/O statements. This interface language is called Data Language/1 or more commonly, DL/1. The specification of parameters to DL/1 is accomplished by means of a CALL[4] statement in the source[5] programming language. During the process of compiling or assembling a program into a form rendering it executable by the computer, a precompiled set of executable instructions for linkage to the DL/1 interface is integrated into the program in its executable form. Interfaces exist for COBOL/DL1, Assembler/DL1 and PL1/DL1. Figure 7–1 provides a schematic of the facilities used in putting together an application program in a DL/1 environment.

PARAMETERS OF THE CALL STATEMENT

Each of the parameters in the CALL statement has a specific function. When performing I/O operations with data bases, as opposed to I/O operations with terminals, four types of parameters can be specified, three required and one optional. The first significant parameter[6] is the function code. Nine of these (GU, GN, etc.) have already been described. The second parameter specifies the PCB, by name. The PCB is a control block. The information in the PCB is transferred to an Application Control Block (ACB),[7] together with other information. It is the ACB from which the program gets its control information when it executes. The third parameter identifies the input/output (I/O) area into which the DL/1 retrieval mechanism is to place the segment that is being retrieved.

---

[4]CALL. A CALL statement is included in the source statements of an application program. During the compilation process, a precompiled set of instructions (in this case a DL/1 linkage) is integrated into the program in its executable form.

[5]Source. In this case, it is the program in the form as coded by a programmer before it is assembled or compiled into a form so that it is executable by the computer. The source language may be either COBOL, Assembler or PL/1.

[6]Actually the first parameter, optional in the COBOL and Assembler statements, but required in PL/1, is a parameter count. This number is merely a count of the number of parameters in the statement.

[7]ACB. Application Control Block. For the sake of technical accuracy, this term is introduced. When a batch application program is to begin executing, one of its first tasks is the generation of an ACB. The information in an ACB is taken from two sources, the Data Base Definition (DBD), which contains information about the data base to be accessed, and the Program Specification Block (PSB). It is the PSB that holds all the PCBs for a particular program. For on-line (transaction type) programs, ACBs are generated off-line and stored in a library from which they can be retrieved by a program as it begins its execution. In the latter case, the ACB library is set up so that the increased overhead of the ACB generation does not get added to the transaction type program's execution time.

The first three parameters are required for any DL/1 CALL statement that transfers segments between data bases and computer storage.

The fourth type of parameter in the CALL statement parameter list is composed of one or more items called segment search arguments (SSAs). SSAs are essentially qualifiers in that they define the scope of the retrieval, or specify the exact identifiers of the retrieval. Segment search arguments can be qualified

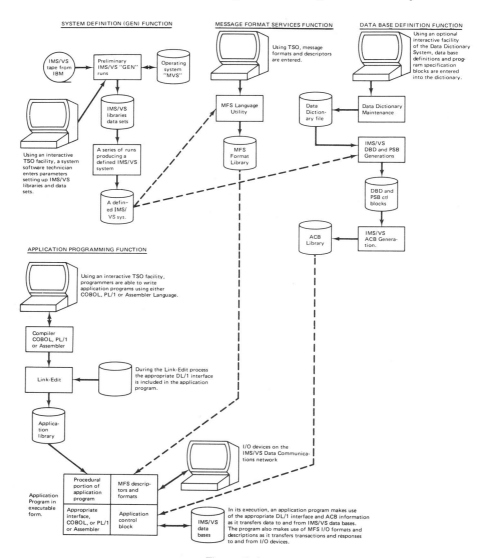

Figure 7–1

or unqualified. Qualified SSAs specify a particular occurrence of a segment, that is, a specific segment from among many of the same type. For example, in an automobile data base, there would be many carburetor segments. A qualified SSA would identify a specific carburetor on a specific engine in a specific vehicle. SSAs for a carburetor might include characteristics like manufacturer, type, year and make of vehicle. Specifically, the SSAs for a GU situation might be: CARTER, two barrel, 1963 CHEVROLET. An unqualified SSA specifies a type of segment rather than a specific occurrence of a type of segment. In the automobile data base, an unqualified SSA would specify any carburetor segment. The exact way in which DL/1 treats an unqualified SSA depends on the function code used. For instance GU with an unqualified SSA will retrieve the first occurrence of the segment type specified, while repeated "GNs" with an unqualified SSA will retrieve sequentially all segment occurrences of the type specified.

It was stated earlier that the specification of SSAs was optional in tne parameter list. It is possible to code CALL statements without SSAs. Again, the manner in which DL/1 handles CALLs with no SSAs depends on the function code that is used. A GU, for instance, with no SSA, results in the retrieval of the first occurrence of the root[8] segment. If a GN function code were specified with no SSAs, every segment in the data base would be retrieved in hierarchical sequence[9] one segment for each GN issued.

STATUS CODES

A further consideration of application programming in an IMS/VS environment is status codes. It is the responsibility of the application programmer to include logic in his program to determine whether or not the function code specified has successfully completed. After an I/O operation executes, the PCB contains, among other things, two characters of data, called status codes, which indicate what has happened as a result of the execution of the function code.

There are a number of status codes with which application programmers need to become familiar. Not all of them apply to each function code. For example, the two values generally expected for the GU operation are either two blanks, indicating a successful retrieval or a GE, indicating that the desired segment was not found. With the GN function code, in addition to the two described, there are status codes GA, GK and GB. GB indicates the end of a data base, GK indicates a new segment type at the same level and GA indicates

---

[8]Root. In a hierarchical structure the root segment is that segment which is subordinate to none, that is, it is the single top segment of a hierarchical structure. It is through this segment that all other segments in the hierarchy are located.

[9]Hierarchical sequence. Within IMS/VS, data bases are structured hierarchically. Hierarchical sequence, in IMS/VS, dictates that these structures be read top to bottom, left to right.

that the segment just retrieved is a level higher than the previously retrieved segment.[10]

There are further status codes that correspond to the other function codes. For instance, while trying to insert a segment, a program might get back an LB status code, which indicates that the segment already exists. When trying to replace or delete a segment, a DJ status code would indicate that a previous GET HOLD function code had not been issued. The examples cited do not constitute a complete list of status codes. Yet, the examples do serve to illustrate the purpose of status codes. It is a requirement that the application program contain logic to interrogate the PCB and to take appropriate action based on the status code found, following an I/O operation.

I/O PCB

When performing I/O operations involving terminals,[11] the type of parameters specified depends on the function code being used. For the GN and GU operations, the name of a control block called the I/O PCB must be specified together with the name of a work area to hold the messages being transferred. Messages can be and often are composed of more than one segment. Therefore to retrieve a message, a GU is issued, followed by successive GN until a QD status code is returned indicating there are no more segments to retrieve. The I/O PCB is used to hold control information needed by IMS/VS after the retrieval of the first segment of a message.

In a terminal I/O operation, as opposed to data base I/O operation, the ISRT function code is used to build output messages. The parameters are similar to those used for the GET function codes and the operation is essentially the reverse of a GET.

NEW TECHNICAL FUNCTIONS

THE DBA FUNCTION

The DBA function, which is the function of Data Base Administration, consists of specifying Data Base Definitions, Program Communications Blocks and programming language data structures to the Data Dictionary System. Individuals performing this function are highly skilled technicians thoroughly trained in the workings of IMS/VS data bases. These technicians, called DBAs,

---

[10]A hierarchical structure within IMS/VS, when processed sequentially, is read one segment at a time from top to bottom, left to right. After reading the last segment occurrence at a level, the next read operation takes in the first segment occurrence at the next higher level, precipitating the GA status code.

[11]I/O operations with terminals in actuality are I/O operations with message queues. DL/1 transfers data between message queues and computer storage. The actual transfer of data between terminals and the queues is carried out by program modules that are part of the Data Communications (DC) features of IMS/VS.

set up both logical and physical data bases, describe logical relationships among segments of various data bases and establish primary and secondary indexes. The DBAs make use of IMS/VS data base structures HISAM, HDAM and HI-DAM, in specifying to IMS/VS the way in which data bases are to be set up.

THE MESSAGE FORMAT SERVICES FUNCTION

The Message Format Services (MFS) function is also performed by highly skilled technicians. This job is related to what is becoming known as the Data Communications Administration (DCA) function. IMS/VS, as do many data base management systems, has a data communications feature. In IMS/VS, the feature is actually called Data Communications (DC) and its purpose is to facilitate application programmer interaction with a teleprocessing network. Within the Data Communication feature of IMS/VS, there are software interfaces that can handle communication with physical I/O devices of a teleprocessing network. In this way, the application programmer is freed from concern about physical device characteristics, line disciplines, protocols and other teleprocessing considerations.

However, even though the application programmer need not concern himself with the data communication aspects of the application, someone has to. Enter the MFS specialist. This individual is responsible for specifying the formats for the physical devices and the descriptions for the application programs. Known as MIDs (Message Input Descriptions), MODs (Message Output Descriptions), DIFs (Device Input Formats) and DOFs (Device Output Formats), these are prepared by the MFS specialist. MIDs and MODs describe messages as they are to appear in a program, stripped of all heading, caption and other edit type information. DIFs and DOFS describe transactions as they are to appear on devices, like CRTs. In this form, the heading, caption and other information is included.

TECHINCAL SUPPORT NEEDED

The last few paragraphs contained a rather brief survey of two new technical functions, Data Base Administration and Data Communications Administration that are required in support of an IMS/VS system. The individuals performing these functions should possess capabilities that are a cross between those of an application programmer/analyst and a systems software technician. In the immediate future, as the involvement with data base management systems becomes more universal, these specializations will become as critical as the systems software specialization has become in the ten years since operating systems were introduced. The expertise required to support and IMS/VS environment is substantial, and while the task of application programming is simplified, there is a significant increase required in the area of technical support.

DATA BASE ADMINISTRATION

FUNCTIONS INVOLVED IN USING IMS/VS PRODUCT

The Data Base Administration function, which is also an important aspect of establishing an IMS/VS data base environment has been described more fully in earlier chapters. Brief mention is made here to show it in the context with other IMS/VS functions. An examination of Fig. 7–1 should give you a reasonably good idea of the functions involving in using the IMS/VS product, together with the auxiliary product Data Dictionary/Directory (DD/D) which is the tool of the DBA.

Figure 7–1 shows the four elements that are essential in using the IMS/VS data base management system. In the upper left is the System definition or GEN function, which is performed by systems software programmers who are thoroughly trained in IMS/VS. To the right are the Data Communication Administration (DCA) functions and the Data Base Administration (DBA) functions. The existence of the Data Dictionary/Directory (DD/D) system is implied for the DBA function. Although not necessarily present, the use of this package or a similar one is strongly recommended to IMS/VS users. The lower half shows the application programming function. The dotted lines illustrate how the various functions are related to one another.

THE APPLICATION DEVELOPMENT FACILITY

Before moving on to treatment of IMS/VS Utilities, there is another tool that should get some attention. It comes in the form of an IBM product that is beginning to achieve some recognition as a more efficient means of developing applications. The product, currently known as IMS Application Development Facility (ADF), is advertised as a means for quickly and efficiently developing application programs for IMS/VS. Included in the facility are program modules that are able to execute DL/1 CALLS, edit input data, format displays for IBM 3270 CRT devices, provide a degree of security and route messages between applications and system users.

Preliminary investigation reveals that the ADF package has, as an objective, the reduction and eventually the elimination of application programming. At this point, the ADF methodology is embryonic, that is, it can be used to replace application programming in only the most basic and straightforward of applications. Basically, the package is composed of a number of functional program modules. These functional modules are able to perform the basic tasks found in most applications. For example, along these functional modules are found a transaction driver, a segment handler, a screen controller, a message sender and an auditor. In addition, there are other programs within the facility containing the logic required to combine the functional program modules into executable IMS application programs. For those applications whose requirements exceed the current capabilities of ADF, exits are provided so that the user can attach modules and subroutines of his own to enhance or to add functions not contained within the facility.

In order to specify what has to be done in an application within the confines of ADF, the programmer (who may be the end user) defines parameters, called "rules," which are coded and entered into the system where they are stored in data tables. As the functional modules execute, they make use of the data in the data tables to tailor the application programs to the user's specific requirements.

SUMMARY

The preceding pages contained a survey of how to "get the show on the road" in support of an IMS/VS system. The individuals performing the functions to provide this support should possess capabilities that are a cross between those of an application programmer/analyst and a systems software technician. In the immediate future, as the involvement with data base management systems becomes more universal, these specializations are seen to become as critical as the systems software specialization has become in the ten years since operating systems were introduced.

8
IMS/VS—The Auxiliary Functions

Data Base Management Systems software packages are equipped with a number of supplemental features. These supplemental features have a couple of functions. Some of them, known as Utilities, are integral to the functioning of the DBMS. Utilities are programs or groups of programs with specific functions. Examples of Utility programs are: Data Base Generators, Recovery and Restart jobs, Reorganization programs and Logging functions.

The other supplemental features are known as Aids. Not integral to the functioning of the system, these programs enhance the Data Base Management System. Examples of Aids include: Data Dictionary packages, Report Generators and Inquiry Systems.

UTILITIES AND AIDS

The material that follows provides some information about the utilities and productivity aids (called simply aids) that can be used in conjunction with the IMS/VS Data Base Management System. As you may suspect, the details of data base management are quite complicated. This section will confirm that suspicion. The information presented is a synthesis of material that spans half a dozen technical manuals. The complexity of the utilities testifies to the complexity of the IMS/VS package itself. The purpose of the following is to provide you with some specific information about the capabilities of the software support that accompanies IMS/VS.

The list below contains a description of some of the utilities and aids that accompany the IMS/VS system.

1. Generation Utilities

2. Data Base Utilities

3. System Log Utilities

4. Performance Reporting and Service Utilities

5. Message Format Services Utilities (MFS)

6. DL/1 Test Program

7. Data Dictionary/Directory (DD/D)

8. IMSMAP

9. Batch Terminal Simulator (BTS)

This distinction between features that are called utilities and those that are called aids is somewhat fuzzy. As new releases of IMS appear, some utilities are redefined as aids. Some other utilities disappear from the utility manual altogether only to reappear in manuals of their own. Regrouping of utilities also takes place from time to time.

GENERATION UTILITIES

These utilities are used to establish the data base control information and structures. It is these programs that set up the framework in which the data is stored. They also accumulate the information needed by application programs to process the data in the data bases.

DATA BASE DESCRIPTION GENERATION (DBDGEN)

This utility creates control blocks from control statements. The control statements (DBD source) are prepared by a Data Base Administrator (DBA). The control statements are compiled by the utility and stored in a library (IMSVS.DBDLIB). When an application program is executed, DL/1 uses the DBD together with a PSB (explained below in PSBGEN) to create internal control blocks. The control blocks contain information necessary for the execution of the program. With on-line programs, the creation of internal control blocks immediately prior to execution of the program is not practical. The alternative is explained below under ACBGEN. The DBD contains the following information about the data base:

1. The physical characteristics of the data base

2. Segment types

3. Physical and logical relationships among segment types

4. Data base organization and access method

PROGRAM SPECIFICATION BLOCK GENERATION (PSBGEN)

A PSB acts as a bridge between the data definition (DBD) and the application program. The PSB statements describe the IMS/VS resources that are needed to execute the program. These resources include:

1. The data base segments used by the program

2. The output message destination

3. The program interface (a function of the application programming language)

4. The program name

The last two resources, the program interface and the program name, are included in a PSB source statement known as the PSBGEN statement. The interface is the means of communication between the IMS/VS language (DL/1) and the application program. Specifying the application programming language (COBOL, PL/1 or ALC) on the PSBGEN statement indicates the appropriate interface module required for program execution. The first two resources, the data base segments and the output message destination, are included in a PSB source statement known as a Program Communication Block (PCB) statement. The PCB statements describe either data base segment sensitivity or output message destination. The word sensitivity is used to define those segments of a data base that are available to a particular application program. Such segments are defined in a PCB through a statement known as a SENSEG statement.

The PSB generation places the created PSB in a library called IMSVS.PSBLIB. When an application program is executed, DL/1 uses the PSB together with DBDs to create control blocks containing information necessary to execute the program.

APPLICATION CONTROL BLOCK MAINTENANCE UTILITY (ACBGEN)

As mentioned above, application programs use DBDs and PSBs to build control blocks for use during execution. The control blocks created by PSBGENs and DBDGENs are merged into an internal IMS/VS format called an Application Control Block (ACB). The purpose of this utility is to effect a reduction in the use of resources in scheduling and executing programs. When an application program is scheduled, the ACBs are read into memory and control is passed directly to the program. The prebuilding of ACBs is required for the DC feature of IMS/VS, although for the DB feature it is optional. The Application Control Blocks are stored in a library IMSVS.ACBLIB.

DATA BASE UTILITIES

This group includes the utility programs necessary for reloading and reorganizing data bases and for recovering damaged data bases. A number of these utilities are used in conjunction with one another. The Data Base Utilities can be sub-divided as follows:

1. Data Base Reorganization and Load Utilities
2. Data Base Recovery Utilities
3. Utility Control Facility

There are eight utility programs in the Data Base Reorganization and Load group, four in the Data Base Recovery group. The Utility Control Facility acts as a controller for the integrated execution of the other data base utilities. These utilities are used to initially load or to reorganize or to reconstruct data bases that are made up of records that are segmented in hierarchical structures. These structures are inherently more complex than conventional records since the segments are related to one another through the use of pointers. The pointers reside in the segments themselves. For instance, an indexed sequential file has another degree of complexity (another set of pointers in addition to those in the index portion of the file) added to it when it is structured hierarchically in an IMS/VS data base. These two degrees of complexity (indexed sequential pointers and hierarchical pointers) only pertain to the physical file structure and organization.

In addition to that, IMS/VS supports logical data bases, which are structures that contain additional relationships between the segments of single or multiple data bases. This is accomplished through techniques such as "logical relationships" and "secondary indexing."[1] These techniques are implemented through the use of pointers also, adding another degree of complexity to the structure. As must be now apparent, reorganization or reconstructing of IMS/VS data base files is an extremely complex task. In the explanations that follow, it will be seen that the utilities that bring about reorganizations or reconstructions interact with one another.

An important note: The initial loading of a physical data base is the user's responsibility. He must write the program and indicate that the data base is being loaded. Appropriate PSBs are required for an initial load.

---

[1]Logical relations and secondary indexing are two methodologies of establishing relationships between segments of data that are stored in a manner quite different from that perceived by the users of those segments of data. Briefly, a secondary index is one where an identifier (key) other than the primary identifier (key) is used to gain access directly to a record. For example, employee number in an employee file might be the primary key, while social security number would be a secondary key. A separate file containing social security numbers and pointers to the main file would constitute a secondary index. A logical relationship is established by establishing a pointer from one segment to another to which it is not already physically related by a pointer.

DATA BASE REORGANIZATION AND LOAD UTILITIES

The Data Base Reorganization/Load processing system consists of eight utilities, four dealing with physical reorganization and four with logical relationship resolution. These eight are described below.

THE HISAM[2] REORGANIZATION UNLOAD UTILITY (DFSURULO) provides the ability to unload and reorganize a HISAM Data Base. The output, in the form of a QSAM (blocked sequential) data set, can be used as input to the HISAM Reorganization Reload Utility or as input to the Data Base Recovery Utility. The HISAM Reorganization and Unload Utility also has the facility to format index work data sets that have been produced by the Prefix Resolution Utility. These formatted index work data sets can then be used by the HISAM Reorganization and Reload Utility to create a secondary index.

THE HISAM REORGANIZATION RELOAD UTILITY (DFSURRLO) has the ability to reload a HISAM data base that has been unloaded by the HISAM Reorganization and Unload Utility. It has the ability to create secondary indexes from formatted index work data sets produced by the HISAM Reorganization and Unload Utility.

The HISAM Utilities are used to reorganize data bases. Structural modifications cannot be accommodated by the HISAM Utilities. In order to reorganize and accommodate structural changes (e.g., adding a segment), HD Reorganization and Load Utilities must be used.

THE HD REORGANIZATION UNLOAD UTILITY (DFSURGUO) is a program that unloads HISAM, HIDAM and HDAM data bases. The unloaded form is that of a QSAM formatted data set. If there are logical relationships in the data base, this utility creates an additional data set that contains prefix information (pointers). This prefix information can be used by the HD Reorganization Reload Utility to create a work data set that is in turn used by the Prefix Resolution Utility to resolve those logical relationships in a reloaded reorganized data base.

THE HD REORGANIZATION RELOAD UTILITY (DFSURGLO) is a program that can be used to reload an HDAM, HIDAM an HISAM data base from a data set created by the HD Reorganization Unload Utility. It can also be used to create a work data set (for those data bases containing logical relationships or secondary indexes) that is used as input the Prefix Resolution Utility. It is the Prefix Resolution Utility that resolves the logical relationships in reloaded data bases containing logical relationships.

---

[2]The terms HISAM and HIDAM, as well as HSAM and HDAM, are used to describe IMS/VS file organizations. Additionally, these terms are used in characterizing the interfaces between the application program and the actual access methods of MVS operating system.

THE DATA BASE PREREORGANIZATION UTILITY (DFSURPRO) produces a control data set that is used as input to other logical relationship utilities. It also produces a list of data bases and segments that must be scanned by the Data Base Scan Utility. The Data Base Prereorganization Utility must be used when data bases being loaded or reorganized contain secondary indexes and/or logical relationships.

THE DATA BASE SCAN UTILITY (DFSURGSO) scans data bases that are not being reorganized to determine the effect of changes in logical relationships caused by a data base that is being reorganized. An output data set so generated is used as input to the Prefix Resolution Utility.

THE DATA BASE PREFIX RESOLUTION UTILITY (DFSURGLO) takes in the work data sets created by other utilities. These work data sets contain information required by the utility to produce output data sets containing the prefix data needed to establish logical relationships and/or secondary indexes in reorganized data bases.

THE DATA BASE PREFIX UPDATE UTILITY (DFSURGPO) uses the output from the Data Base Prefix Resolution Utility to update the prefix (pointers) of the segments that were affected by a reorganization or reloading of the data base.

DATA BASE RECOVERY UTILITIES

Conceptually, the Recovery Utilities processing system is quite simple. It consists of copying the physical data base from time to time and maintaining a log of all changes made to the data base in the intervening time between copying. If the data base becomes damaged, it can be restored by restoring the data base from the copy and then applying all the logged changes (since that copy was made) to the restored data base. The following sections describe these recovery utilities.

THE DATA BASE IMAGE COPY UTILITY (DFSUDMPO) copies data set groups.[3] This utility can copy multiple data sets on mixed device types. Also the user can specify whether one or two output image copies are to be created.

THE DATA BASE CHANGE ACCUMULATION UTILITY (DFSUCUMO) produces a summarized sequential data set from log data sets. The output contains only that information that is necessary for recovery. The user specifies a purge date and as the log data sets are processed by the utility, all records prior to that date are eliminated from the process. The records that are kept are sorted by data set within data base.

---

[3]Data Set Group. Alternative grouping of segments according to other schemes in addition to hierarchical structure, for example, size or frequency of use.

THE DATA BASE RECOVERY UTILITY (DFSURDBO) is used to restore a data set that has been damaged physically. This utility does not provide recovery from errors caused by application program errors. The accuracy of the data in the data bases is to be ensured by the user of the data bases. The inputs to this utility are typically an image copy, a change accumulation input or logs or some combination of the three.

THE DATA BASE BACKOUT UTILITY (DFSBBOOO) is used to effect the restoration of data bases from a point at which updates have been applied to a point before the program causing those updates was initiated. It also can restore back to a checkpoint. This utility obviously has a number of uses, depending upon the error that precipitates its invocation. This process produces a log data set. This log must be used in subsequent recovery (Data Base Recovery Utility) as the records on the backout log match corresponding entries on the update log data set. The matched records from the update log are used to negate the updating effect on the data base being recovered. In this way, a data base can be recovered and updates that have been applied as part of an erroneous process can be removed.

THE UTILITY CONTROL FACILITY

The basic function of this utility is to control the execution of multiple utilities that are included in the Data Base Reorganization and Load and/or the Data Base Recovery groups. Use of this utility to combine the execution of other utilities presupposes, of course, a knowledge of the other utilities. In addition, there are some restrictions on the use of this utility.

THE UTILITY CONTROL FACILITY (DFSUCFOO) is a semi-automatic (one job, one step, one scheduling) process that provides procedures for performing most data base utility operations and maintenance utility functions that precede recovery and reorganization of data bases. It can also handle data base recovery and manipulations associated with reorganizations. It can be used to effect the combining of data base changes into composite change records in the Change Accumulation process. The control statements that drive this utility can be coded in a free form manner. Multiple control statements can be input causing the Utility Control Facility (UCF) to execute multiple utilities.

In the mode known as Normal Processing, UCF requires control statements for all the utility functions that it is to perform except for Data Base Scan, Prefix Resolution and Prefix Update. All required statements for these three functions are generated automatically, unless an unload or reload only is specified. In that case the user must specify that these utilities are required.

The control statements are used to build control data sets. The entries in these data sets are cross referenced to unify the correctness of user specifications. UCF executes the utilities in a particular sequence. In this way the user is safeguarded against some operational problems that might possibly occur.

SYSTEM LOG UTILITIES

The system log data set is an output of the IMS/VS control program. The information placed on this log has many uses, such as statistics, accounting, restart and recovery of data bases. The log contains an entry for all input messages and all output messages, as well as an indication of messages processed, the number of data base references, the type of data base references and processing time. From this data can be governed statistics about message volume by line and by terminal type and accounting information by application programs. Within the IMS/VS control program is a routine known as the system recorder. This routine places on the system log the data used for restart, recovery, statistics and accounting.

THE SYSTEM LOG RECOVERY UTILITY PROGRAM (DFSULTRO)

This utility program is used to create a usable log data set from one that cannot be used. The input can be either a single log data set or dual log data sets. Any errors that cannot be corrected by the utility can be investigated manually and entered onto the newly created log data sets by way of control statements. The utility can be run in a couple of ways. Using duplicate (DUP) mode, the utility, can be run using a single or dual log data sets as input. An interim log data set is output. Unreconciled errors can be corrected through the use of control statements entered as input and the utility is run again in replace (REP) mode and a corrected log data set is output. If a valid corrected log data set is produced from dual log data set input, then it is not necessary to run the REP facility of the utility.

THE SYSTEM LOG TERMINATOR UTILITY PROGRAM (DFSFLOTO)

This one is used to recover log data that were lost as a result of a system failure. Using a "dump" tape, the program locates the log work area, buffers, control blocks; positions the log tape properly; writes the remaining log data and closes the log data set.

THE IMS/VS STATISTICAL ANALYSIS UTILITY

The analysis utility is composed of multiple parts, the Sort and Edit Pass 1 (DFSISTSO), Edit Pass 2 (DFSIST20), Report Writer (DFSIST30) and Message Select and Copy or List (DFSIST40). Sort and Edit Pass 1 selects those records from the log data set that are used by the statistical programs. It pulls together message segments of multi-segment transactions, enqueues and dequeues records associated with transactions and edits records and puts output messages behind the input messages that triggered that output. Edit Pass 2 extracts records from system messages that are needed to run the statistical reports. Report Writer is the program that produces the final statistical reports. The types of statistical reports are:

1. Messages Queued But Not Sent—By Destination

2. Messages—Program To Program—By Destination

3. Line and Terminal Report (a loading report)

4. Messages Queued But Not Sent—By Transaction Code

5. Messages—Program To Program—By Transaction Code

6. Transaction Report (loading by transaction code and time of day)

7. Transaction Response Report

8. Application Accounting Report

9. IMS/VS Accounting Report

10. Operating Information

The Message Select and Copy or List is an optional program. It is used to place selected messages from Edit Pass 2 on an output data set or to print them.

THE FILE SELECT AND FORMATTING PRINT PROGRAM (DFSERA10)

This print program is used to aid in the examination of data from the IMS/VS log data set. Using this utility, the entire log data set can be printed, multiple log data sets can be selected and printed, selected log records can be printed or selected log records can be processed by routines entered from available user exits.

THE MIS/VS LOG TRANSACTION ANALYSIS UTILITY (DFSILTAO)

This analysis utility is used to gather specific information about individual IMS/VS transactions. Information such as transaction identification, message processing program, time transaction received, the time of the message call, the time the message processing program is terminated, message class and the like. The utility uses this data to calculate response time, time on input queue, processing time, time on the output queue. These calculations assist on installation in finding system bottlenecks and to evaluate if transaction classes have been properly assigned.

THE IMS/VS LOG TAPE MERGE UTILITY (DFSLTMGO)

This utility can merge up to nine log tapes into one log tape. The use of this utility is restricted to operation in Multiple Systems Coupling (MSC) environments, where more than one IMS/VS system is running.

PERFORMANCE REPORTING UTILITIES

THE DATA BASE (DB) MONITOR REPORT PRINT PROGRAM (DFSUTR30)

This is an off-line utility that organizes and prints data on DB system performance. The data is collected by the DB Monitor (DFSMNTBO) while the DB system is in operation. The reports that are produced are as follows:

1. Buffer Pool Statistics (Data Base)

2. Buffer Pool Statistics (VSAM)

3. Program I/O Report

4. DL/1 Call Summary

5. VSAM Statistics

6. Monitor Overhead

7. Distribution Appendix

These reports contain categories and summaries of IMS/VS activities traced at various levels of detail. In order to use these reports, one must have an understanding of the units of information contained in the reports. The elements used in the reports are:

1. Elapsed time

2. IWAIT time

3. Not IWAIT (Elapsed time—IWAIT time)

4. CPU time

5. Schedule to first DL/1 Call

6. Elapsed execution time

7. Maximum time

8. Total time

9. Mean time

Each of these terms has a specific meaning, which is contained in the manual describing the utility.

THE DATA COMMUNICATION (DC) MONITOR REPORT PRINT PROGRAM (DFSUTR20)

This print program is also an off-line program. It takes data accumulated by the DC Monitor (DFSMNTRO) and organizes it and puts out reports and displays containing that data. The elements used in the reports are similar to those in reports produced by the DB Monitor Report Print Program.

The following is a list of reports produced by the DC Monitor Report Print Program:

1. System Configuration (data about OS/VS and IMS/VS systems used)

2. Buffer Pool Statistics (Message Queue)

3. Buffer Pool Statistics (Data Base)

4. Buffer Pool Statistics (VSAM)

5. Buffer Pool Statistics (Message Format)

6. Region (data on timing, IWAITs, and DL/1 calls presented by region)
   Region Summary
   Region IWAIT

7. Program (data on timing, IWAITs, DL/I calls, scheduling and dequeueing that is presented by an application program)
   Programs by Region
   Program Summary
   Program I/O

8. Communication (data on communication subtask timing, IWAITs, transmitted and received blocksizes, inter-system traffic and queueing)
   Communication Summary
   Line Functions
   MSC Traffic
   MSC Summaries
   MSC Queueing Summary
   Communication IWAIT

9. Transaction Queueing (data on queue lengths and scheduling occurrences presented by transaction type)

10. DL/I Call Summary (statistics on all DL/I calls issued by every program)

11. Distribution Appendix (statistical distribution of above data)

Again, it must be pointed out that a knowledge of the elements in the reports is a prerequisite to using the reports. In the case of DC Monitor, the elements with which one must be familiar are too numerous to list here.

THE IMS/VS PROGRAM ISOLATION TRACE REPORT UTILITY (DFSPIRPO)

This routine lists all transactions that had to wait because transactions had accessed the data base record. Both the waiting transactions and the transaction holding the record are printed. A TRACE ALL option will cause the elapsed time of the wait to print also. The input to this utility is the system log tape.

THE SPOOL SYSOUT PRINT UTILITY (DFSUPRTO)

The print utility is used to provide for the copying of messages produced by the on-line control program from its data sets to a system output device. Output from this utility is a printout of status information, followed by a printout of the contents of the spool.

THE MULTIPLE SYSTEMS VERIFICATION UTILITY (DFSUMSVO)

This utility is used to verify consistency and compatibility of systems definition in an environment where there is more than one IMS/VS system defined. It is run in two phases. The first phase validates the input and the second verifies the multi-system control blocks.

DL/1 TEST PROGRAM

There is another utility found in the IMS/VS Application Programming Reference Manual, under the title of Application Programming Testing Aids. Known as the DL/1 Test Program (DFSDDLT0) and called "dee el tee zero" by those who use it, this utility is an IMS/VS application program that issues calls to DL/1 based upon information in control statements. Optionally it can compare results of the calls with expected results that are also provided in control statements. In this way it is used to test DL/1.

The program uses different types of control statements in order to produce specific kinds of results as indicated in the following list:

1. The STATUS control statement establishes printing options and determines the PCB against which subsequent calls are made.

2. The COMMENTS statement allows for the printing of comments.

3. The CALL statement identifies the type of call that is to be made and supplies information required by the call.

4. A DATA statement supplies the segment information for certain types of calls.

5. The COMPARE statement is quite powerful; it can be used for PCB comparisons or the comparison of user I/O areas.

6. The OPTION statement is used to set the SNAP option and establish the number of unequal comparisons before aborting the step.

7. A PUNCH statement creates an additional output data set that can be used as input to later DLT0 runs. This is helpful in regression testing.

This utility can be used to load a data base, display a data base, do regression testing, aid in debugging and verify how a call is executed.

OTHER FACILITIES

DATA DICTIONARY/DIRECTORY

Conceptually a data dictionary is a centralized repository of information about data resources. A directory is an index that contains information about the locations of data resources and the interrelationships among data resources. A dictionary package of some sort is virtually indispensable in documenting and thereby keeping track of the complex, interrelated and changing information and data in data base systems. The IBM package is known as the Data Dictionary/Directory (DD/D). Chapter 6 dealt with this product.

IMSMAP

IMSMAP/VS is a documentation aid that produces pictorial layouts of both physical and logical data bases. It consists of two programs: DBDMAP and PSBMAP. DBDMAP produces layouts or maps from DBDs and optionally can print the descriptive characteristics of the data base description. PSBMAP produces layouts from DBDs and PSBs combined. It maps the sensitive segments, that is, those segments contained within the PSB.

This tool should be used when a data base is created or modified. It is useful in letting a programmer visualize the physical and logical relationships. It is a good reference document and can be useful also for training.

BATCH TERMINAL SIMULATOR (BTS)

Batch Terminal Simulator II (BTS II) is a program that allows on-line terminal programs to be tested in a batch environment without the use of teleprocessing hardware. It stimulates the key functions of the IMS/VS Data Communications (DC) feature.

BTS II facilities include provision for checking program logic by keeping track of all data base calls and recording pertinent information that can later be printed. It maintains statistics that can be used to determine the cause of system resource contention problems or to evaluate the impact of new applications on the existing system. BTS II also allows the formatting of IBM 3270 CRT displays, permitting the testing of control blocks generated by the MFS Utility.

OTHER PACKAGES

There are other packages available that are associated with IMS/VS. The problem is that a list of these packages becomes obsolete rather quickly because as new levels of IMS/VS are released, some of the functions are absorbed into the IMS/VS utilities. Some of the utilities from an earlier level are modified. It all gets a little confusing. However the list that follows provides an idea of what is available. An IBM Sales Representative can usually provide more detailed information. Other packages are described below.

DATA BASE DESIGN AID (DBDA)

A data base designer enters input, output and processing requirements into this package. Output is in the form of a series of reports that show:

1. The data elements of the data base

2. The defined relationship using those elements

3. A relative measure of the frequency of use of the relationships

4. A grouping of the elements into suggested segments

5. A suggested hierarchical organization of these segments

6. A suggested list of secondary index segments

DBPROTOTYPE/VS

This is a design evaluation tool that provides statistics from a basic "bare bones" IMS data base design. The designer can make adjustments to his basic design and analyze the results from successive runs and then select the design that appears best. DBPROTOTYPE/VS is an enhanced version that evolved from DBPROTOTYPE, an earlier 360 DL/1 version of the product.

DCANALYZER

This aid is used in the evaluation of prototype data bases. It produces reports that reflect message processing timings while the application and the data base are still in the prototype state and before data communications are installed.

TEST IMS UTILITIES (TIMS & TIMS/VS)

This aid and its virtual storage (VS) extention consist of programs that can create IMS data bases and OS sequential data sets. Programs are also included for listing and comparing IMS data bases. The VS extention provides support for VSAM and enhancements for the subsetting of production data for a testing environment.

OTHERS

In addition to the above products, there are a number of user developed pacakages, some of which are available through IBM, others through organizations such as GUIDE. Others can be obtained from other corporations that are using IMS/VS.

9
Staffing, Educating and Organizing for an IMS/VS Shop

The material presented in this chapter reflects the author's direct experience with a divisionalized corporation (CBS) making use of specific data base management system software (IMS/VS and DD/D). Therefore the chapter will be of more direct benefit to those in divisionalized corporations who elect to use IMS/VS and DD/D. And yet, there is much information that has general application to any user or potential user of a Data Base System. One may have to apply some inductive reasoning, but it is possible to formulate some general guidelines from the particular facts that are presented here.

THE BATTLEFIELD APPROACH VERSUS THE TEXTBOOK APPROACH

Organizing, staffing and educating can be approached in two ways, by the book or under battlefield conditions. The textbook approach has already been written. It will not be duplicated here. My exposure to the tasks of organizing, staffing and educating a Data Base System staff took place after the decision to use a Data Base Management System had been reached. My experience is a combination of direct participation, consultation and observation.

The textbook approach to these tasks is outlined in an illustration in Martin's book, *Principles of Data Base Management.*[1] Just beyond the title page is an illustration showing a roadway with milestone markers spotted in various places along the road. Each milestone (there are over thirty of them) has a caption. The milestones outline the textbook approach to the successful implementation of a comprehensive information system. The first milestone is captioned "Top Management Comprehension and Commitment." It does not take long for Martin and me to part company. I am firmly convinced that any company that waits for top management comprehension and commitment to an information system will never get it. Every systems course I ever took and every systems book ever written contains the admonition to get top management commitment. It simply cannot be done. Top management is made up of men who have a combined experience in marketing, finance and accounting. It seems unlikely that there will be any great changes in that structure. These men know that they want information, but they do not wish to comprehend how they get it. It is the middle managers who must comprehend both top management's needs and the general specifications of information systems.

SETTING UP A STAFF TO EVALUATE POSSIBLE DATA BASE SYSTEMS

One of the next steps which Martin recommends is the selection of a Data Administrator. The individual, as opposed to the Data Base Administrator whom we will describe a little later, is to be the guardian of the data. Martin sees him as a member of the top management team. It all starts to remind me of the situation as envisioned by the academicians in the early and mid-sixties when MIS was going to save the world, and within ten years the top men in many companies would be those with an MIS background. Unfortunately MIS did not live up to its billing and is presently trying to recover from a rather dismal track record. In any event, waiting for the Data Administrator to be appointed will be incrementally more futile than waiting for top management commitment.

The next couple of milestones set up by Martin call for selection of a "data-description language" and the setting up of a team of top system designers. These steps are significantly more realistic. Assuming that someone or some group in the organization has made a decision to evaluate the possibility of using Data Base technology, a committee can be set up to study the alternatives available. At this point in our discussion, two assumptions are going to be made. These assumptions are made so as to restrict the scope of the presentation. *Assumption 1:* The organization that has chosen to evaluate the technology has made a rational judgment, and there is at least a potential need for the technology.

---

[1]James Martin, *Principles of Data Base Management,* Prentice-Hall, Englewood Cliffs, N.J., 1976, inside title page.

Assumption 2: The organization is large enough and has, or is prepared to get, sufficient staff to pursue an investigation and to install a Data Base System in order to evaluate it. As a rule of thumb, the staff commitment should include about ten people. Their expertise should consist of the following talents: one proven director or manager with knowledge of Data Base Systems, two individuals with a knowledge of file structures, two individuals with systems software backgrounds, two systems analysts familiar with the application to be used as a test vehicle, an individual with knowledge of data processing standards, an individual with project management experience and a systems programmer with communications software experience.

THE WORK OF THE INITIAL EVALUATION COMMITTEE

The initial committee should consist of a cross section of about five of the above individuals. A preliminary study should reduce to two or three the number of DBMS's to be investigated in detail. Reducing the number, arbitrarily if necessary, to two or three is necessary since Data Base Management Systems are extremely complex. Investigating more than two or three in detail is neither economically nor practically feasible, unless the organization doing the investigating can afford, or for that matter, find the number of technically qualified individuals required to conduct the study. A study of this type should take four to six months. It should include a detailed examination of the published functional specifications, consultations with organizations already using the systems under investigation and a determined effort to ascertain the organizational need for a data base management system. This study should be concluded as quickly as possible. The system eventually chosen by the committee can then be obtained and installed as a test vehicle. Without going into details, it should be pointed out that various leasing and purchasing arrangements for Data Base Systems can be, in themselves, complicated. It takes some time for the various administrative details to be straightened out. *A warning:* The easier it is to get a system in, the harder it is to get it out, if you decide you don't want it. A final *observation:* Because of the complexity of the various Data Base Systems, it is impossible, unless your organization has virtually unlimited resources, to do a detailed evaluation of more than one system concurrently.

THE FINAL SELECTION

A diverting but very enlightening anecdote connected with the above recommendations and observations concerns CBS. At CBS, the original committee report included a detailed evaluation of two Data Base Systems with a recommendation that the organization use Brand X. The recommendation was made by the committee based on the technical judgments of the committee members. These judgments were taken into consideration when IMS/VS, which had fared second best in a field of two, was chosen. The selection was made based on political and organizational considerations, rather than the technical ones. Although a couple of the members of the committee were puzzled by the action, most realized that the choice was made partially based on their findings together with other non-technical information from other sources. The decision was not made in spite of their findings.

INSTALLING THE TEST SYSTEM

Martin's milestones continue and they reflect rather well the sequence of events as they should take place. What follows in this presentation is the sequence of events as they actually did take place in a particular organization. In the chronicle that follows, some of it is expressed in the first person singular. Since I was "present at the creation," so to speak, the material reflects my particular perspective as Director of Data Base Systems for CBS.

THE CORPORATE STRUCTURE

CBS is a divisionalized corporation in which the divisions in similar types of business are organized into groups. There is a Broadcasting Group, a Records Group, a Publishing Group and others. A division of the Publishing Group made the decision to use a Data Base System when redefining their Management Information Systems. Since this division was one of many users of a centralized CBS Data Center, the cooperation of the Corporate MIS Department was required. Individuals from this group together with divisional representatives made up the committee to study and recommend a particular Data Base System.

STAFFING

It was after the selection of IMS/VS as the vehicle that I was appointed to my position. However, prior to that time I had been requested to present some ideas on the Data Base Systems function and organization within CBS. My initial attempts at organization, job positions, titles and descriptions reflected knowledge that up until that time had been largely theoretical. However, as time passed, they were modified as additional information and practical experience were combined with the theoretical. Job descriptions were made up for Data Base Administrator, Data Base Communications Specialist, Data Base Configuration Specialist and others. A sample of two of these job descriptions can be seen in Fig. 9–1.

DATA BASE ADMINISTRATOR

As has been seen elsewhere, the description of a Data Base Administrator is as varied as the textbooks written on the subject of Data Bases. Within CBS, there are two separate Data Base Administration functions; each have individuals with the title of Data Base Administrator (DBA). There is a divisional DBA whose function it is to interface among the divisional users of the data that is to be in the data bases: the application programming project leaders who supervise the writing of programs that store, manipulate and retrieve the data; and

TITLE: Data Base Configuration Specialist

REPORTING STRUCTURE: Reports to the Manager, Data Base Systems

GENERAL RESPONSIBILITIES: Responsible for the definition (GEN), installation, maintenance, support and enhancement of the Data Base Configuration for non-communications systems. Also responsible for the utilities associated with the Data Base System.

PREREQUISITES:
A. EDUCATION: Bachelor's Degree or Associate Degree desirable, preferably in Computer Science or Data Management.
B. EXPERIENCE: To be qualified the candidate for this position should have had four years experience in some combination of data base systems programming, communications systems programming, or system software programming.

RESPONSIBILITIES:
- Establishment of the Data Base configuration necessary for the support of non-communication based data base systems.
- Ability to describe the concepts, relationships of data and access methods of a Data Base System.
- Testing of new releases of the IMS/DB feature.
- Utilize procedures and utilities to perform maintenance functions on Data Bases.
- Describe physical storage for a given data base in terms of the access methods of the Data Base System.
- Ability to back up and recover a Data Base.
- Participate in the installation of non-communications based data base applications.
- Creation and maintenance of test data sets for testing new releases of IMS/VS.
- Evaluate the relative merit of various access methods for particular applications.
- Familiarity with the security facilities of the Data Base System.
- Ability to implement a secondary index providing access to data in a different sequence.
- Provide security for data under his control.
- Be familiar with the responsibilities of the Data Base Data Communications Specialist and the Data Base Data Dictionary Specialist so as to provide backup for those positions.

RELATIONSHIPS:
- Interfaces with Corporate and Divisional Data Base designers in conforming design to standards
- Interacts with Systems Software Programming personnel
- Works with Data Base Data Dictionary Specialist and with Data Base Data Communication Specialist

Figure 9–1.

ACCOUNTABILITY:
This individual, by using his technical expertise, can effect a reduction in the amount of MIS resources (hardware and software) required to sustain efficient user interaction with a data base. Errors on his part can appreciably diminish the efficiency of the interaction of a user with his data base.

TITLE: Data Base Data Communications Specialist

REPORTING STRUCTURE: Reports to the Manager, Data Base Management Systems

GENERAL RESPONSIBILITIES: Responsible for the definition (GEN), installation, maintenance, support, and enhancement of the Data Base/Data Communications System.

EDUCATION:

PREREQUISITES:
A. EDUCATION: Bachelor's Degree or Associate Degree desirable with preference for Science (BS), Computer Science, Data Management or Statistics.
B. EXPERIENCE: To be qualified for this position, the candidate should have five years experience in systems software programming, including data communications programming and data base systems programming.

RESPONSIBILITIES:
- Generation of the Data Base Systems, that is, the installation of a working data base management system that can be utilized by Division MIS systems and programming personnel.
- Maintenance of a Data Base System facility which controls multiple data bases and a total data communications network.
- Ability to describe the concepts, control and flow of the Data Base Communications System.
- Define queues, buffer pools, message processing regions, batch processing regions, job priorities and classes of jobs.
- Participate in the design and implementation of Logical Terminal Networks.
- Specify recovery and checkpoint/restart procedures.
- Participate in the design and implementation of appropriate security measures.
- Utilize procedures and utilities to monitor the performance of the data base systems.
- Participate in the design of data base structures.
- Stay abreast of technical nuances in the field of Data Base Management Systems.
- Act as backup for the Manager Data Base Management Systems, who is his immediate supervisor.
- Thorough familiarity with Data Base Management System utilities.

Figure 9-1 *(cont.)*

- Be familiar with responsibilities of the Data Base Configuration Specialist and the Data Base Data Dictionary Specialist so as to provide backup to those positions.
- Define requirements to both Corporate and Divisional Data Base Administrators for descriptive parameters for terminals, transactions, data bases and program specification blocks.
- Make major contribution to the tuning of Data Communications and Data Base subsystems aimed toward making efficient use of computer resources.
- Provide important parameters to the scheduling functions which facilitate a smooth flow of work from an operational perspective.

RELATIONSHIPS:
- Communicates with Corporate MIS Management and Corporate Data Base Administrators.
- Interfaces with technical personnel in the area of computer operations, communications, and system software programming.
- Interfaces with Divisional data base administration, data communications administration and programming personnel.
- Communicates with technical personnel in other corporations as a member of technical groups like GUIDE, SHARE, and IMS users groups.
- Interfaces with DBMS vendor representatives for the purpose of achieving optimum utilization of the DBMS.

ACCOUNTABILITY:
Using his expertise, this individual can install computer support software that can substantially reduce the amount of time that users of MIS resources must wait to get information from data bases. He also can save precious computer resources by using his technical judgment. On the other hand, a mistake on his part can result in the shutting down of an entire Data Base Management System, resulting in operating divisions losing access to their Data Base for a prolonged period of time. Bad technical judgment on his part can lead to serious misuse of computer resources.

Figure 9-1 *(cont.)*

those individuals on the corporate MIS staff who actually create the data structures that reflect the most efficient way of storing the data.

There are two basic specializations in the corporate MIS staff group. There are the systems software technicians who install, maintain and fine tune the data base system programs and procedures, and then there are the Corporate Data Base Administrators who define the physical and logical relationships among the data elements that reflect the combined judgment of the divisional DBA and their own.

The objective of the divisional DBA is to balance the access and security requirements of the data from the divisional users' point of view. The objective of the corporate DBA is to balance the wishes of the divisional DBA and the efficient allocation and use of Data Center resources. I suspect that this last function gave rise to Leo Cohen's comment about the requirements for a DBA being those found in "an experienced kamakazie pilot."

OTHER POSITIONS

The staffing for the jobs that became available proceeded along the following lines. The division positions were filled with individuals already employed in the division. Two people were appointed to handle the divisional DBA function; they reflected a balance of the technical and the political. They complemented each other. One of them dealt primarily with users and divisional management, while the other dealt primarily with corporate DBAs and systems software specialists. Both of them worked closely with the application programming project managers.

The corporate staffing took a little longer because of some understandable confusion at the outset. Having established the required functions, systems software specialists and DBAs, the reporting structure had to be established. After some discussion, it was agreed that the systems software specialists functions would be established as a function of the CBS Data Center Systems Software department and would report to MIS Corporate Data Center operations management, and the DBA function would report to the Corporate MIS Staff management. Initially this appeared to be purely a political judgment, but whether or not it was became unimportant.

THE FIRST APPLICATION

The organization turned out to be an effective one. Essentially it works as follows: the first application to be put on the system as a job under IMS/VS was IBM's Data Dictionary/Directory (DD/D). Among other things, this package acts as a central repository for such things as Data Base Descriptions (DBDs), Program Specification Blocks (PSBs), Data Elements' Names and other required documentation information. In addition to that, DD/D is a system of programs that produces, among other things, the source statements that are inputs to the IMS/VS "DBDGEN utility" and the COBOL, ALC and PL/1 structures for the application programs. These structures can be stored in an operating system library (copy lib) from which they can be accessed by application programmers for inclusion in their programs.

The corporate systems software technicians and the corporate data base administrators cooperated closely in installing the DD/D package under IMS/VS. Once installed, the corporate DBAs contacted the divisional DBAs. The latter, working with the application programming team project managers, formulated the relationships among the data elements and forwarded them back to the corporate DBAs. The corporate DBAs and divisional DBAs cooperated in coding parameters signifying such data base characteristics as storage structure (HDAM, etc.), data base names, segment names, field names and so forth. So doing, they prepared input for the DD/D.

In due time, output from the DD/D was entered as input to IMS/VS and the data base structures were established. All this was accomplished initially in close cooperation with the systems software technicians who closely monitored the system to make sure that it was functioning properly. It should be pointed out that all this initial work was done with IMS/VS functioning on "four out of eight cylinders." Only the Data Base (DB) feature was used initially. All work was in "batch." Initial experiences were good. The software functioned well. Interaction between IMS/VS and MVS and VSAM, two other new system software products being installed concurrently in the CBS Data Center, was accomplished with only minor difficulty.

ADDING THE DC FEATURE

The next step was to "cut in the other four cylinders," and invoke the Data Communications (DC) feature. This step required significantly more effort. Close cooperation was required between the individuals of divisional DBA function and the individuals of the systems software technical group. The DC feature serves as the software that services the communications network as it interfaces with the data base management software. In order for the systems software technicians to define this feature, a significant amount of specific information was required from the divisional DBA function. This information included such things as: transaction codes, logical terminal names, type of terminal, addresses of terminals, communications (telephone) line numbers, transaction priority and so on.

TIME FRAME

The task of completely defining and specifying the IMS/VS DB and DC features, together with a functioning DD/D that had the ability to support limited divisional testing, took about nine months elapsed time. This period of time can be reduced to one month, with sufficient staff assuming the knowledge and experience. In other words, the first time, with our lone systems software technician, who initially had no formal training in data base systems, it took nine months. Since that time he has been thoroughly trained, as has one other individual. It is now possible to define a new release of IMS/VS, including testing of the facilities, in approximately two weeks using two systems software technicians. The difference is in the knowledge, the size of the staff and the experience.

AN EXPERIENCE WITH ASSEMBLING A SYSTEMS SOFTWARE TECHNICAL STAFF

Before getting to the specifics of education, permit me one additional subjective excursion. For whatever help it may be to you, let me share with you the way the systems software technical staff was put together.

About six months after the division had begun development of its systems, a few individuals within the Corporate MIS Department activated the plan for supporting Data Base Systems. I was appointed Director of Data Base Systems at the CBS Data Center. I have no way of really knowing why I was chosen except for the fact that I had some theoretical data base work in my background (my master's thesis written in 1969 and accepted in 1970 by the Baruch School of Business, CCNY, was on the subject of file structure and information systems), and I possessed a reasonably good track record of accomplishment at CBS. My first task was to build a staff of systems software technicians who would be able to install and support the IMS/VS Data Base Management System. From six persons interviewed (all CBS systems software technicians from existing departments), I chose an extremely capable and conscientious individual by the name of John Talley. He had four years experience in communications systems software. I felt I was off to a good start when a couple of the individuals, who had been in competition with him for the job, acknowledged to me that I had indeed chosen the best man for the job.

For the next five months, John combined formal training with "OJT" as he defined the system and installed the DB feature. During this time, he and I interviewed a number of candidates for a second systems software technician to work with us and unanimously chose one.

Also during this time, because of the amount of work that had to be done, we brought in a consultant from an outside firm, who possessed intimate knowledge of and had worked with the IMS/VS product at other locations. He was of inestimable value to us because he had the "hands on" experience we lacked. By the time his services were no longer needed, we had spent almost $20,000 in fees for his efforts, but all those involved in the project agreed that the money had been well spent.

ESTABLISHING CORPORATE STANDARDS' PROCEDURES AND GUIDELINES

Concurrent with these developments was the organization of the corporate Data Base Administration staff. This group consisted of three individuals with experience and training in file structures and standards. In addition to taking several IMS/VS and Data Dictionary courses, one of the first tasks of this group was the establishment of a set of corporate standards, procedures and guidelines. The undertaking of this task early made a significant impact on future development.

At first, standards were issued piecemeal. A process was set up whereby a subcommittee consisting of individuals from the IMS/VS Systems Software group, the corporate and divisional DBAs sat down together and hammered out the standards, one functional area at a time. The sessions took place about five or six times a month resulting in the establishment of preliminary standards in three or four functional areas. Following a session in which a standard was set, one of the corporate DBAs assumed the responsibility of getting it typed and distributed. This method served well in establishing preliminary standards quickly.

At the same time, two other procedures were initiated, one temporary and one that became permanent. The temporary procedure involved handling revisions to the standards. It was really quite simple. All it involved was numbering the cover memorandum covering the standard being issued. Those using the standards were always able to identify the latest revision by the number on the cover memo. However, this process was only temporary. It was only needed for about ten months.

The second procedure, or perhaps job is a better word, that was initiated was the establishment of a permanent set of IMS/VS standards. A complete set was produced just ten months after the first session for the purpose of producing standards was held.

The Appendix (found at the end of this book) contains the table of contents of the standards and procedures established by the corporate DBA staff. Subsequent pages contain selected sections from those standards. These selections are included in order to provide some insight into the kind of standards that should be quickly implemented so as to establish basic ground rules to be followed when installing a DBMS and a Data Dictionary System. Standards of this type should be set up regardless of the DBMS used. Granted IMS/VS is complex, but the standards are intended to regulate the user of the DBMS, not the DBMS itself. All Data Base Management Systems attempt to offer all kinds of flexibility. Unregulated use of this flexibility is quite likely to lead to chaos. Standards are designed to contribute to the establishment of a stable environment by reducing, and in some cases eliminating entirely, the esoteric solutions to mundane problems. The author acknowledges a debt to the CBS-MIS department for permission to use these standards. Although published and issued by the corporate DBA staff, these standards represented a collective effort on the part of a number of the individuals involved in the project: IMS Systems Software personnel, divisional DBAs and application programming Project Managers. The corporate DBA group is able to see to it that the standards are observed since it is their function to prepare the data for entry first into the Data Dictionary/ Directory and subsequently to the IMS/VS system.

STAFFING

STAFFING THE MASTER TERMINAL OPERATOR POSITION

Another job that should be specified is that of the Master Terminal Operator. Master Terminal Operation is an integral element in the successful utilization of an IMS/VS system. A skilled operator is needed to tend the system while it is in operation. The operator, known as the Master Terminal Operator (MTO), performs as an IMS/VS system resource controller. In this way, he carries out functions not unlike those carried out by an Operating System console operator. Since IMS/VS is like an operating system, running under an operating system, the MTO has some control over resources such as: application programs, transactions, communication lines, programs, classes of jobs, message regions, data bases and physical and logical terminals. The amount of control and degree of control given over to the Master Terminal Operation function is determined by the particular operating environment, that environment's use of other software products and its operating procedures and standards.

For example, in an environment using VTAM, the degree of control over communication lines and terminals by the MTO is somewhat more vague than it would be in an environment using BTAM, the former being a more sophisticated teleprocessing access method than the latter. Also, the amount of control by the MTO would be greater in an environment where there are fewer automated procedures for functions like "dynamic back-out," and "data base recovery." In the environment where there are many automated procedures, the amount of control exercised by the MTO would be less.

Staffing the MTO position can be somewhat paradoxical. A skilled individual, knowledgeable in IMS/VS operations, is required to do the job properly. In those cases where something goes wrong, the skill and knowledge of this individual are needed to minimize "outage time" and to prevent damage to data bases. Yet, when everything is working well, the job is incredibly dull.

To address the paradoxical nature of the situation a few basic suggestions are offered. First, in addition to a CRT master terminal, a printer should be employed as a hand copy output device. All messages are written to the printer as well as to the CRT. The printer "makes noise," the CRT does not; so the printer attracts attention and can trigger a response in the event that a message to a temporarily unattended "noiseless" CRT is not noticed. This is particularly helpful when everything is working well; the CRT master terminal might be unattended, but the noise of the typewriter terminal would attract attention.

Some operators seem to take an immediate interest in a new product like IMS/VS. This kind of individual should be encouraged and given training and on-the-job exposure during the developmental stages of the implementation of IMS/VS. This individual should then be given the opportunity to help to train others in the MTO function.

OTHER STAFF POSITIONS

While all of this activity was taking place, an organization was taking shape and specific jobs and responsibilities were being established. For example, John Talley's position was given the title of "Data Base-Data Communications Specialist." This title was developed in an attempt to define his skills and responsibilities as accurately as is possible in a job title. The second technical position was given the title of Data Base Configuration Specialist as was the other position in the department, which at the time was budgeted but vacant.

The jobs of Data Base-Data Communications Specialist and Data Base Configuration Specialist were defined and forwarded to the personnel department. These job descriptions were written in fairly general terms, so that individuals in the personnel department would not be buried under a pile of "buzz words," which they could not understand.

SUMMARY OF ORGANIZING AND STAFFING

Before getting into the specifics of education, let me pause here to recap.

1. An organization has been established so that a divisionalized company is able to make effective use of specific data base management system software, i.e., IMS/VS and DD/D.

2. The organization, in addition to the management positions, has functions in three sections of the company.
   a. Corporate MIS
   b. Divisional MIS
   c. Corporate Systems Software

3. The corporate DBAs produce and enforce standards. These individuals prepare and enter "data" into the data base management system. This "data" is used to define the structure of the data base. The information underlying this "data" is provided by divisional DBAs.

4. The divisional DBAs interact with individuals in the user departments, the systems and programming project leaders and divisional MIS management. From this inter- action they are able to specify information for the corporate DBAs, enabling them to define the structures of the data bases.

5. The system software technicians perform the function commonly known as a GEN. The GEN function is one in which the system (IMS/VS) is defined (tailored for a specific installation's hardware and software configuration). Since the hardware and software configuration of most installations is usually dynamic, the systems software technician's efforts are also dynamic. He must work with a base that is constantly changing. In addition there are a host of tasks associated with support of IMS/VS once it has been GENed. Many of these tasks come under the heading of "fine tuning" the system. For example, the setting of buffer pool sizes, allocation of storage space for specific functions and monitoring the performance of system utilities are but a few of the tasks of the systems software technician.

6. The Master Terminal Operator function must be established. Initially the systems software technician must perform this function as the system is GENed for the first time. Once the system becomes relatively stable, a Master Terminal Operator should be trained. The rub with this job is that it has the potential of being extremely critical and at the same time extremely dull. As yet there is no "pat" solution to this problem.

EDUCATING

Concerning education, one thing should be pointed out at the outset. It is going to be expensive. Assuming that you must start from ground zero to train indi- viduals in the various aspects of Data Base Management, the cost could run to $100,000 over a two-year period. If that number shocks you, let me spell it out for you. IMS/VS will be used as an example. There are other systems on the market and the educational requirements for their use may be less; however, there are two qualifications. First, IMS/VS combined with DD/D is quite a comprehensive data base management facility. Many of the others are not quite as comprehensive and therefore not as complex. It follows that the educational requirements would be less. Second, most DBMS sales representatives will not dwell on educational requirements, but rather on capabilities of the system. In effect, these sales representatives say "trust me, my system will do exactly what the specifications say." You can do that if you wish, but if you want to get the knowledge of the DBMS into the heads of your own technicians, you're going to have to pay handily for education.

IBM's PLAN OF EDUCATION

The IBM Corporation lays out a plan of education for the individuals who are to perform the various functions required by IMS/VS and DD/D. A note on DD/D: It has become axiomatic that an organization that decides to use a Data Base Management System must also use a Dictionary/Directory System. Therefore the educational outline that follows includes educational requirements for DD/D. The increased cost is incremental.

The following material is a summarization of the recommended Data Base System education curriculum as set down in the IBM Customer Education Catalog and Schedule (G320-1244), which is published semi-annually and updated quarterly.

SPECIFICS OF EDUCATION FOR INDIVIDUAL POSITIONS

Education is required for the following individuals:

Master Terminal Operator (MTO)

Corporate DBAs

Divisional DBAs

Divisional Programmer Analysts

Systems Software Specialists

Data Base Systems Management

MIS Management

EDUCATING MIS MANAGEMENT

Let's take care of the easy part first. After a preliminary introduction to Data Base Systems, MIS management personnel can be educated by the managers of the Data Base Systems functions. It is one of the responsibilities of these managers to present the concepts and techniques of DBMS to MIS management and to user management. If MIS managers, directors and vice presidents cannot understand the principles of Data Base Systems as presented by the managers of Data Base Systems, then there is good reason to doubt the comprehension capabilities of the Data Base Systems managers themselves. The expenditure of "out of pocket" dollars, therefore, to educate MIS management and user management should be nominal.

EDUCATING DATA BASE SYSTEMS MANAGERS

The education of Data Base Systems Managers is another problem. As with the advent of most new technology, there are a number of charlatans around in the field of Data Base Systems. As a rule, the knowledge of DBMS and the capability of managing a DBMS project vary inversely with the quantity of "buzz words" used. It is well to be wary of the individual who intimidates because of his apparent fluency, but who in reality leaves you impressed, but not informed. In selecting an individual for the job, the better course is to choose an individual with a known managerial "track record," from within your organization than to hire an unknown individual who knows all the words. If you can find a person with both a good managerial "track record" and a background in DBMS, that individual would be an ideal choice.

The Data Base System Manager may require some detailed Data Base theory courses such as "Data Base Design and Administration," an IBM course in the Systems Science Institute, which costs about $1,000. In addition, he should attend the latest James Martin Seminar and Leo Cohen's seminar, each one costing about $700.00. Martin's seminar opens to view the full panorama of the capabilities and possibilities of Data Base technology. The Data Base Systems Manager should be exposed to this so as to be aware of some of the euphoria associated with the potentials of Data Base technology. Cohen's seminar is somewhat more pragmatic in that it provides some guidelines for the manager to help him evaluate alternatives from among the various Data Base Management Systems in the marketplace.

Another course that gives an excellent overview of the fundamentals of IMS/VS is called DL/1 Application Analysis, costing $435.00. In addition to the tuition costs, provision should be made for travel and living expenses, since it is possible that Data Base Systems Managers might have to take some of the courses in localities remote from their place of business. This is true not only for managers, but for other individuals as well. So much for management, let's now look to educating those who work for a living.

EDUCATING THE SYSTEMS SOFTWARE SPECIALIST

The most expensive individual to train is the Systems Software Specialist. The cost for educating one person can be itemized as summarized in the table.[2]

---

[2]This table reflects costs as of 1978. IBM is constantly restructuring its curriculum making it difficult to pin down exact costs.

COST OF EDUCATING SYSTEMS SOFTWARE SPECIALIST

Course	Cost
IMS/VS Concepts and Facilities	–0–
IMS/VS Data Base Implementation I	$798
IMS/VS Data Base Implementation II	725
IMS/VS Data Base Performance and Tuning	1005
VSAM Coding for OS/VS	365
OS/VS VSAM for Systems Programming	645
IMS/VS Data Communication Implementation	1391
DL/1 Application Programming	357
IMS/VS Data Communication Application Programming	262
IMS/VS Message Format Services (MFS)	337
DB/DC Data Dictionary/Directory	370
IMS/VS Data Communications Performance Analysis	820
IMS/VS Data Base Design and Performance Workshop	1310
IMS/VS Data Base Systems Control and Flow	485
IMS/VS-VTAM-SNA Implementation	535
Total	$9405

The cost for the above is over $9,000. It is my considered opinion that this curriculum is necessary to develop a System Software Specialist who is up to the task of supporting a working IMS/VS system in an "MVS," virtual storage environment.

EDUCATING DIVISIONAL PROGRAMMER/ANALYSTS

The educational requirements for divisional Programmer/Analysts consists of a subset of the courses given to the Systems Software Specialist and the Data Base Systems Manager. A suggested curriculum for these individuals follows:

1. IMS/VS Concepts and Facilities

2. DL/1 Application Analysis

3. DL/1 Application Programming

4. IMS/VS Data Communications Application Programming

5. IMS/VS Message Format Services (MFS)

DIVISIONAL DBA

The educational requirements for the Divisional DBA include:

1. The latest James Martin Seminar

2. IMS/VS Concepts and Facilities
3. Data Base Design and Administration
4. DL/1 Application Analysis
5. DL/1 Application Programming
6. IMS/VS Data Communication Application Programming
7. IMS/VS Message Format Services (MFS)
8. DB/DC Data Dictionary/Directory

CORPORATE DBA

The educational curriculum for the Corporate DBAs consists of the following seminars and courses:

1. Data Base Design and Administration
2. Leo Cohen Seminar
3. IMS/VS Concepts and Facilities
4. DL/1 Application Programming
5. IMS/VS Data Base Implementation I
6. IMS/VS Data Base Implementation II
7. IMS/VS Data Communications Application Programming
8. IMS/VS Message Format Services
9. DB/DC Data Dictionary/Directory
10. IMS/VS Data Communication Implementation

MASTER TERMINAL OPERATOR

Last to be presented, but by no means last in importance, is the Master Terminal Operator (MTO). This individual must also receive some training. His education should include:

1. IMS/VS Concepts and Facilities
2. IMS/VS Master Terminal Operations
3. On-the-job training with Systems Software Specialists from the time of the first stable "GEN."

In addition to the courses just specified, there also exists a number of courses devoted to instruction in the use of the various "Aids and Utilities" packages associated with IMS/VS. These courses can be added to the necessary curricula as the need for them arises.

10
Comparison of IMS/VS to Other Systems: TOTAL, IDMS, SYSTEM 2000, ADABAS, DATACOM

This chapter is offered to highlight *some* of the differences among *some* of the Data Base Management Systems that are on the market. It is not intended to be a comprehensive look at each DBMS, as other authors like Leo Cohen have already provided. The purpose of this chapter is to highlight some of the ways in which several of the available Data Base Management Systems differ. In order to do this, I acknowledge several pages of somewhat redundant information on IMS/VS. My intention is to provide you with a quick recap of the IMS/VS product, and then to let you compare the other products to it.

Leo Cohen has devoted an entire book to a comparative analysis of Data Base Management Systems.[1] It is a comprehensive study to which I have made frequent reference in preparing that which follows. Having spent several years in analyzing and working with Data Base Management Systems, I have reached the conclusion that it is virtually impossible to do a complete comparative analysis on Data Base Management Systems software packages. There are too many of them, they are too complex, and they are in a constant state of revision and improvement. Yet there are some basic distinctions that can be made. In this chapter, some fundamentals of a number of these Data Base System packages are put forth. The material describing IMS/VS and DD/D with which this book deals comes from my first hand experiences. The material describing the other

---

[1]Leo Cohen, *Data Base Management Systems*, Q.E.D. Information Services, Inc., Wellesley, Mass., 1976.

DBMSs comes from research and reading. I, therefore accept complete responsibility if there are any misconceptions or misrepresentations conveyed in my review of these other systems.

SOME GENERALIZATIONS

Let's begin with some generalizations. A few of the general observations that follow here become rather axiomatic once you become familiar with a number of Data Base Systems packages. Yet, these observations are not immediately discernable prior to gaining that familiarity. It is for that reason that they are stated early.

AXIOM #1

No Data Base Management Systems software package can be all things to all people. This is true in spite of the fact that each package is marketed as though it were.

AXIOM #2

Data Base Management Systems software packages provide mechanisms for the rapid retrieval of information from Data Bases. There is a price that must be paid for this. File maintenance, that is, updating, is a time and resource consuming process relative to conventional systems. For a number of years, using conventional systems we had relatively slow information retrieval mechanisms; however, these systems possessed capabilities that permitted files to be updated relatively quickly. With Data Base Systems, we have the opposite—relatively rapid information retrieval mechanisms with relatively slow updating capabilities.

AXIOM #3

Each Data Base Management System comes complete with its own jargon. Although there are close similarities among some of the packages, there is enough dissimilarity to cause a great deal of confusion to the novice. This is true even among those who are technically trained, although many of those individuals would be loathe to admit it.

AXIOM #4

The old electronic data processing maxim, "the space-processing trade-off," is still in effect. There is much in Data Base Systems design oriented toward reducing the amount of space required to hold data. Yet as the space requirement goes down, the processing complexity and its associated "overhead" goes up.

AXIOM #5

The "name of the game" still seems to be: getting enough resources, both equipment and personnel, to support the desired software. This observation can work either of two ways. If you are one of those privileged few who can get enough equipment to perform a detailed comparative analysis on a number of different Data Base Management Systems packages, you'll still nevertheless have difficulty in locating and selecting personnel in sufficient quality and quantity to conduct the evaluation. If, on the other hand, you are like most users of computer equipment, you're always trying to get ten pounds of feathers into a five pound bag. In this case, a detailed comparative analysis is totally impossible, since the installation of only one DBMS consumes a substantial quantity of resources.

Lest this axiom seem to mitigate totally against the use of DBMS software, permit me to offer the following explanation. The estimation of the actual resources required has been made more complex than ever with the introduction of virtual storage. This technology itself has an architectural resemblance to Data Base Management Systems technology. The promise of virtual storage is like the promise of the politician, i.e., the providing of resources that aren't there, but making more efficient use of the resources that are there. The scarcest resource at this point is massive amounts of in-line computer storage. As a result, peripheral storage devices are used as a substitute. The manufacturers of computers and peripheral storage devices maintain that they can provide a better mechanism for swapping or paging *program modules* and *data records* between peripheral storage devices and computer storage than you yourself can. In general terms, they can.

The developers of DBMS, who in some cases are the same as the manufacturers of computers and peripheral equipment, believe that they can provide better software mechanisms for the swapping and paging of *data elements* or data segments between peripheral storage devices and in-line computer storage than you can. In general terms, they can do this better also. As a result, you are left somewhat at the mercy of the vendors, since several different technologies are involved. No single individual or even group is familiar enough with these differing technologies to take all factors into consideration. So, you have to "make an act of faith," in a sense; make a choice, pick a DBMS and go with it.

REVIEW OF SOME TECHNICAL PROPERTIES OF VARIOUS DBMS

An act of faith, however, does not necessarily imply a "blind leap of faith." There are some elements of information available on each of the packages that can contribute to "making an 'intelligent and informed' act of faith." The following pages, containing a review of some of the technical properties of the various Data Base Management Systems software packages, are intended to provide information to assist you in making your act of faith both intelligent and informed.

The packages receiving attention include IMS/VS, TOTAL and IDMS as well as SYSTEM 2000, ADABAS and DATACOM. Other packages being reviewed indirectly, since they are quite similar to those receiving close attention, include IMAGE, IDS II, DMS 1100, DMS II and RAMIS. IMS/VS, probably the most comprehensive DBMS, has already received a thorough treatment elsewhere. Following the treatment of these Data Base Management Systems, there is a final look at Data Dictionaries and Data Directories as part of Data Base Management Systems.

SIMILARITIES IN DATA MANAGEMENT TECHNIQUES AMONG SYSTEMS

In a number of ways, although there are architectural differences among the various Data Base Management System packages, there is much similarity in the data management techniques used. These techniques include the use of lists, chains and pointers, file or data set inversion, indexing, physical and logical relationships and the segmentation of data. Each of the Data Base Management Systems, although referring to these techniques by different terms, uses several of them in varying fashion. It is my intention to describe each of the techniques once. If a technique is used in a DBMS being examined subsequently, then the technique is *not* described in detail a second time. For example, a technique "file or data set inversion" is described before any specific DBMS. Therefore when this technique is encountered within the context of the DBMS called TOTAL, a familiarity with inversion of files or data sets is assumed. Inversion of data sets, having already been described, is not explained in detail a second time.

For those who are interested in pursuing detailed descriptions of the techniques in the context of each Data Base Management System package, I recommend Leo Cohen's book *Data Base Management Systems.*[2] (This publication can be obtained from Performance Development Corporation of Princeton, New Jersey.) Cohen's book contains excellent detailed descriptions of IMS/VS, TOTAL, IDMS, ADABAS and SYSTEM 2000. My thrust will be to describe only as much detail as necessary to make the systems' features intelligible and to permit them to be contrasted against one another.

QUICK REVIEW OF FUNDAMENTALS

DATA VERSUS INFORMATION

Before getting into the individual packages, let's review some fundamentals. First, the distinction between data and information should be established. The following is an example of data:

16, 4

11, 7

14, 9

17, 10

13, 14

---

[2]Ibid.

This tabular representation is nothing more than two columns of numbers signifying nothing in particular. However, Fig. 10–1 is an example of information as reflected by those numbers:

MIS VERSUS DATA BASE SYSTEM

As has been stated elsewhere, a function of a Data Base System is to transform data into information. Yet one might observe that the function of a Management Information System (MIS) is to transform data into information. What's the difference between a Data Base System and an MIS? The question is a valid one. A Data Base System is a functional part of an MIS. The following schematic (Fig. 10–2) shows an MIS.

The entire schematic is an MIS. Splitting the schematic in half, right down the middle of the interface block, will result in a Data Base System being represented by the right half of the schematic. The DBMS is a function of a Data Base System. A Data Base System, including the DBMS, is a tool. The responsibility for the use of the tool belongs to the one who uses it. Nails, a hammer, a supply of lumber, paint, brushes, paint thinner can produce a functional and esthetic addition to a house if used properly. The point is that a DBMS is a tool that can be used in producing a functional improvement to an existing MIS or a tool that can be used to a functional part of a newly developed MIS. Emphasize the word *tool*.

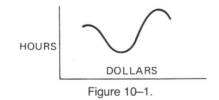

HOURS

DOLLARS

Figure 10–1.

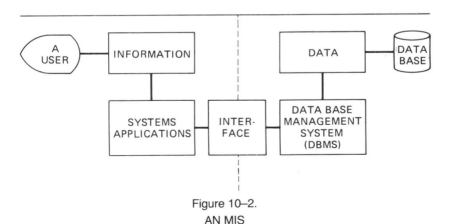

Figure 10–2.
AN MIS

CALL STATEMENT, A COMMON PROPERTY

One thing that all Data Base Management Systems have in common is that their retrieval capabilities are invoked by means of an application program issuing some kind of CALL statement. This CALL statement is essentially a high level programming language macro instruction containing parameters that specify to the DBMS software how to get the data that is desired and what to do with it.

OBSOLESCENCE AND SOME BASIC ELEMENTS FOR COMPARISON

Unfortunately when attempting to describe the technical characteristics of a number of Data Base Management Systems software packages, a qualification is necessary. The material presented here is subject to a degree of obsolescence. The packages described are themselves in a state of transiency. Each year several new releases of these systems become available. Most frequently the new releases contain only minor architectural changes, yet occasionally they do contain major changes. I must therefore qualify my presentation in that sense.

Looking at the Data Base Management packages in general, there are some basic elements which can serve as a basis for comparison. These basic elements include:

1. Type of System
2. Data Base structure
3. The retrieval function, query capabilities
4. File or data set organization
5. The data base management system functions

TYPE OF SYSTEM

The descriptions of the various Data Base Management Systems that follow concentrate on the essentials of each system as they differ with one another. The descriptions are not intended to be exhaustive. The earlier detailed examination of IMS/VS was intended to provide the reader with a thorough look at just how complex a Data Base Management System can be, as well as to provide a base to which other DBMSs can be compared. At this point, IMS/VS seems to be the most comprehensive DBMS in the sense that it contains many features and facilities, is extremely flexible as well as complex, supports complex data structures and has data communication capabilities as an integral component.

Leo Cohen distinguishes two types of DBMS. This seems a reasonable distinction. There are the designer type and the end-user type.

IN DESIGNER TYPE SYSTEMS, changes to file structure necessitate changes to programs. These types of systems provide greater flexibility of use,

ind as a consequence they are more complex and require a greater learning
curve. Of this type, IMS/VS is probably the most flexible and the most complex.
TOTAL and its look-alike, Hewlett-Packard's IMAGE, are probably the simplest.
IDMS lies somewhere in between. IDMS look-alikes include Honeywell's IDS
II, Univac's DMS 1100 and Burroughs' DMS-11.

THE END-USER TYPE OF PACKAGES usually requires large amounts of
computer storage relative to their capabilities since they represent the "high
level languages" of the DBMS world. Included in this group are SYSTEM 2000,
ADABAS and DATACOM. Yet since they are oriented toward the end-user,
they are relatively easy to use and the educational curve is relatively short
compared to that of the designer group. Also, the end-user type systems are not
tunable; they cannot be speeded up or slowed down. They just give solid, steady,
mediocre (from a resource utilization standpoint) performance. Designer type
systems, on the other hand, are tunable. IMS/VS is probably the most tunable,
and quite complex. It has, figuratively speaking, lots of knobs.

DATA BASE STRUCTURE

As we have seen, the term Data Base can have many definitions, all of
which are similar and correct, each reflecting a specific point of view. In examining packages, let me use the following:

A Data Base is a collection of data elements selected or organized so as to satisfy
a specific class of user inquiries.

Examples of a data base that could fall under this definition would
include:

an encyclopedia

an airline flight guide

a yellow pages telephone book

a white pages telephone book

a Sears catalog

A REVIEW OF STORAGE TECHNIQUES

In computerized data bases, storage space is allocated for each data set
required. This storage space, often referred to as data space, is typically allocated
on disk, around the track and down the cylinder. In other words, the data space
is allocated track 1, top platter 1; track 1, bottom platter 1; track 1, top platter
2; track 1, bottom platter 2, . . . track 1, bottom platter n; track 2, top platter
1; etc., rather than across one platter surface at a time like a phonograph record
(see the two views as shown in Fig. 10–3).

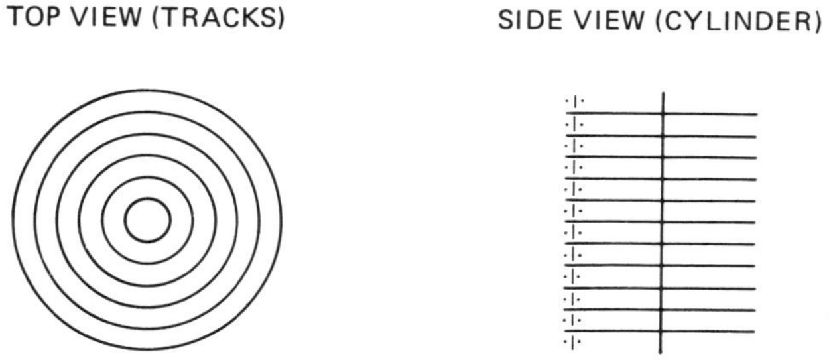

TOP VIEW (TRACKS)   SIDE VIEW (CYLINDER)

Figure 10–3.
TWO VIEWS OF DISK STORAGE

There are three basic ways in which data is stored in Data Bases by Data Base Management Systems, sequentially, directly and arbitrarily. Sequentially, that is, where one or more fields of a record are used to represent a key, and the records are ordered according to that key. In sequential storage processing, one record is stored in the available storage space immediately following the preceding record. This method of storing data reduces wasted space to a minimum, but makes updating cumbersome. Insertions require that the entire data set be recopied if physical sequence is to be maintained. There is a sequential storage technique known as indexed sequential that obviates the need for complete recopying. This technique maintains the logical sequence of the data set through the use of an index containing the keys of the records. This index is kept essentially in physical sequence (although not completely), while the remainder of the data set is maintained in logical sequence. Frequent reorganization of indexed sequential data sets is necessary.

In Data Bases, data sets can be stored directly or randomly by record. In the direct or random storage of records, a randomizing algorithm is used to perform a calculation on the key of the record. The result of the calculation is an address of a location that falls within the boundaries of a specific area of data space. This technique results in more wasted space than sequential, but reorganization requirements are minimal, and it is generally possible to retrieve individual, specific data elements more quickly.

The last method employed for storing data in the Data Base could be best described as arbitrary. No portion of the record (no key) is used to determine the location of that record in the Data Base. Typically, the records might be stored in the next available location from the end of the data space or the next available location from the beginning of the data space. This methodology is also somewhat wasteful in terms of data space.

Each of the Data Base Management Systems packages uses one or more of these storage techniques.

THE RETRIEVAL FUNCTION, QUERY CAPABILITIES

The retrieval functions of the packages should be evaluated according to their capabilities in being able to access across file or data set boundaries with a minimum number of physical access to peripheral storage devices. This factor is most complex. The efficiency of this method can be impacted by the way in which data sets are logically structured and physically stored. The whole Data Base Administration function is devoted to balancing the trade-offs in this complicated area. In addition to that, however, there are some DBMS packages that may be more suited to your specific application than are others.

FILE OR DATA SET ORGANIZATION

File (data set) organization and Data Base Modelling are two concepts between which a distinction should be made. The Data Base Model represents the view of a Data Base that reflects the perspective of the user of the data. The user's view of the data sees it as information. This view can transcend file (data set) boundaries. In other words, a data base model is a logical file organization that is independent of the physical distribution of the data elements or records. In the view of the Data Model, a set of data elements or records may be logically related and then be given any physical distribution. A Data Model can be implemented using any number of file (data set) organizations. A given file (data set) organization, on the other hand, may represent any number of data models. Examples of Data Models are Hierarchical Structures and Networks, which have been treated elsewhere.

In the area of files (data sets), there are several methodologies used by Data Base Management Systems software packages. These include simple lists, chains, partially inverted files, fully inverted files and ring structures. A very good readable paper on the subject is "The Elements of Data Management Systems," by G. E. Dodd, *Computing Surveys* (ACM) June 1969. Lists and chains, as well as the concept of inversion have been treated elsewhere. At this point, the distinction between fully inverted and partially inverted files is presented, followed by illustrations of a ring structure and then an examination of specific Data Base Management Systems packages.

BOTH PARTIALLY INVERTED AND FULLY INVERTED FILES use keys. Inversion takes place when an index is set up to locate data elements that have a key value in common. It is actually the keys that are inverted. A key is partially inverted when the index (key value file in Fig. 10–4) points to a list of data elements which contain a common key value.

A key is fully inverted when the index (key value file in Fig. 10–5) contains a tabulation of the data elements that contain a common key value. To state it a little differently, the partially inverted file has a pointer in the key value file to the first record in the list in the object file. The first record in the list points to the second, the second to the third, and so on. In the fully inverted file, the pointers in the key value file point to each of the records in the object file.

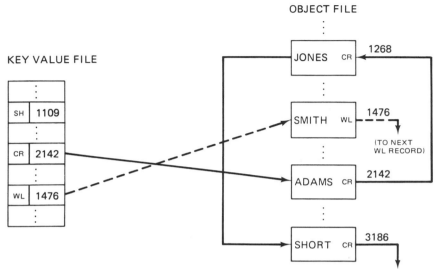

Figure 10–4.
PARTIALLY INVERTED KEY

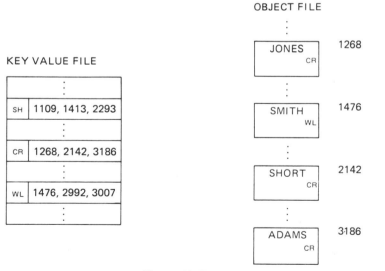

Figure 10–5.
FULLY INVERTED KEY

There are trade-offs between fully and partially inverted files. In a fully inverted file, queries involving many attributes can be serviced rather quickly since physical accesses can be minimized because so much information is kept in one file, the key value file. Paritally inverted files lend themselves to processing that is associated with retrievals according to a primary or single key.

A RING STRUCTURE is one in which the records or data elements are connected in a continuous loop. Any element in a ring structure can potentially be the beginning of the list. Figure 10–6 has a ring structure with one way pointers. It is also possible to have ring structures with two way pointers as seen in Fig. 10–7.There are other variations of ring structures. Some of the Data Base Management Systems that use ring structure support the more elaborate structures as a user specified option. The selection of a more elaborate structure is usually the function of a particular application. It should be borne in mind that there are always trade-offs, and elaborate structures will usually degrade

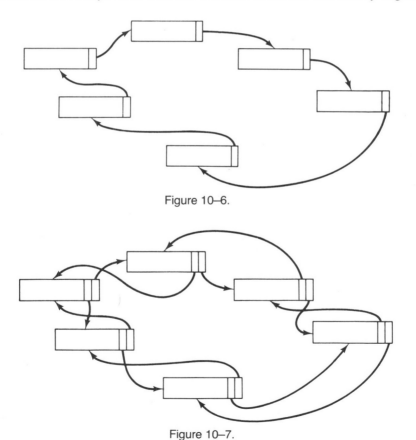

Figure 10–6.

Figure 10–7.

either query response time or updating speed. For a comprehensive review of file organization and data base modelling, the reader is referred to James Martin's excellent book, *Computer Data Base Organization,* published by Prentice-Hall, second edition, 1977.

THE DATA BASE MANAGEMENT SYSTEMS FUNCTIONS

The data base management systems functions are dissimilar from package to package. In addition to the basic differences between designer type and end-user type packages, there are additional differences between the packages within those two categories. One of the main differences is in the terminology that is used. Each DBMS uses its own terms to describe its own functions. This in itself makes comparative analysis cumbersome. Despite these difficulties, however, some comparisons are possible. In subsequent pages, each DBMS will be described in its own terminology. Wherever possible, comparisons will be made, one system against another, using a common terminology. Since I personally am more familiar with IMS/VS than the other packages, the common terminology will most often be that of IMS/VS.

Recalling any earlier statement that "No DBMS can be all things to all people," I shall now proceed to describe the various DBMS packages. I would also like to mention that as the packages are examined, the space devoted to each one should diminish. The explanations of each succeeding package can rest upon much of what is said about the preceding packages. This chapter is intended to be read as a whole and therefore much of what is presented in earlier pages represents foundation material for that which follows. Little would be gained from redefining redundant terms and concepts within the context of each package.

IMS/VS RECAP

Since IMS/VS is given thorough treatment elsewhere, it will merely be surveyed here. The summary presented here provides a sketch of what is probably the most comprehensive and complex of all the Data Base Management Systems.

OBJECTIVES OF IMS/VS

The stated objectives of IMS/VS are typical of any Data Base Management System. These objectives include: the elimination (reduction would be a better word) of redundant data, rapid response to queries against large volume data bases, the reduction of program and data maintenance, the independence of data, high level programming language interface for data retrieval and the fostering of an environment suitable to the phased implementation of projects. In designing IMS/VS, a system designed to facilitate user implementation of a Data Base system in a batch and/or on-line environment, supporting a wide variety of applications, the IBM Corporation developed a comprehensive set of facilities for doing so. In their design philosophy, they included facilities:

ı. to assure program and Data Base integrity

ɔ. for complete Data Base management

:. for Data Base recovery and reorganization as a system function

ꓸ. for separate logical and physical data structures

DATA STRUCTURE

As far as data structure is concerned, IMS/VS uses hierarchical structures for its logical data bases. These logical data bases could be thought of as modules of data, or data modules. The hierarchical structures are relationships among segments of data, a segment containing one or more fields of data. There is provision within the segments for several pointers that can be used at the user's option to establish multiple hierarchical relationships among numerous segments. Using these capabilities, several logical views of the same physical data base are possible. The language of IMS/VS is called Data Language/1 or DL/1. It is an input-output language consisting of instructions for sequential processing of segments—GET NEXT; direct processing of segments—GET UNIQUE; and selective processing within a hierarchical structure—GET NEXT WITHIN PARENT. It also allows for updating of segments with a GET HOLD version of the three instructions above as well as INSERT, DELETE and REPLACE instructions.

FILE STRUCTURES

The IMS/VS package supports four basic file structures. One of them is sequential (HSAM), one is indexed sequential (HISAM), one is direct with randomizing algorithm (HDAM) and there is also direct with an index (HIDAM). These structures are also called access methods, but they are not access methods in the commonly accepted sense of the term. They do not bring about the actual transfer of data, but rather they interface with the access methods of the operating system under which IMS/VS is running as a job or a task.

UTILITIES

The IMS/VS package comes complete with a substantial number of utilities, among which are those enabling the user to specify the physical and logical structures of the various data bases and data base views that the user defines. There is a utility to generate data base definition (DBD) control blocks for both logical (data models) and physical data base structures. Another utility is available that generates control blocks for the numerous logical views required by the various programs of the application. These views are known as Program Specification Blocks (PSB) in IMS/VS.

There are two techniques within IMS/VS that permit the establishment of relationships among segments that transcend file or data set boundaries. The techniques are secondary indexing and logically relating segments. Secondary indexing is closely akin to inverting a file, while logically relating segments is not unlike superimposing network kinds of structures over existing hierarchical structures.

In addition to these comprehensive Data Base Management System facilities, IMS/VS also contains extensive Communications Network Management System facilities. What the IMS/VS Data Base (DB) feature does for data bases, the IMS/VS Data Communications (DC) does for a communications network. Included in the DC feature are facilities such as: physical terminal support, centralized control of the system through a Master Terminal Operation function, message or transaction processing facilities, data and terminal security capabilities, system commands, system recovery programs and logical terminal operations.

In addition to the utilities mentioned above, there are also a number of other packages, commonly called Aids, which have been specifically designed to be used with IMS/VS.

OTHER IMS/VS FEATURES

Two additional features of IMS/VS, which did not receive any attention in the detailed explanation, are the Multiple Systems Coupling (MSC) feature and the Fast Path feature. IBM, with their eye no doubt on the "distributed systems" of the future, has developed the MSC facility. Also, in typical fashion, a new "buzz acronym" has also been coined. The MSC package uses the existing IMS/VS facilities but enhances their capabilities to operate on two or more IMS/VS systems on two or more IBM 360 or 370 computer configurations. Later releases of IMS/VS are introducing greater capabilities and also more "buzz acronyms" such as TDS, UDS and PDS.[3] These capabilities include IMS/VS support in a "distributed environment" for selected IBM terminals, both programmable and non-programmable. Detailed explanations of these capabilities would ensnare us in a quagmire of IBMese. Suffice it to say, the support for "distributed processing" exists and can be used. Yet, in keeping with other IMS/VS facilities, the expertise must be learned from IBM on IBM's terms, in IBM classes and in an IBM environment.

The other feature, known as "Fast Path," is defined by IBM as "a compatible extension of IMS/VS that is designed to enable the user to select either improved performance for simply structured transactions or full function for complex transactions, depending on the requirements of particular applications."[4] Again, a detailed explanation would involve a great deal of IBMese. Some of the new terms include Main Storage Data Base (MSDB) and Data Entry Data Base (DEDB). An MSDB is a root only fixed length segment data base

---

[3]TDS—transmit data set; UDS—user data set; PDS—print data set. These terms are names used beginning with IMS/VS Release 1.1.4.

[4]International Business Machines, *Service for Consultants*, IBM, White Plains, N.Y., August 1977, p. PPA 2.6.

hat resides in main storage. A DEDB contains records with root segment types
or holding fixed and summary data and sequential dependent segment types of
he roots, which contain detail information. The idea is to provide fast access
o selected data. Yet it should be made clear that both "Fast Path" data bases
and applications are separate and distinct from "non-Fast Path" data bases and
applications in an IMS/VS environment. In other words, "Fast Path" data bases
are exclusively avilable to "Fast Path" applications. Any other IMS/VS DL/1
data bases are not available to "Fast Path" applications, nor are "Fast Path"
data bases available to IMS/VS-DL/1 applications. Installation of the "Fast Path"
feature involves a normal IMS/VS system definition together with the required
extensions needed to define the specifics of the user's desired "Fast Path"
system, its data bases and application programs.

A final note, the use of "Fast Path," Multiple Systems Coupling and other
enhancement features that IBM periodically announces quite often requires interfacing with other IBM products not normally within the sphere of Data Base
Management Systems technology. These products include facilities like VSAM,
VTAM-NCP, MVS and SNA. It is possible for a user to make a commitment
to a feature in IMS/VS technology and not realize at the time that that commitment
implies a further commitment to another software feature quite apart from IMS/
VS.

There are a host of aids and other packages that a user can purchase or
rent, which can help in a typical IMS/VS environment. A sample of these appears
below.

IMS/VS Batch Terminal Simulator (BTS II)

IMS/VS DB Prototype

IMS/VS Space Management Utilities

Application Development Facility (ADF)

Data Dictionary/Directory

There are other features and aids with costs that correspond approximately to
their complexity and what they can do for you.

RESOURCE ESTIMATES FOR IMS/VS

Making resource (storage and DASD space) estimates for IMS/VS is extremely
difficult since it is such a comprehensive system containing so many options
and features, which may or may not be included in the system definition.
Compounding the difficulty is the installation of IMS/VS in a "virtual storage"
environment. In this kind of an environment, with the paging back and forth
between DASD and computer storage, there is created something of a moving
target that is very hard to hit. There are published resource requirements in the
IBM technical manuals and journals. These together with requests for infor-

mation from individuals who have already used the IMS/VS system represent the best source of information on resource requirements for IMS/VS. My experience has shown that even these are quite nebulous, since there are so many variables involved.

CONCLUSION

The preceding outline of IMS/VS should serve to bring back into focus the detailed material from an earlier chapter. Let us now proceed to look at the next package. I have arbitrarily chosen IMS/VS as the base against which to describe other systems features and facilities. For example in describing IDMS, when I introduce the term sub-schema, I would say that this is like a PCB in IMS/VS. I have elected to do this because of the divergent terms found in the various packages.

TOTAL

TOTAL might well be the simplest of the designer type Data Base Management Systems available. As such it is rather easy to learn to use it.

DESCRIPTIVE LANGUAGE

Before describing the package, the descriptive language of TOTAL should be reviewed. Going through these descriptions, one of the causes of the confusion in understanding DBMSs will become immediately apparent. One of the descriptive terms that is used has a different meaning in the context of the TOTAL system than it has generically. The term "Data Element" is usually synonymous with the term "field." In TOTAL this is not the case.

The basic element of data in the TOTAL package is called the DATA ITEM. A DATA ITEM is a field of data. As previously stated, a field of data is often referred to in DBMS technology as a "data element." But this is not so with TOTAL. Within TOTAL, a collection of one or more DATA ITEMs is called a DATA ELEMENT. A collection of DATA ELEMENTs is called a DATA RECORD. A DATA RECORD in the TOTAL Data Base Management System is, in essence, a record in the conventional sense. A DATA SET or a DATA FILE in the TOTAL Data Base Management System is a collection of records of the same type or essentially of the same structure. A TOTAL system DATA BASE is a collection of DATA SETS. For conceptual clarity, the DATA ELEMENT in the TOTAL Data Base Management System is the equivalent of a SEGMENT in the IMS/VS system.

FILE SYSTEMS

The TOTAL system provides the capabilities of a partially inverted file system. It contains basically two types of files, Single Entry Files or Data Sets and Variable Entry Files or Data Sets. The Single Entry Data Set is not unlike ı "master" file. The DATA RECORDS of this kind of file (data set) contain the keys that are addresses of a comprehensive and cohesive set of information that is distributed among DATA RECORDS in Variable Entry or "detail" Data Sets.

The DATA RECORDS of Single Entry Data Sets also called Master Data Sets are stored and retrieved directly using a system supplied randomizing algorithm and the key fields of the DATA RECORDS. The DATA RECORDS of the Variable Entry Data Sets are stored serially in the first available position of the Data Sets allocated data space. The DATA RECORDS of the Variable Entry Data Sets are retrievable through chains (pointers) related to the Master Data Sets.

KEYS AND CODES

The keys and codes of TOTAL are the final elements of descriptive language to be examined prior to describing the other aspects of the package. There are two types of keys in the TOTAL Data Base Management System. The Control Key is a value that uniquely identifies a DATA RECORD in a Single Entry Data Set. Before defining the other key, the Linkage Key, it is first necessary to define Linkage Path. A Linkage Path is a bidirectional chain that is used to connect the DATA RECORDs of a Variable Entry Data Set. There is a forward and backward pointer in each Variable Entry Data Set DATA RECORD that links it with the DATA RECORDs preceding and following it in the data set. A Linkage Key is a value that links DATA RECORDs in a Variable Entry Data Set with a unique DATA RECORD in the Single Entry Data Set. Since the DATA RECORDs in the Variable Entry Data Sets can be associated with one or more unique DATA RECORDs, in Single Entry Data Sets, there is a Linkage Key containing a Control Key value for each Linkage Path with which a Variable Entry Data Set DATA RECORD is associated.

A Variable Entry Data Set DATA RECORD having three Linkage Paths and associated with three Single Entry Data Set DATA RECORDS can be illustrated as in Fig. 10–8. Figure 10–8 is a simplified schematic used merely to help convey the concepts of Control Keys, Linkage Paths and Linkage Keys. In actual fact, the records in a TOTAL DBMS are slightly more complex than those pictured.

One of the components of the Variable Entry Data Set DATA RECORDs that is not pictured is the Record Code. This code is a two character field used to identify the format of a Variable Entry Data Set DATA RECORD.

So much for descriptive language. Let's now examine the package from a more pragmatic viewpoint.

HOW IT WORKS

It must be apparent by now that the Linkage Path and Linkage Key facilities of the system make it possible for the TOTAL DBMS to support both logical

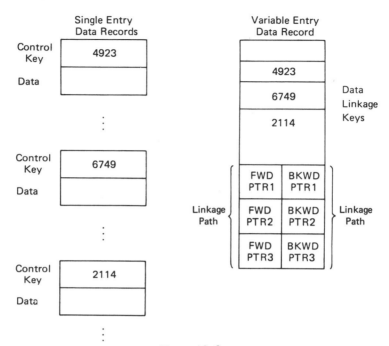

Figure 10–8.

and physical data bases. Both of these structures can be defined by a Data Base Definition Language. The Data Sets, once defined, are accessed through a Data Manipulation Language. As with IMS/VS, the accessing is done through a CALL statement, which is supported in many programming languages. Since the CALL statement was not examined in great detail in the explanation of IMS/VS, the following typical COBOL CALL statement is illustrative:

```
                            1       2     3     4        5
CALL DATBAS USING      READV,  STAT, EMP, EMPREF, CLP-PAYROLL
        6          7        8       9
    PR-EMP-KEY,   EMPLIST,  EMPREC,  ENDP.
```

The CALL Parameters are as follows:

FUNCTION	one of the allowable TOTAL commands
STATUS	area for communicating the disposition of the CALL
DATA-SET	the name of a field that contains the name of the data-set to be operated upon

REFERENCE	the name of a field for communicating the internal reference point within a Variable Entry File
LINKAGE-PATH	name of a field containing the name of the linkage path utilized in the CALL statement
CONTROL-KEY	name of a field containing the value of the key for the linkage path specified in the CALL
DATA-LIST	name of the start of a list that contains the names of the elements to be read or written by the CALL
DATA-AREA	name of an area that either contains the elements to be written or will receive the elements to be read
END	name of a field that contains the value "END"

This command will read a record from the Variable Entry file "EMP" along the linkage path "PAYROLL" using the value in field "PR-EMP-KEY." The fields specified in "EMPLIST" are moved from the Variable Entry Record retrieved to the area "EMPREC."

The instruction repertoire of the Data Manipulation Language DML of TOTAL contains a few more mnemonics than IMS/VS, yet it also is only an input/output language. The instructions include SINON and SINOF through which an individual signs on and off the system. There are open (OPENX) and close (CLOSX) commands for opening and closing files. There is a sequential read (RDNXT) and a direct read (READM) for DATA RECORDs in Single Entry or Master Data Sets. There is also instruction for updating DATA RECORDs (WRITM), adding DATA RECORDs to (ADDM) and deleting DATA RECORDs from (DEL-M) Single Entry or Master Data Sets. Similar instructions exist for Variable Entry or Detail Data Sets. The RDNXT instruction is used for serial processing of both Single Entry and Variable Entry Data Sets. Selective reads are also used in Variable Entry Data Sets. READV, READR and READD are used to access DATA ELEMENTS either serially (READV and READR) or directly (READD). There are also instructions for updating DATA RECORDs (WRITV and WRITD), or adding DATA RECORDs (ADDVC, ADDVB, ADDVR and ADDVA) to Variable Entry Data Sets. There is also a FINDX instruction that is used to locate records. Searching is done by key or serially from a specific position in Single Entry Data Sets and through Linkage Paths in Variable Entry Data Sets. Three other instructions are in the repertoire: RQLOC, which permits the user to place updates in the same physical order as the data set, and FREEX and ENDTO, which are Multi-tasking operators.

There are numerous installations where TOTAL is installed. There are also a number of releases in use in these installations. The capabilities of these releases is a variable factor. The TOTAL DBMS can be implemented on many configurations, IBM 360, 370 and System 3 equipment, PDP-11's and computers from Varian, NCR, CDC, Honeywell, Burroughs and Univac.

CONSIDERATIONS FOR THE POTENTIAL USER

The following are some overall observations on the TOTAL Data Base Management System that should be considered by the potential user.

SECURITY

Security is provided at the DATA ITEM (field) and DATA ELEMENT (segment) levels. Fields are assigned password security names, which are eight characters in length. It is these names that are used by the Data Manipulation Language (DML). When CALLs are issued, only those DATA ITEMs or DATA ELEMENTs specified by the user are returned. Further security procedures are the responsibility of the user. The system provides an exit call, DATBSXT, through which the user can implement his own security checks if he desires.

As far as data integrity is concerned, TOTAL performs no check on data format. It is the responsibility of the user to see that decimal data is not placed in a field that has been defined as binary, for example. TOTAL, however, assumes full responsibility for the integrity of the structures (i.e., the linkages that relate the elements in the logical and physical data bases).

SOFTWARE SUPPORT

There is some software support that can be used together with the TOTAL DBMS to enhance its performance.

One of the packages is called SOCRATES. This package is an information retrieval facility that incorporates conjunction and disjunction (AND, OR and NOT) logic. Using this package, the job of the application programmer is simplified in the area of fabricating searches requiring multiple parameters. Without the SOCRATES package, the skill required by the programmer is significantly greater since he must thoroughly understand the architecture of the data bases against which he is making queries. With SOCRATES, the user, not necessarily a programmer, need only be aware of what he is looking for and be able to prepare the SOCRATES retrieval statements.

There is a communication package that can be used with the TOTAL Data Base Management System. Called ENVIRON/1, it is a real-time general Teleprocessing Monitor. It has stand alone capabilities. When it is used with TOTAL, it controls a single partition or region in which TOTAL and several application programs can reside. ENVIRON/1 contains a logging function, which supplants the logging function of TOTAL, providing checkpoint or point of failure restart facilities. The ENVIRON/1 monitor supports the concept of logical terminals, as does IMS/VS-DC. Within the region controlled by ENVIRON/1, there are facilities to support concurrent independent tasks, each associated with a particular logical terminal. Each program is written as if it were a single-thread module for one terminal, although multi-thread capabilities are present. Application programs are written in reentrant mode so that the same copy can be used to handle transactions from multiple terminals. The multi-threading, therefore, is a function of the ENVIRON/1 system, not of the application.

There is another package called COBOL-XT, which is a COBOL-like language that generates reentrant load modules of 512 byte pages. The architecture of ENVIRON/1 supports modules of this size, which do not modify themselves in any way. Because of this restriction, some statements in COBOL like ALTER that allow this are eliminated from COBOL-XT.

There is also a batch terminal simulation facility available which, like the BTS II package of IMS/VS, allows for the simulated testing of terminal application programs in a batch environment. Simulated messages are read in from tape and processed. A log is kept on another tape. The testing, in simulation, of multiple tasks in concurrent execution is possible with this facility.

Security in the ENVIRON/1 package is left to the user. Since both the Master Terminal routine and the Sign On routine are written by the user, as many or as few security procedures can be added as the user wishes.

There are "restart and recovery" facilities in the ENVIRON/1 package. In the event that a program that only reads from a data base terminates abnormally, the system provides a "dump," and the program can be restarted once the error condition has been diagnosed and corrected. In the event a program that is updating data bases terminates abnormally, the entire region controlled by ENVIRON/1 is cancelled. Restoring is somewhat more complicated in this case. Two files are needed, a "roll file," which maintains terminal status, and a log file, containing a copy of transactions and "before" and "after" copies of the updated data base records. In order to facilitate a restart where an updating program has failed to run to completion, the taking of periodic checkpoints is another facility required in addition to the log and roll files. In the case when it happens, the system is quiesced, the log tape is processed backwards to restore the system to its status at a checkpoint. Effectively, the process "backs out" of the data bases those incomplete updates that took place before the program failed. At that point, the system can be restarted, all programs can be re-restarted except the one that terminated abnormally. That program should be corrected before it is restarted.

IDMS

The initials IDMS represent Integral Data Base Management System. IDMS is structured to conform to CODASYL[5] suggested guidelines. CODASYL-compliant Data Base Management Systems are those conforming to the uses of terminology and programming needs that were recommended by the CODASYL committee for Data Base Management Systems. This committee is known as the Data Base Task Group (DBTG).

---

[5]CODASYL: Conference of Data Description Languages. The commercial language COBOL was developed by this group. They are now working on a comprehensive, manufacturer-independent data base language.

184

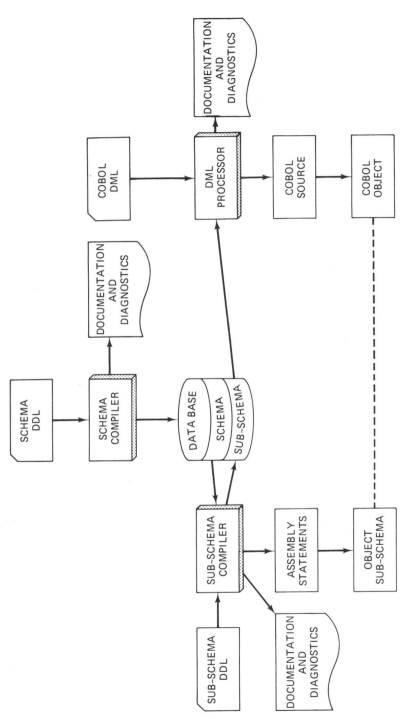

Figure 10-9.

LANGUAGE

The IDMS Data Base Management System has a language for data base (schema) and data base subset (sub-schema) descriptions. This language is known as a data description language (DDL). IDMS also has a language that is used to store data in and retrieve data from data bases. This language is called a data manipulation language (DML). The DML verbs or operations can be imbedded into application programs written in commonly known programming languages such as COBOL, PL/1 and FORTRAN. Preprocessors are used to generate "CALLs" to IDMS. There are Assembler Language MACRO instructions that allow data base manipulation instructions to be used in Assembler Language programs.

Figure 10–9 illustrates the flow within IDMS of the DDL and the DML.

DATA GROUPINGS

Within IDMS, the following CODASYL terms are used to represent data groupings. A DATA-ITEM is the smallest unit of named data. This definition conforms with TOTAL's, and it defines that which IMS/VS defines as a field. The next significant collections of data in the CODASYL and hence IDMS data description language are DATA-AGGREGATEs and RECORDs. Both are similar in concept to the Segment of IMS/VS. Within the context of the explanation of Segments and Data Bases in IMS/VS, it was indicated that the concepts of files and records that were used in conventional systems are gradually being replaced by segments and data bases. In the CODASYL data configuration, this is true to an even greater degree.

A DATA-AGGREGATE is defined as a named collection of DATA-ITEMS within a record. A DATA-AGGREGATE can be either a VECTOR, which is a DATA-AGGREGATE of identical DATA-ITEMS; or a REPEATING GROUP, which is a DATA-AGGREGATE of dissimilar DATA-ITEMS. A RECORD is a named collection of DATA-ITEMS or DATA AGGREGATES. In IDMS, the next collection of information is called a SET. Within a SET, there is a named collection of records that form a two-level hierarchy, with one record type as the "owner," and one or more record types as subordinate "members" of the SET. Finally, there is the DATA BASE, which is a named collection of records and the set relationships between them. There may be multiple DATA SETS in a system.

DATA DESCRIPTION LANGUAGE

Let's take a closer look at the Data Description Language (DDL). The DDL provides a method of defining all DATA-ITEMs, RECORDs and SETs in a DATA BASE. There are actually three DDL compilers in the IDMS system, two associated with schema (global data base definition, describing all data elements in the user's data resources) and one associated with sub-schema (views of portions of data bases as seen by individual programs). These are similar in concept to the DBDGENs, PSBGENs and ACBGENs of IMS/VS. A degree of security is made possible through the application of sub-schema DDL.

The first of these compilers, the schema compiler, is used to compile a complete schema definition. In a typical application there may be one "live" schema and some "test" schemas. These schemas contain descriptive information about every record type in the data base as well as set structures relating to those records. Furthermore, a user may define a number of areas into which a data base can be logically segmented. Again there is a potential confusion because of terminology. The concept of a segment in this context is not the same as it is within the context of IMS/VS. The logical segmentation spoken of here is more like the concept of a "data set group" of IMS/VS. This definition of area involves a subset compiler of the Data Definition Language. Known as Device/Media Control Language (DMCL), it gives the user the facility to map a schema into a group of data sets. This kind of grouping allows a user to have parts of a data base on- or off-line, as required, and also permits reorganizations to be done piecemeal when required. The third compiler is the sub-schema compiler. This compiler allows for the definition of subset of records, data-items and areas to be specified that are to be used by specific application programs.

STORAGE

Within IDMS, physical storage is in fixed direct-access blocks, which are called pages. Within these pages, data is available in the form of RECORDs. A page contains pointers to the individual RECORDs stored on that page. The RECORDs themselves are composed of a data portion and a pointer portion. The pointer portion (called PREFIX) is used to establish the relationships that are specified by the user through his data base administrator. IDMS supports both fixed and variable length RECORDs. Within a page, RECORDs are stored from "the top down" and the index entries for the RECORDs are stored from "the bottom up." Some free space is left for growth. There are 32 bytes of overhead in each page for such information as an indicator showing the first position of free space in the RECORD data area. The schematic (Fig. 10–10) helps to convey this idea.The IDMS page management routines always keep RECORDs at the uppermost portion of the page, so that there is no fragmentation of the RECORDs within a page. If a RECORD is deleted, all other RECORDs are moved up and the 8 byte line pointers at the bottom of the page are adjusted accordingly.

When defining a schema, a data base administrator establishes the method with which each record is to be placed in the data base. Within IDMS, there are three storage and retrieval methodologies that are used. They are all based on the overal strategy of IDMS's data base structure. These methodologies are known as "location modes" within the context of IDMS. They are named CALC, DIRECT and VIA. Here again, the potential for confusion. Within IDMS, the CALC location mode is similar to what is commonly known as direct or random in conventional systems as well as in some Data Base Management Systems such as IMS/VS. The CALC location mode is defined as that which

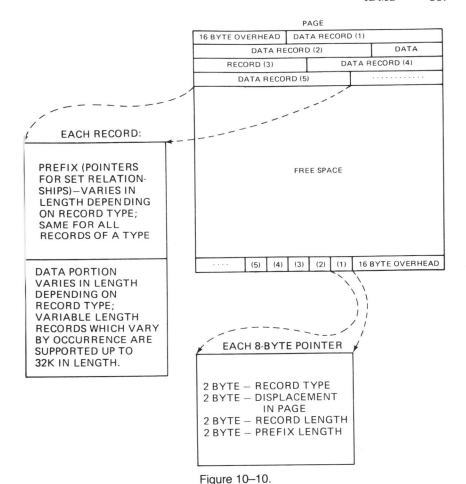

Figure 10–10.

places RECORDs in and retrieves RECORDs from a DATA BASE on the basis of randomization on a specified key field. The DIRECT location mode, in the IDMS context, is a convention in which a location in an IDMS DATA BASE is specified as a specific page and line within that DATA BASE. The VIA location mode is one in which RECORDs are stored in a DATA BASE on the basis of their physical proximity to the owner RECORD of the SET in which they are members.

A typical page is a physical block between 1500 and 4000 bytes in length. A number of pages are required to fabricate a DATA BASE. A collection of pages within an IDMS DATA BASE is referred to as an area. A particular value for a RECORD in the DATA BASEs is called an occurrence. In those cases where the system is not able to store an occurrence in a page, a synonym handling routine is invoked. A separate inventory of pages, known as space management pages (SMP), is referenced. These special pages are spread at determined intervals throughout the DATA BASE. They are used for storage of occurrences that cannot be kept in the intended page. A linkage is established, however, between the index of the intended page and the occurrence so that retrieval is through the intended page.

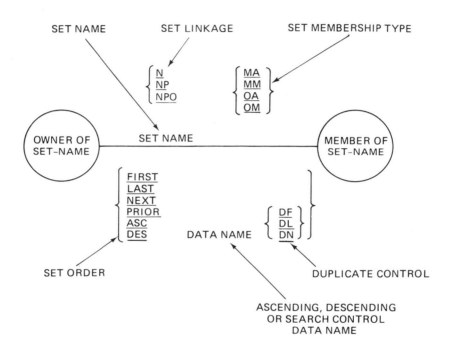

Figure 10–11.

ABBREVIATIONS

ASC — ascending order based on data-name
DES — descending order based on data-name
DF — duplicates first
DL — duplicates last
DN — duplicates not allowed
MA — mandatory automatic
MM — mandatory manual
N   — next
NP — next and prior
NPO — next, prior and owner
OA — optional automatic
OM — optional manual

FLEXIBILITY AND COMPLEXITY

The IDMS Data Base Management System contains a great deal of flexibility and consequently a certain degree of complexity. A number of options are available with which the user can establish a number of SETS and DATA BASES of varying complexity. The Data Definition Language is used to describe Networks and Hierarchies through the establishment of set relationships. Figure 10–11 is a schematic that portrays the concept of how these set relationships are established.

ASC	ascending order based on data-name
DES	descending order based on data-name
DF	duplicates first
DL	duplicates last
DN	duplicates not allowed
MA	mandatory automatic
MM	mandatory manual
N	next
NP	next and prior
NPO	next, prior and owner
OA	optional automatic
OM	optional manual

OPTIONS

Specifying the various options can result in the establishment of some of the following:

SPECIFYING "N" FOR SET LINKAGE would result in a chain where the owner would point to the first member, the first member would point to the second and so on, with the last member pointing back to the owner to complete the loop. In picture form see Fig. 10–12.

SPECIFYING "NP" FOR SET LINKAGE would result in a chain with bidirectional pointers and a closed loop—both directions. Graphically see Fig. 10–13.

IN THE "NPO" OPTION, a bidirectional closed loop would result with all members pointing back to the owner. Pictorially see Fig. 10–14.

IDMS CONTAINS ANOTHER SET OF OPTIONS governing the mechanics of Set membership, another example of unique terminology. These options are Automatic, Manual, Optional and Mandatory. These options are used combinations as follows:

Mandatory/Automatic   (MA)

Mandatory/Manual   (MM)

Optional/Automatic   (OA)

Optional/Manual   (OM)

These options are best understood in the context of some IDMS commands that are contained in application programs. The commands STORE and CONNECT are used to add new data RECORDs and/or to establish additional SET rela-

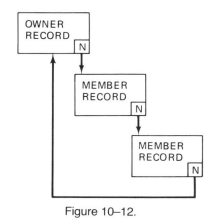

Figure 10–12.

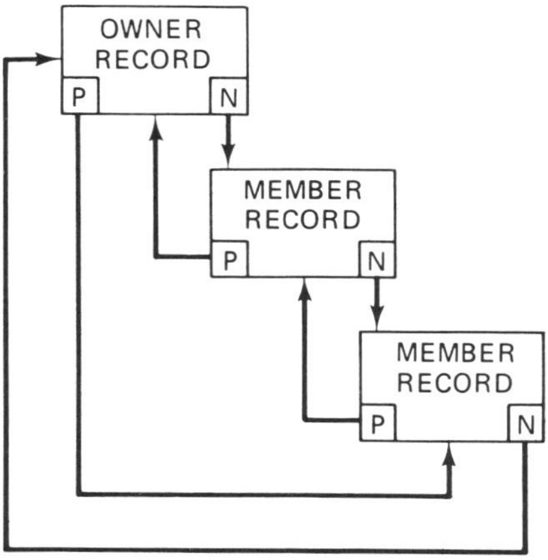

Figure 10–13.

tionships. DISCONNECT and ERASE are commands used to remove RECORDs from specific set relationships and/or to remove RECORDs from DATA BASEs. The MODIFY command allows the changing of DATA ITEMS within REC-ORDs. SETs are defined when the schema is defined and one of the above options describing the method in which member RECORDs participate in the SET is specified at the same time. The use of these options describes RECORDs as belonging to a specific set membership type. Each option has its own rules. The Manual SET has RECORDs added to the data base by a STORE command, but not made a member of the predefined SET until a subsequent CONNECT command establishes it as a member of the SET. The Automatic option requires the RECORD to become a member of the SET when it is stored. The Mandatory option stipulates that once a RECORD has been established as a member of a SET, it cannot be removed unless it is deleted from the DATA BASE. The ERASE command accomplishes this. The DISCONNECT command can remove a RECORD from membership in a SET with the Optional specification.

The remaining options stipulate where in the chain a member RECORD is to be placed. It can be inserted FIRST, LAST, NEXT (after NEXT) or PRIOR (to NEXT). It is also possible to sequence the members of a SET using the parameters ASC for ascending and DES for Descending. Duplicate control is possible with the DF duplicates first, DL duplicates last or the DN duplicates not allowed options.

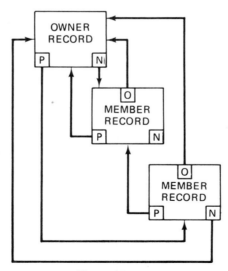

Figure 10–14.

OTHER CONSIDERATIONS

With the set concept of IDMS, it is possible to contruct a number of different types of data models. It is possible for RECORDs to be both owners and members making possible the structuring of both networks and hierarchies. The variations are virtually limitless. The schematics (Fig. 10–15) illustrate a few of the possibilities.

The basic structure supported by IDMS is that of partial inversion. Since it is possible to enter an IDMS data base at any point (a property of chaining), and since any member can be the head of one or more lists itself, a user is given great flexibility in design potential. Realizing this potential falls to the Data Base Administrator.

RETRIEVAL COMMANDS

In addition to the file maintenance commands above, there are three basic retrieval commands in IDMS. In order to define these commands, there are two final IDMS terms that should be described first. In IDMS, an executable program is known as a "run unit." During the running of the system, a tabular arrangement of information is kept by IDMS for its own use. The information includes

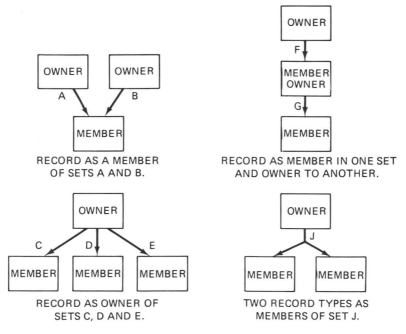

Figure 10–15.
POSSIBLE VARIATIONS OF OWNER AND MEMBER RELATIONSHIPS

the last record accessed in an area, the last record accessed by a program (run-unit), the last occurrence of record type and the last record occurrence of set type. This information, a status indicating the most recently located record for the program, the area, the record type and the set type, is called "currency."

The three retrieval verbs are FIND, GET and OBTAIN. The FIND verb locates the specific record on which currency is to be established, the GET verb brings it into working storage. The OBTAIN verb performs a combined function of FIND and GET.

SECURITY

IDMS is competitive in the area of privacy, security and recovery. The sub-schema offers a degree of security in much the same way as the PSB offers it under IMS/VS. It would also be possible for the Data Base Administration function to have a DBA program written to intercept and examine record occurrences that have been retrieved during the execution of application programs. This DBA program, if it found that an application program had retrieved a record that it was not entitled to, could override the retrieval and return an error status code to the application program.

It is possible to restrict sub-schemas by defining them as read-only, thereby reducing the potential for structural damage that could take place if maintenance instructions like STORE and ERASE were permitted. Furthermore, pointer information in the prefix portion of the record is stripped off before data is made available to the user.

Recovery of IDMS data bases is made possible through a number of utility programs like a dump (copy to tape), a restore utility, a journal (one page segments), roll forward and roll back utilities. Roll forward is a utility that applies "afterlook" copies of pages to a partially restored data base in order to bring it up to a correct point in time. Rollback is a utility that is used to back out updates that have been made by a program that has abnormally terminated.

SUPPORT PACKAGES AND VARIATIONS

IDMS has a number of support packages with which it can be interfaced. However, a recent announcement of the Cullinane Data Management System (CDMS) indicates that if you wish you can get it all from one vendor. Figure 10–16 illustrates the possibilities. In the center of the schematic is IDMS, which has just been described in broad terms. The CDMS package contains, in addition to the basic IDMS, an IDMS-DC Teleprocessing Monitor called SHADOW II, an integrated Data Dictionary, an on-line query facility, a report generator package called CULPRIT, back end facilities for interfacing PDP/11 and IBM 370 computers in a DBMS environment, an IDMS for PDP/11 computers called IDMS-11 and an EDP-AUDITOR package.

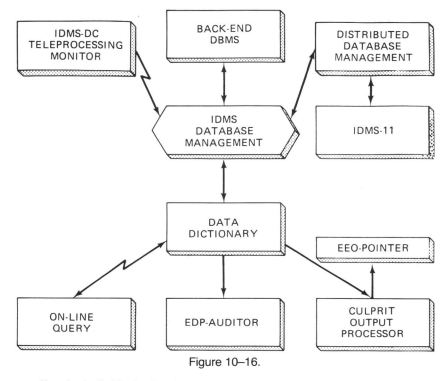

Figure 10–16.

For the individual who does not wish to get it all from one vendor, there are alternatives. Although the original IDMS was designed as a batch system, there is a multi-user version available. This version called the Central Version, contains Generalized Communications Interfaces (GCIs), which contain the necessary routines to run with CICS, INTERCOMM, Taskmaster, Cullinane's own SHADOW II or virtually any other commercially available teleprocessing monitor, including a "home-grown" version. Also included in this multi-user version is an additional module called the Central Activity Monitoring Program (CAMP). This program monitors and controls the accesses to the control function of the IDMS Data Base Management System, letting the requests for the system resources through as they can be accommodated. Automatic roll back and recovery facilities are also part of the Central Version. The automatic versions of these facilities are invoked in an on-line environment to detect abnormally ending application programs. These are then inhibited from running and their effects on the data base are removed. When this action is completed, the other application programs in the system can continue processing. The capability of interacting with the system through the console in the use of the roll back, roll forward and special journal file procedures permit rapid recovery of a DATA BASE in cases involving system failure, operating system malfunctions, etc.

SYSTEM 2000

Users of the S2000 Data Base Management System have the facility to structure and process hierarchically structured data bases that can be fully inverted if desired. You might think at this point that the terminology from the systems that we've already examined would suffice so that no new terms would be required. Unfortunately, that is not the case. It would seem that no self-respecting DBMS development team is able to fabricate a system using existing terminology. It seems that each system comes up with its own terms, exclusive to itself. S2000 is no exception. Yet, at this point, some of the terms introduced begin to bear a relationship to terms used before.

FILE STRUCTURE

LANGUAGE

The file structure of S2000 is quite elaborate. In order to describe it, some basic terminology must be examined first. A data base in S2000 is made up of six (6) files. Semantics become troublesome immediately, since the term "data set" cannot be used synonymously with file in S2000, as it has a completely different meaning. Within S2000, the term "data set" is used to define a group of data elements. It is the rough equivalent of an IMS segment occurrence. Another basic term is repeating group, often abbreviated as RG. The repeating group defines the components which contain the elements making up a data set. An illustration may help in clarifying these three concepts. Consider the hierarchy in Fig. 10–17.

In the illustration the ROOT, DEPT and SKILL blocks correspond to the term repeating group. A single occurrence of a particular RG is a data set; for example the ROOT RG for the individual "JONES, 23 RIVER ROAD, PASSAIC" would comprise a data set. The elements within the RG would be NAME, ADDR and CITY. In other words, elements define data sets and a collection of data sets make up a repeating group.

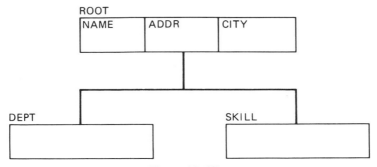

Figure 10–17.

Since data bases in S2000 are structured hierarchically, some other structural nomenclature is offered. The term "Family" describes a single hierarchical path between data sets, each one of which is on a different level. The concept is similar to the DATA-AGGREGATE of IDMS. Since it only encompasses a single path, it is *not* equivalent to a record. A "Parent" is a data set that has one or more data sets subordinate to itself in the hierarchical structure. "Ancestors" are those data sets in a "Family" in the levels above the "Parent." A "Dependent" is a data set that has a "Parent." "Descendents" of a data set are those data sets that occur at levels below in the "Family," that is, in the hierarchical path. A "Logical Entry" is a structure of data sets that all ultimately relate to a data set at the highest level. This term is the equivalent of a logical record. "Siblings" are all the data sets of the same RG type that share a common parent. This concept is similar to the IMS/VS concept of TWINS.

PHYSICAL FILE STRUCTURE

Let's now look at S2000 physical file structure. As has already been stated, an S2000 data base is made up of six (6) files. The files are integrated to produce an overall physical file organization. These six files are

CDEFIN	The Data Base Definition Table is a file containing descriptive data and two tables. The first table contains, for each repeating group, a pointer that references the first data set of that RG that resides in CFIND (described below). In the second table are contained references to the indices for keyed elements. It is, in essence, a value directory, called CVALDR.
CVALUS	is a file containing one entry for each unique value of a keyed element. Associated with these entries is a pointer to a block of addresses in another file called CENTS (described below). These blocks of addresses reference data sets in CFIND (described below). CFIND itself has no data in it, but rather points to the actual data located in CDATA (described below). CVALUS is arranged in ascending sequence.
CENTS	contains pointers to CFIND for those values that have more than one occurrence. For values that have only one occurrence, then the pointer in CVALUS points directly to CFIND rather than to CENTS.
CFIND	records contain no data, just pointers. It contains pointers to CDATA, where actual data content is stored. It also relates to other CFIND records that relate to it; for example, a particular data set represented in CFIND is related to its "Sibling," its "Parent" and its first "Dependent."
CDATA	is a file in which actual data contents are stored.
CNAME	is an overflow file that handles overflow from CDEFIN, CVALUS and CDATA.

Perhaps the best way to show the configuration of the component files of an S2000 data base is through illustration. Figure 10–18 is a schematic picturing each of the files and the relationships among them.

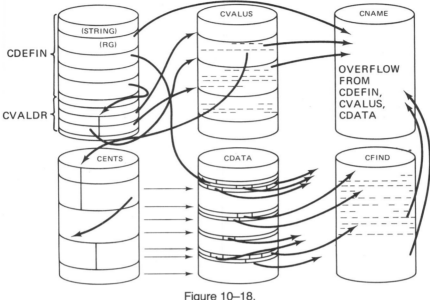

Figure 10–18.

The inverted file structure of SYSTEM 2000 lends itself to information retrieval involving complex queries, that is, queries to which response involves retrieving data elements from more than one source. In the language of conventional systems, this would describe queries that would result in data being retrieved from more than one file. The user desiring these increased retrieval capabilities should weigh them against the increased resources and time required to do data base file maintenance and updating.

PROCESSING

SYSTEM 2000 has two data manipulation modes of processing. Processing can be done either in "batch" or in "teleprocessing." There are two methods of doing the processing, that is, there are two languages, Natural Language and Procedural Language. The Procedural Language can be used exclusively in the "batch" mode of processing, whereas the Natural Language can be used in either the "batch" or "teleprocessing" mode. When using the Procedural Language method, interface with the data base is made through a programming language supported by the host computer. Figure 10–19 illustrates this.

Within the Procedural Language, the user is better able to "fine tune"[6] the performance of the system as far as use of resources is concerned, since he

---

[6]"Fine tune"—This term as it is used here does not have the same connotation as it does when used in conjunction with designer type systems. In this case, the amount of impact on system performance is limited to the DBA and the application programmer. There is little, if anything, that can be done by way of "fine tuning" by the systems software specialist.

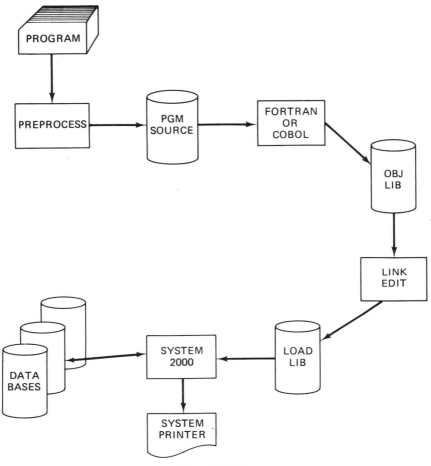

Figure 10–19.

has more control over the placement of data within and his own application program's position in the data base.

The Natural Language can be used in either a batch or in a conversational on-line mode of processing. Again, a schematic (Fig. 10–20) is employed to illustrate.

In supporting the Natural Language, the system is completely user-oriented, in that its primary function is making it as simple as possible for the user to formulate requests and get responses quickly. In this method of processing there are no ''fine-tuning'' opportunities for the user. The system provides the services in its own most efficient manner, and the user cannot make any adjustments to

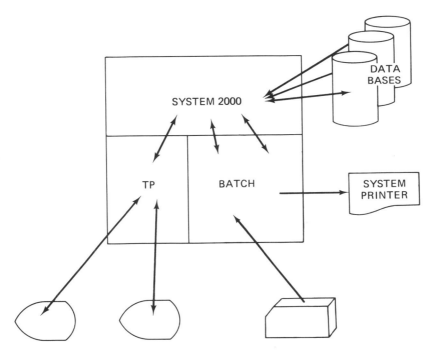

SYSTEM 2000

DATA BASES

TP

BATCH

SYSTEM PRINTER

Figure 10–20.

improve the performance of the system from a resources point of view. In the Natural Language environment, the user is in virtually the same position as a Time Sharing customer.

COMPETITIVENESS AND INSTALLATION

SYSTEM 2000 is competitive with other DBMS packages in that it is able to be interfaced with some communications packages, such as the TP facilities of Univac and CDC, IBM and MRI's own TP-2000. It also has restart and recovery facilities.

As far as installing SYSTEM 2000 is concerned, MRI usually has its own technicians install it in your shop in less than a week. Once installed, data base specification and loading are the responsibility of the user. When application programs are written in a programming language, the "CALLs" to S2000 are embedded in the application programs. The program is passed through a "pre-compiler" that converts the "CALLs" into higher level programming language (like COBOL and FORTRAN) statements, which are then compiled into object modules together with the rest of the program, using the appropriate compiler. S2000 is similar to IDMS in this respect and unlike IMS/VS, TOTAL and ADABAS.

ADABAS

The acronym is an abbreviation for Adaptable Data Base System. This Data Base Management System package also makes use of inverted file technology, but unlike SYSTEM 2000, it does not make use of hierarchical structures. It is the product of a German firm, Software AG. United States offices for the firm are in Reston, Virginia.

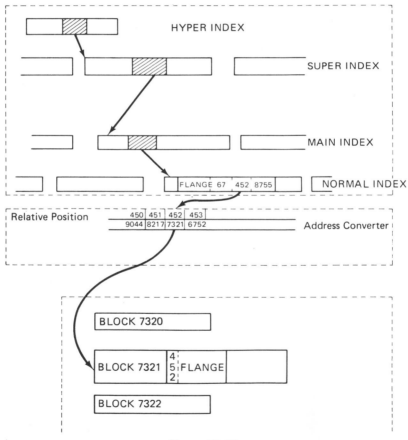

Figure 10–21.

LANGUAGE

From prior material, it is known that inverted files make use of tabular indexes to retrieve data based upon key fields of particular data records. ADABAS, true to form, uses its own special language. In ADABAS, a key is called a descriptor. Within ADABAS there are three kinds of files: indices, address converters and the data files themselves. Each of these file types has nomenclature. The index files are in levels, from Hyper (highest level) to Super (next level) to Main and finally to Normal index. The Normal index contains descriptor occurrences and pointers to the address converter file. The address converter file is made up of relative position identifiers of data records and pointers to specific locations (addresses) of the data. The data record itself contains the data. Figure 10–21 provides illustration of this ADABAS structure.

Some of the language of ADABAS is that which defines the files just described. The address converter file for example is called the "Associator." Since there is no hierarchical structure to an ADABAS data base, terms like segment, twin, repeating group, single entry records, etc., which appear in other Data Base Management Systems, are not needed. This does contribute to making ADABAS a somewhat more simple system to understand.

In ADABAS a record is a record in the commonly understood sense. When a record is entered into an ADABAS data base, it is given an "internal sequence number," an ISN, which is then used to identify the record for all operations. An "Associator Network" is an ordered list of the values that were assigned to the ADABAS descriptors (keys). Related to each descriptor value is an ordered list of ISNs for that value. The ISNs do not reference a physical location, but rather a relative entry in the "Associator," the address converter table. This table contains the pointer that references the physical location of the data record. In ADABAS there is a way to couple files through the use of a descriptor common to the file to be coupled, so that complex queries can be serviced. The technique of using an address converter reduces the overhead required for file maintenance and updating.

APPLICATION SOLUTIONS

There are several ways in which application solutions can be implemented in ADABAS. It can be done through programs written in host languages like COBOL, PL/1, FORTRAN or Assembler Language. Using this method, the host language invokes a data base operation through issuing a subroutine "CALL" to ADABAS. The schematic (Fig. 10–22) illustrates this.

ADABAS also has query language capability. It is called ADASCRIPT and allows for commands to be addressed to an ADABAS data base. These commands are essentially natural language in format. ADASCRIPT is usually employed by non-programmers and is a conversational mode of processing. The facility does syntax checking and report formatting for the user. There is also

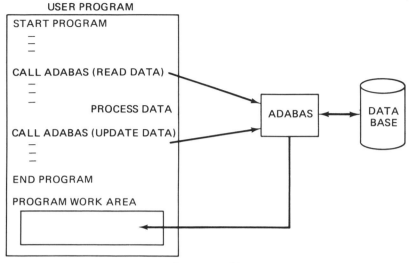

USER PROGRAM

Figure 10–22.

a report writer facility that is also part of the ADABAS Data Base Management System package, called ADAWRITER.

UTILITIES

The ADABAS system also has a number of utilities available with it. Included are routines designed to perform the specialized data base management system functions. There are utilities for the following:

1. Loading of files into the data base
2. Deletion of files from the data base
3. Coupling and Uncoupling of files
4. Definition of fields within files
5. Declaration and Deletion of descriptor fields within files
6. Logical Reordering of files
7. Saving and Restoring of the data base
8. Restoration of the data base to a particular checkpoint status
9. Establishment and maintenance of data security information
10. Physical expansion of a data base
11. Status reporting
12. Restart, Recovery, Backout, etc., included in an automatic restart function

In the area of telecommunication support, there are modules available that enable ADABAS users to interface it with CICS, INTERCOMM, TASKMASTER and TSO. In addition there is a Software AG product known as COM-PLETE that supports telecommunications.

ADVANTAGES

A distinct advantage of the ADABAS system is that fewer new concepts are introduced than there are on the other systems. It is relatively easy to learn to use it. Another advantage is that ADABAS's file structure permits it to use variable length data records. This fact together with a "Null Value Suppression" routine allows data compression to take place, resulting in reduced auxiliary storage requirements.

DATACOM

The final DBMS to be examined is DATACOM. This review is the most sketchy since the facilities of the package are similar in some respects to those of the packages already examined. One of the distinguishing characteristics of DATACOM is that it was originally a telecommunications package. The data base management capabilities were later added.

Somewhat like IMS/VS, DATACOM is composed of two basic features: DATACOM/DB (DB meaning Data Base) and DATACOM/DC (DC meaning Data Communications). Unlike IMS/VS, in which the DC feature requires the DB feature, the DATACOM features can each be implemented separately.

LANGUAGE

The terminology of DATACOM parallels a few of the other systems. A DATACOM data base is a collection of files (maximum 240) that is managed by the system as a unit under a single index. In this environment, data in separate data bases are not related. There are levels of indices, not unlike the ADABAS model, but minus the address converter. A DATACOM file contains fixed length logical records of similar format. Because of a compression feature, the records can be of variable length physically.

A DATACOM key is a record identifier and is inverted within the index of the data base. Within a DATACOM data base, there are two types of keys that can be specified. A "Native key" is one used to store records sequentially. A "Master key" can be established as a uniqueness identifier for records in the file. The "Master key" and the "Native key" may of course be different data elements. A "data element" is a named set of contiguous positions, not unlike an IMS/VS segment, within a record. An "element list" is a user supplied list of data elements (16 maximum) that represent a request for information from the data base.

A schematic of a DATACOM Data Base appears in Fig. 10–23.

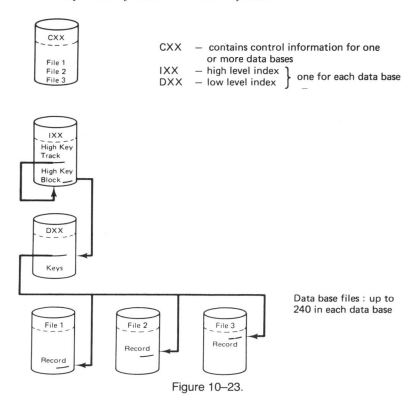

CXX — contains control information for one or more data bases

IXX — high level index ⎱ one for each data base
DXX — low level index ⎰

Data base files : up to 240 in each data base

Figure 10–23.

INDEX

The index contains references to all the occurrences of a data element and therefore a DATACOM data base is fully inverted. By way of contrast, the processing of a single file is faster in DATACOM than in ADABAS because the overhead of handling the address converted is absent in DATACOM. As a trade-off however, processing of a complex query requiring access to data in multiple files is faster in ADABAS because of the address converter. In DA-TACOM, the facility for processing complex queries is accommodated by merging indices. A merged index simply establishes logical relationships between records of different files in the data base. The process works like this: A unique identifier is assigned to each key. When the same unique identifier is given to keys of more than one file, it makes them in effect the same type of key. The values for these keys are then merged into a separate area of the index, creating, in essence, a new index. Retrieval is then achieved through this new index.

DATACOM also has a data compression feature that can be selected for use on individual files. The feature removes unneeded zeros and blanks from records when they are stored.

Data base access in this DBMS are completed through CALLs. Control
s passed to DATACOM/DB from an application program, which can be written
n COBOL, FORTRAN, PL/1 Assembler Language or RPG II. The retrieval
anguage of DATACOM includes both direct access and sequential reads as well
ıs add, update, and delete instructions.

DATA DICTIONARIES (AGAIN)

Having provided an overview of a number of Data Base Management System
software packages, let us briefly reexamine the concept of the facilities that are
currently known as Data Dictionaries and occasionally, as Data Directories.
Both of these facilities have received more detailed attention in Chapter 6. The
facility known as a Data Dictionary is simply a documentation tool that resides
"on a computer." Data Dictionaries are increasing in importance from
"nice-to-have" with conventional systems to virtually indispensible with Data
Base Systems. Dictionaries contain information such as names of data bases,
files, records, segments, data elements, descriptive data about the various data
groupings just mentioned, programs, systems, etc. In addition, current enhancements have given many Data Dictionary software packages the facilities capable
of producing data definitions that can be used by both Data Base Management
Systems and application programs. These facilities permit programmers and
DBAs to prepare input statements for only the Data Dictionary, with the Data
Dictionary System software itself preparing input data definitions for the DBMS
and data structures for application programs.

The facility known as a Data Directory is an index or a table of data
elements, segments, records, files or data bases names that also contain a pointer
or some other mechanism that is able to locate those data elements, segments,
records, files or data bases. More recently it has also come to define a table that
gives the relationships among items of data. It is the addition of this facility that
leads to the belief that Data Dictionaries and Data Directories will be merged
into one, and the resulting Data Dictionary/Directory facility will subsequently
become part of DBMS software. The "Data Dictionary/Directory (DD/D)" package represents the first step in that direction by IBM.

My personal conclusions regarding the evaluation of Data Base Management Systems and Data Dictionary packages are few and fairly simple.

1. Comparison of DBMS specifications by those individuals who are uninitiated as far
as DBMS fundamentals are concerned is virtually an impossibility. The generic
terminology of DBMS is difficult in itself. Compouding the situation even further
is the fact that the terminology and techniques employed by the many different
DBMS packages is often dissimilar. There are a number of potential solutions to
this problem. Among them are:

Expose a few of your better technical and managerial personnel to an education
in the fundamentals of DBMS.

Since some packages are better suited to specific problem solutions than are others, define your problem and establish a solution and then try to choose a package.

Use a reputable consultant early in the game. Be sure that he can explain DBMS principles in terms understandable to management personnel.

Make an attempt to learn the language and the concepts of Data Base technology. It is here to stay, and if you don't control it, it will soon control you.

2. A detailed benchmark of several DBMS packages is not economically feasible unless you've got a lot of excess computer capacity to play with. The resources required to "GEN," test and develop applications for each of several DBMS systems is in most cases just not practical. Just trying to have your personnel become familiar with the complexities of each system mitigates against benchmarking several of them. There are ways of getting around this problem also.

Visit other DBMS users, as many as possible. Question them about their experiences with things like installation, resources required, size of data bases and files, response time and "busted chains," and "pointers to oblivion."

Arbitrarily eliminate some of the packages from contention.

When you finally select a package, make it clear to everyone involved that there will no doubt be some second guessing later on, but that the choice has been made and there's no turning back. The chosen package is going to be used and that's that.

11
Integration of Data Base With Other Contemporary Technology

IMS/VS is merely an example of one type of an electronic data processing technology that continues to evolve. There are several other Information Processing technologies that are developing concurrently with data base systems. It is becoming rather obvious that these technologies overlap one another to some degree. A number of terms, like Office of the Future, Electronic Mail, Distributed Processing are quite familiar. These terms are but a sample of contemporary technological developments that are expanding simultaneously with data base management system technology. This chapter contains an examination of some of those technologies. Examined are those technologies that are actually integrated, to some extent, with data base systems. Included in this chapter is treatment of the following subjects:

1. Distributed Processing
2. Minicomputers
3. Microcomputers
4. Word Processing

Let's first look at Distributed Processing.

DISTRIBUTED PROCESSING

To the chagrin of some, the following simple definition is offered. Combinations of computer technology, data base management systems and teleprocessing technology result in something that is currently being called distributed processing, distributed systems or distributed data bases. Unfortunately, no matter what various authors may state, these terms in and of themselves define some concepts that are general in nature. Furthermore, these terms are used rather indiscriminately within the MIS profession, which does not help at all in clarification. In general, all these terms have something in common in that they are used to describe an orderly fragmentation of storing, processing and retrieving of data, using devices that may be geographically remote, but electronically interconnected with one another. Yet there are some basic distinctions that can be made between the terms. The term "distributed processing" describes an orderly fragmentation of processing among two or more computers with the processing controlled by a centrally located computer commonly known as a host. The term "distributed data bases" indicates an orderly fragmentation of data bases or files among the peripheral storage devices of one or more computer configurations. "Distributed systems" describes the hardware and/or software configuration of a system in which distributed processing takes place.

There are a number of kinds of distributed systems that can be configured. The following pages will illustrate and explain conceptually a number of these alternatives.

ANATOMY OF A DISTRIBUTED SYSTEM

The basic components of a distributed system could be illustrated as in Fig. 11–1.

COMPONENTS

This illustration merely shows the components and how they are typically linked. A distributed system may contain some or all of these components or multiples of those components. With the exception of the terminal devices and the remote job entry terminal, all the components in the distributed system above are computers, in spite of the fancy names. The names describe the function of what the computer is doing, but the device is a computer. For that matter, the term "intelligent terminal" describes terminal devices with computers built into them. If the above distributed systems were to contain "intelligent terminals," then every device in the illustration would be a computer. In addition to the computers shown in the illustration, there are also peripheral devices such as disks and tapes connected to the computers. Conceptually, the idea of distributed systems (processing or data bases) is simple. However, specific systems can be quite complex; that complexity being a function of either the specific system or the "nuts and bolts" technology of networks, data bases and operating systems.

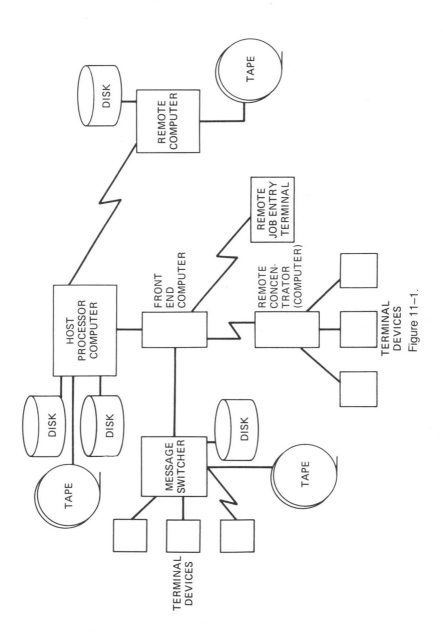

DISK

REMOTE
COMPUTER

TAPE

REMOTE
JOB ENTRY
TERMINAL

HOST
PROCESSOR
COMPUTER

FRONT
END
COMPUTER

REMOTE
CONCEN-
TRATOR
(COMPUTER)

DISK

DISK

TAPE

MESSAGE
SWITCHER

DISK

TAPE

TERMINAL
DEVICES

TERMINAL
DEVICES

Figure 11–1.

209

DATA PROCESSING ACTIVITIES

Within distributed systems or networks, as they are sometimes called, specific kinds of data processing activities are supported. These could be called:

1. Device sharing
2. File (Data Base) sharing
3. Program sharing
4. Module sharing

DEVICE SHARING would be the ability to gain access to and use devices that are remotely located as if they were located locally.

FILE OR DATA BASE SHARING would provide the ability to transfer and process data located on remotely located devices as if the data were on devices that were locally located.

PROGRAM SHARING would allow programs to be run on remotely located computers.

MODULE SHARING would provide the capability of dividing large tasks into smaller ones by establishing an interactive relationship between computers in the network so that both data and program modules could be transferred between those computers.

KINDS OF NETWORKS

As stated earlier, there are a number of ways in which a distributed system or network can be set up. The exact network configuration is dictated by the particular application or applications that are to be supported. However, there are some basic configurations that can be considered generic and can be described conceptually apart from a specific application.

The simplest type of network is the point to point network where there is one device communicating across a communications line to a computer. The device may be a terminal or an "intelligent terminal." There can be more than one point to point facility on a computer. Each is a separate point to point arrangement (see Fig. 11–2). Increasing slightly in complexity is the multipoint (multidrop) connection. It is conceptually similar to a party line telephone arrangement (see Fig. 11–3).

More complicated network structures include a mixture of computers and terminals that are interconnected. Each of the following configuration names is somewhat descriptive of the functions of the particular network. The following is not an exhaustive list of possibilities, and other concepts could be added. At the very least, they should provide the reader with a feel for the kind of networks that are possible as well as the functions for which each is best suited.

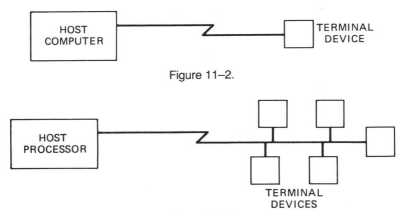

Figure 11–2.

Figure 11–3.

A CENTRALIZED NETWORK is one in which a number of satellite computers and terminals communicate with a central computer. The central computer has supervisory control over the system. The satellite stations can communicate with each other through the central computer which, in addition to other things, can act in this case as a message switcher. Control over the network is simplified in this type of configuration, shown in Fig. 11–4.

A TREE STRUCTURED OR HIERARCHICAL STRUCTURED NETWORK (shown in Fig. 11–5) is one where there are levels of computers, each level exercising some supervisory control over the level beneath it. Functionally, the processing at the lowest level may be either quite simple or perhaps specialized. The next level of processing includes some supervisory and control functions over the lowest level as well as reporting statistics to the highest level. The highest level uses the information reported to provide management with information.

A DISTRIBUTED NETWORK is one where there are several computers that can exercise supervisory functions. Also, connections exist between each computer and several other computers in the system (see Fig. 11–6). The main consideration is that of performance. It is this type of system that virtually guarantees one hundred percent availability of computer resources. There is usually a cost involved for some redundancy in both data and equipment. Continuing traffic analysis can be used to monitor the system so as to assure the proper balance between performance and economics.

OTHER CONCEPTS RELATED TO DISTRIBUTED SYSTEMS

Related to distributed systems are some other concepts, which come complete with their own terminology. These other concepts include: Message Switch-

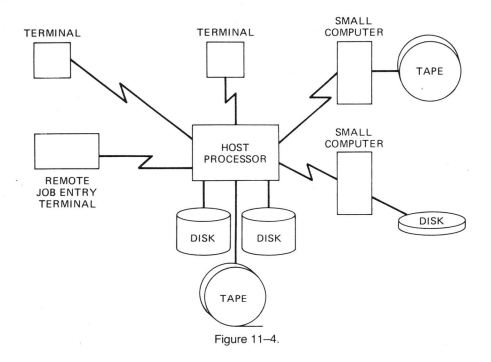

Figure 11–4.

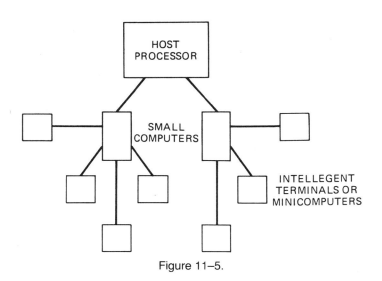

Figure 11–5.

212

ng, Packet Switching, Front-end Computers, Remote Concentration and Remote ob Entry.

MESSAGE SWITCHING is a process whereby a transaction finds its way hrough the network from its source to its destination. A transaction has as part f its contents a header that contains routing information. This routing information is put onto the transaction header by the network. In this type of environment, the destination to which the transaction is to go is sometimes busy handling another transaction. A function of the network software is to store this transaction until the intended destination point is able to take it. "Store and forward" is a term that is often heard to describe that function. In some configurations, one computer handles message switching for a host computer. All messages come into the switcher from numerous locations. The switcher communicates them to the host, sometimes but not always, through a front-end computer. The switcher also receives response transactions from the host and routes them out to the appropriate terminal device.

PACKET SWITCHING is a form of message switching. It involves a process f dividing long messages into fixed length sections called packets. Each packet s forwarded across the network toward its destination along the best possible route at that time. Since the various possible paths can be idle or busy at any

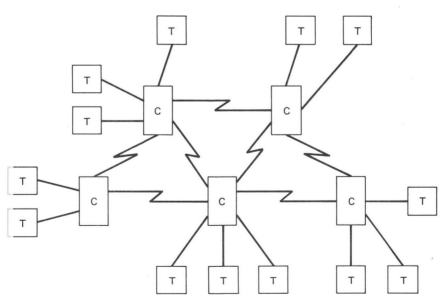

C — COMPUTER
T — TERMINAL

Figure 11–6.

given time interval, the packets may travel different routes to their destination. When they all arrive at their destination, they have to be put in order and reassembled into the original message.

A FRONT-END COMPUTER is a computer that is used to relieve a host computer of some of the work it has to do. For instance, in a certain environment there might be fifteen communication lines coming into a host. There is a certain amount of software overhead that must be resident in the host to support those fifteen lines. It is possible, rather than having those lines come into the host, to have them come into a front-end computer and put the associated software into that front-end machine. One path is established between the front-end computer and the host. This one path replaces the fifteen, and the host is relieved of a considerable amount of work, which is now done by the front-end computer. The host is generally a large scale computer, and the resources that had been dedicated to servicing the lines can then be devoted to other work.

A REMOTE CONCENTRATOR is also a computer. Its function is to concentrate transactions from a number of remote terminals and forward them to a host computer site. The purpose for doing this is to reduce the number of communication lines from remote terminal sites to the host computer site. For example, terminal sites at Los Angeles, San Diego, Palo Alto, San Francisco and San Jose might all be connected to a concentrator in San Jose that has a communications line to the host site in New York. The alternative of having five lines from each of the five cities to New York would be far more expensive. The assumption is made here that the one line from San Jose is sufficient to handle the traffic volume from all five cities.

A REMOTE JOB ENTRY TERMINAL is a device that handles "batch processing" applications. Batch work usually consists of high volume input and output transactions that are processed in batches where there is no need to respond to individual transaction on a one-to-one basis. These jobs usually consist of long report listings like ledgers and payroll registers or the reading and processing of large files that are in some sequence. A remote job entry terminal is the facility that permits this kind of work to be done at a site remote to the host computer. For example, at the end of the month, closing journal entries are entered through a remote job entry (RJE) terminal device. These entries travel electronically across the communications line to the host computer where a final balancing takes place. The host responds to the terminal indicating the ledger is in balance. A request to print the ledger is then made through the CRT. The host begins sending the ledger electronically across the communications line to the RJE terminal's printer where it is listed.

INFLUENCE OF TELEPROCESSING

Distributed Systems rely completely on an older technology known as Teleprocessing or Telecommunications. Teleprocessing uses communications lines to allow computers and terminal devices or other computers to interact with one another. This technology is out of the "state of the art" category and is used almost as universally as computers are.

However, there are a couple of myths that should be put to rest. The first of these is the improvement that satellite communications is going to make in telecommunications. A misconception exists in this area that should be cleared up. Satellite communication introduces a delay into telecommunications. That delay is real and is not going to be eliminated by architecture (SNA) or protocol (SDLC) or an access method (VTAM). Superimposing all those things on top of the problem tends to confuse the issue. The reason for the delay is the distance the signals have to travel (to satellite and back to earth). All the architecture, protocols and access methods in the world are not going to change the fact. Now satellite communications, *on the average,* will improve telecommunications because of wider data paths and lower error rates. However, individual transactions, such as real-time inquiries, are going to take longer.

The same effects can be expected with application of data concentrators. Unless the speed of the lines and modems is increased, concentrators will result in individual inquiries being slowed down, simply because they will have to make their way through more equipment. The big improvements in telecommunications by using satellites and concentrators will be in remote batch processing where large amounts of data are passed across communications lines.

DISTRIBUTED PROCESSING TECHNOLOGY

The technology of Distributed Processing, using the older technology, Teleprocessing, has been developing concurrently with the development of data base technology. A couple of other technologies, "Minicomputers" and "Microcomputers," have also been developing at the same time, "Minis" in the late 1960s and early seventies, and "Micros" in the mid and late 1970s. In order to gain a perspective on the evolution of these two technologies, let's go back a few years.

BACKGROUND

An interesting idea regarding EDP evolution is the one developed by Cyrus Gibson and Richard Nolan. They organized and articulated things that most EDP users already know. Their HBR article[1] brought into focus the stages of growth of EDP resources and costs that took place during the years 1960 through 1975. A summary of that article follows. Basically, the hypothesis is this: An "s" shaped curve shows four basic stages in the growth of EDP resources and costs. Graphically, this is shown in Fig. 11–7.

In addition to costs and resources, this curve reflects other things like growth in the number of applications and growth in EDP dependent functions.

---

[1]Cyrus F. Gibson and Richard Nolan, "Managing the Four Stages of EDP Growth," *Harvard Business Review,* Vol. 52, No. 1, January–February 1974, pp. 143–152.

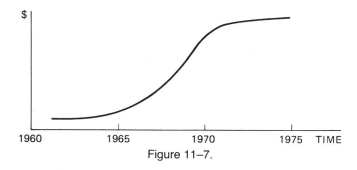
Figure 11–7.

The hypothesis continues; four causes exist for the growth process:

1. Development of application portfolio (early 1960s)
2. Building of an EDP organization (middle and late 1960s)
3. Bulding an EDP management control system (early 1970s)
4. Developing user awareness (middle and late 1970s)

Four basic *stages* parallel the above four causes:

1. Cost reducing accounting applications (early 1960s)
2. Proliferation of applications in all functional areas (middle and late 1960s)
3. Moratorium on new applications: emphasis on control (early 1970s)
4. Data base applications (middle and late 1970s)

Certain organizational characteristics became manifest during the evolution of these stages.

STAGE I TOOK PLACE IN THE EARLY SIXTIES, and management was lax as new applications went onto the computer rather smoothly. As the mid-sixties approached, management noticed that EDP resources, primarily the computer itself, were not being used to full capacity. Using their managerial prerogative, they pushed to fully utilize this resource as they would any other resource. In this case, however, they did so without understanding the concept of software. Controls were lacking, and there was no charge-back of costs to the user.

EDP managers were moved up in organizations, and there was a proliferation of applications as bright young people with multi-colored view-graphs made presentations to superficially enthusiastic users. During the height of Stage I activity, one might have observed the following scenario: youthful EDP specialists; multi-colored view-graph foils; user, who still is not being charged for computer usage or services, nods or grunts; programmers work for a year; specialists return to user and say "Here it is." User says "No, it isn't." These happenings were isolated from one another and ignored by all but a few "Cassandras."

THE BEGINNINGS OF STAGE II were evidenced by the running out of resources, primarily hardware. In the rush to use up idle capacity, applications of all kinds had been taken up. To the original efforts on Payroll, Accounts Payable, Accounts Receivable and Billing were added General Ledger, Budgeting, Forecasting, Sales, Inventory Control and others. One day, it was discovered, that with a staff of twenty systems and programming people working feverishly on six new applications, as well as maintaining four existing applications, there was no more room on the computer. Meetings were hastily called, and a number of alternatives were presented.

Alternative one could have been the cancellation of one or more of the applications, but it was found that no one could any longer live without his application.

A second alternative that may have occurred was the suggestion that applications be modified so as to streamline them, but that alternative was discarded for one or more of the following reasons. Preliminary investigations disclosed that there was no documentation for the applications. Further investigation showed that the applications programs would never work, but somehow they did, twice a week, under the careful guidance of the programmer. This alternative was finally "put to rest" when the realization that the required modifications would take three to six months and that the resources to do that were not available.

A third alternative, "buy our way out," or "get a faster machine," or "get another machine," seemed to be a viable alternative. Scenario: EDP Manager gets specifications, costs of machines, costs of present manual system, consequences of alternatives; prepares multi-colored view-graphs, makes presentation. It was during this presentation that some vice president made the comment on what a fine job the EDP Manager had done and said that he wished that others would do the same quality homework on their presentations. With this, the entire room was filled with a feeling of victory that comes with conquering a mighty foe. The proposal to get more equipment received wholehearted approval, and Stage II was well under way.

On the surface nothing had changed except that there was more and it was bigger. Users still had a free ride. However, as Stage II progressed, rumblings, minor at first but growing more pronounced, were heard beneath the surface. When problems arose, the only responsible person that seemed able to correct the problem was a programmer. The resources dedicated to the maintenance of existing applications were consuming a growing percentage of the systems and programming staff. This, in turn, caused an enlargement of total systems and programming staff, as new applications requests increased from a trickle to a torrent. There were many repetitions of the "buy our way out" scenario described above, and more equipment and staff were added, until . . .

STAGE III DAWNED GRADUALLY. The vice president who had originally commented on the quality of the first study had since departed. One day, as the EDP Manager was going through the Nth iteration of the same old proposal, somebody noticed that he was using the same multi-colored view-graphs as were used six months ago. This individual voiced his observation. Perhaps he was a "bright young MBA" from the Wharton School of Business. His initial observations had resulted in his becoming the object of everyone's attention. The question he then asked was the question that began Stage III in most companies. "How much money are we spending on EDP?" To which the EDP Manager responded, "Oh, maybe about seven million dollars." The "bright young MBA," with all the self-confidence associated with one who either had "a full house, aces high" or had everyone believing that he did, said, "I think it's more like thirty million." Stunned silence.

Stage III saw a period of consolidation, soul-searching and non-growth EDP budgets. The "MBA's" question received its first answer. Nobody really knew how much money was being spent on EDP. Looking at the general ledger, it was found that EDP costs were buried all over the place. Attempts were made to pull them out. In the meantime, no additional money was forthcoming for the EDP function.

The EDP Manager was put under extreme pressure to consolidate. He began turning down requests for modifications to existing systems and new applications, using for excuses a mumbo jumbo of jargon that nobody understood. Users, still not paying for EDP services, were not concerned about limitations of core, CPU cycles, access times and the like. The users took their "out of joint noses" to their superiors and up the line went the complaints. At the level in the organization where the reporting structure of the EDP function and the user functions came together, the complaint received attention, and down the line came the edict "Do it."

With no additional funds for more resources and with additional work still coming, the EDP Manager, in many cases having either become a Vice President or having been replaced by one, began to take steps to centralize. Simply stated, it was, he believed, more economical to do many jobs in a few large computers at one central site than in many small computers at a number of local sites. Also in Stage III, controls and standards were instituted and enforced. Systems for charging users for the resources that they used were formalized.

Most companies in the 1974–1975 time frame were in Stage III. Large centralized data centers were handling the needs of many users. The personnel in these data centers were engaged in making them more efficient. Sharing of common resources, system facilities, hardware and software were all geared to increasing efficiency. However, bigness of itself tends to create some inefficiencies, and a fourth stage in the process had appeared. Some were already into it, others were anticipating going into it, and still others didn't believe that it existed.

STAGE IV INVOLVED A RESTRUCTURING of the application portfolio. There was a tendency to use application software packages that were more generalized. The user began to be recognized as a full partner in EDP activity. As the Stage IV scenario unfolded, factors not exactly new, but hitherto only partially recognized, began making themselves felt. These factors were "Minicomputers" and later on "Microcomputers," Data Bases and Distributed Processing. Additionally, there were other technological changes taking place both within and outside of the EDP community in tandem with these factors. These changes could have been stated as observations by the mid 1970s. They are as follows:

1. Processing unit performance had increased by a factor of 200, memory by a factor of 20 and cost by a factor of 3. Computers were getting faster, smaller and cheaper. This trend continues, but there are technological limits beyond which it seems impossible to go. Although there are currently computers that operate in nanoseconds (billionth of a second), the technology to go beyond this to picoseconds (trillionth of a second) is up against a theoretical limit, i.e., the speed of light, where matter becomes energy when it moves that fast. Also, it seems that there is little that can be done technologically beyond the tiny bubble memory that is being developed.

2. EDP technology has merged with Telecommunications technology.

3. The Centralization/Decentralization question, in the 1975–76 time frame, had become not a technological, but a political question. Distributed systems may provide a political compromise.

4. The current Centralized Organization structure has been made possible, largely because of Telecommunications and Teleprocessing technology. Distributed systems can use some of the hardware already in place to migrate.

5. The existence of "Microcomputer" and "Minicomputer" technology has complicated the Centralization/Decentralization question, from both a political and a technological point of view.

6. The Systems Analysis/Systems Design function has had added to itself the Data Base function. The importance of the Systems Analysis function, after a ten-year lull, is again on the ascendancy. The Data Base Administration function is the manifestation of this ascendance.

7. The Systems Software function has become stronger and more important. One of its more important tasks has been to keep "in tune" the large number of boxes and software packages that must interface with one another.

MINICOMPUTERS

Around 1970, just when many organizations were going from Stage II to Stage III, another phenomenon made its presence felt: the "Minicomputer."[2] Looking at "Minis" in the context of contemporary computing is quite enlightening in that it indicated, in spite of much activity and fluttering about, that minicomputers are nothing more than computers.

CHARACTERISTICS

The term "Minicomputer" is little more than a clever marketing gimmick. Let me suggest the following:

1. A definition of a "Minicomputer" is rather vague. Some other characteristics of a "Mini" are that it is *relatively* small in size, *usually* requires no special environment, is *relatively* simple to operate and *generally* comes packaged including software. This last characteristic is *often* a total application package and is known as a *Turnkey System*.

2. "Minicomputers" are still being used for the same kind of work as they were in the past, that is, for "Front-end Systems," and "Data Concentrators," as well as for stand alone applications.

3. Since some "Minicomputers" are not "mini" in terms of processing power, they can, in sufficient quantity, do the same work as larger computers. Whether or not an organization should use "Minis" or a large computer is a decision based on economics, organization and politics; not on technology.

In the early 1970s, when "Minicomputers" first began to really catch on in the commercial environment, they really represented a giant step backwards, with respect to processing capabilities. "Minis" at that point in time had the processing capabilities of the IBM 1400 series computers of the early 1960s. The advances that minis offered were that they were smaller, "cheaper" and frequently did not require a specially controlled environment in which to operate, relative to what the 1400 series computers had needed.

ATTRACTIONS

In the early 1970s, Stage III of Nolan's theory was well along. Large scale computer mainframes, with their speed and the ability to handle many jobs concurrently, were doing virtually all the data processing for those corporations able to afford computers. The trend had been toward centralization of computers in large corporate data centers. Remote job entry and teleprocessing develop-

---

[2]It is this treatment of "Minis" that I believe gave rise to the reviewers' comments that I am biased against "Minis." I am not biased against "Minis," I merely question their existence. My article in July 1978, *Insosystems*, "Where have all the mini's gone?" articulates my question.

ments helped make this possible. With all this sophistication, who would want an obsolescent 1400 series computer even if it was small, inexpensive and easy to install? Well, there were a few types of individuals who did. Those, who until this time had not been able to afford computers or data center services, were one type. Another type was the individual who had become dissatisfied with data center service. Another type of individual was the person who was given complete profit and loss (P & L) responsibility for his operation (department, division, group, or whatever). The last type of individual began to investigate the claims of "Minicomputer" manufacturers that they could "do it cheaper."

By 1974, "Minis" had gained a fair amount of acceptance by commercial users. There were a few casualties along the way, but that's true with any new enterprise. The biggest problems had been software, or perhaps I should say the lack thereof and the initial inexperience of both "Mini" manufacturers and their OEMs[3] in selling to businessmen rather than engineers.

The motivations that spurred organizations to get "Minis" were generally economics and the desire to maintain control. The economic question was a tricky one, and some caution had to be exercised before commitment was made to a "Mini" as an inexpensive solution to a problem. Although "Minicomputers" were indeed inexpensive, peripheral equipment was quite expensive. Some peripherals, such as mass storage disk and high speed line printers, ran up the cost quickly. Software was also another expensive addition to the original cost of a "Minicomputer." The most important area in which caution had to be exercised was in the area of problem definition. If an organization had a problem, and an existing inadequate manual system was fouling things up, then all a "minicomputer," or any computer for that matter, was able to do was to foul things up more quickly. It was in this area where potential savings were sometimes frittered away and additional expense actually incurred.

In the area of control, there was little argument to offer. No doubt a locally situated "Mini" offered a department or a division complete control of its use. However, recalling some of the difficulties that arose in Stage I and II of Norton's hypothesis, it was in this type of local environments that those difficulties arose. In a local environment expediency often has the upper hand over longer range objectives. In these environments are seen a lack of controls, inadequate documentation and other such shortcomings, which cause consternation in the long run. If it is the judgment of management that this price can be paid, then it should be so documented, so that when the price is exacted in the long run, there are no recriminations.

---

[3]OEM: original equipment manufacturer. Enterprises would purchase equipment from various manufacturers and combine it into one product, which they subsequently marketed. It was often combined with software and marketed as a complete working system. These systems are known as "Turnkey Systems."

CAPABILITIES

Before 1975, most "Minicomputer" applications were essentially single thread systems, that is, one job at a time ran in the computer. In many ways it was reminiscent of the early sixties before the introduction of multiprogramming and operating systems on large scale systems. These applications were single thread in concept, but technological improvements made the cathode ray tube (CRT) an inexpensive way of entering data into a computer. Historically, the single thread methodology allowed for one path of input to enter the system; one item of input was entered, processed and filed and some output was written before processing began on the next item of input. Once CRTs were introduced, there was a requirement within the system that the software support the CRTs. Multiple CRTs permitted several input paths. Items were entered intermittently. The software was designed so that interleaving of input, processing, filing and output was possible. "Minicomputer" software, when supporting this type of processing, was in actuality a "Mini" operating system. Gradually during 1975 and 1976, these "Mini" operating systems became more sophisticated and at the same time "Mini" hardware became more powerful and the distinction between "Mini" and "non-Mini" became more blurred.

"MINIS" AND LARGE COMPUTERS COMPARED

In my opinion, a computer is a computer. They come in different shapes and sizes, but they are all computers. However, since a number of them are marketed as "Minis" some attempt should be made to define them. Word length in "Minis" is generally 16 bits, maximum memory size is 250K (K = 1024) words. There are several exceptions to this which keep it from becoming an absolute distinction. The "Minis" generally have a slower processing unit cycle time and a slower memory cycle time that do the larger computers. The instruction repertoire of "Minis" is generally smaller than that of larger machines. Exceptions to this also exist, again complicating the attempt at a clear-cut distinction.

Input/output data transfer rates in "Minis" are equal to the machines in the lower end of the large scale line. Most "Minis" have only one data channel or bus, through which peripheral equipment is connected to the "Mini." The large scale machines have multiple channels. The memory path between memory and the processing unit is of equal width in both "Minis" and the machines in the low end of the large scale line. Large scale machines support a larger range of peripheral equipment than do "Minis."

Reliability of both kinds of computers is high, but generally higher in "Minis." Vendor support is generally better in the large scale line, but this is changing also. The purchase cost in the upper range of large scale computers is millions of dollars; in the lower range it is hundreds of thousands, and with "minis," it is tens of thousands of dollars.

Operating requirements for large scale computers are greater. Physical facilities requirements, such as air-conditioning and electrical power, are often greater for large scale computers than they are for most "Minis." Large scale computer installations generally require a staff of skilled operators as well as a staff of support personnel. The operation of a "Minicomputer" can often be handled by the department in which it is installed with no increase in staff.

The large scale computer can currently do more than a "Mini" in two areas. It can do more computations per unit of time than the "mini" because of its faster cycle times and larger memory capacity. It can also carry on more asynchronous activity concurrently because of its bigger and faster components. Multiprogramming by means of an operating system is another way of saying "carry on more asynchronous activity concurrently." In this environment, the large scale computer gives the illusion of doing six or seven things at the same time. The reason for the further clouding of the distinctions between large scale computers and "Minicomputers" is that in the area of architecture, i.e., speed (cycles), memory size, word lengths multiprogramming, etc., that the "Minis" manufacturers have made improvements. Many "Minis" now do what large scale computers were doing in 1974–1975.

That about sums up as briefly as possible the distinctions that can be made between the computers called "minis" and those that are not. The distinctions are not clear, and a look into the future indicates that it will become less clear as "Minicomputers" begin to overlap further into the domain of the large scale computer.

SUMMARY

The trend in systems for which "Minis" are suited seems to be for "Distributed Systems," as you have seen, and for stand alone applications. The limitations for "Minis" should continue to be in the area of large scale computations and accessing large amounts of data. There is a great deal more that could be said about "Minicomputers," but within the context of this book, our primary concern is describing them as functions within Distributed Processing or Data Base applications.

MICROCOMPUTERS

Around 1975, when "Minis" had become an accepted part of the EDP/MIS landscape, "Micros" began to make their presence felt in a big way. And yet, microcomputer and microprocessor technology was to have an even greater impact on the "status quo" than did "Minis." With "Micros" as with "Minis," a computer is a computer. It has the same five basic components: memory, processor, input, output and control as does any other computer. It is an extremely small configuration. Although input/output devices like CRTs and printers must be big enough to be usable, the other components are virtually microscopic. Figure 11–8 gives you an idea of relative sizes.

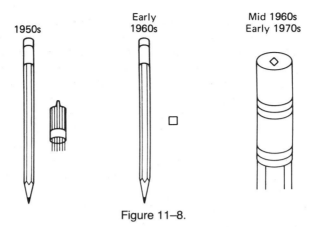

Figure 11–8.

A treatment of "Microcomputers" is beyond the scope of this book. Most of you reading this book are aware of the many uses to which "Micros" have been put. They are used in braking systems on automobiles, in hand-held programmable calculators and in childrens' games. More important, however, in the light of this book's scope, are their uses in computer terminals and in other computers.

"Micros" are used in large scale computers in helping them to move data across channels between peripheral devices and computer memory. Some of the more mundane internal "housekeeping" jobs done by large scale computers that were at one time handled by software are now done by "Micros." Putting a "Micro" into a terminal device like a CRT provides that device with some basic computing capabilities. Devices like this are sometimes known as "intelligent terminals." Without going into a lot more detail about them, you should be able to see, in view of the other material, that "Micros" have the potential to enhance the capabilities of Distributed Processing by making the components more productive at less cost.

WORD PROCESSING

Concurrent with the arrival on the scene of these low cost, highly flexible "Micros" has been the rapid increase in their use for "Word Processing." Basically, "Word Processing" uses computers for the processing of words to produce textual information in the same way that computers have been used in the past to process basically numerical data into quantitative information.

Commercial and scientific data processing applications have essentially concerned themselves with the manipulation of numerical data. Although textual information is often used in reporting numerical information in these applications, the words used were just carried along. They were rarely processed or manipulated in any way. The use of textual information was kept to a minimum and was often considered a nuisance to analysts and technicians. This fact is not meant as an indictment against anyone, for it is an undisputable fact that it is a lot easier to manipulate numbers than it is words—unless you have virtually unlimited resources.

During the 1970s, the amount of computing resource available began to advance geometrically. The virtually unlimited resource arrived somewhere around 1975–1976. It arrived in greater quantities and in smaller packages—"Minis" and "Micros," or whatever you want to call small computers. Many of the techniques for handling numbers can also be used for handling words. It is being done by organizations of all shapes and sizes. Exxon is into it as are many smaller companies.

Hey, so what? What has all this got to do with IMS/VS? Well IMS/VS or some other Data Base Management System is part of current EDP technology and the contemporary MIS environment. Information Processing is made up of Data Base, Distributed Systems, DBMS, "Minis," "Micros," Teleprocessing, Data Processing and Word Processing. For this reason, these subjects were considered.

Appendix A
Some CBS IMS Standards and Procedures

This appendix contains examples of a few of the standards and procedures developed by the CBS IMS/VS Project Team. Although geared specifically to CBS' organizational makeup, they are included here to give you not only ideas, but actual examples of the kind of standards that are required in an IMS/VS environment.

The first page of the appendix contains an index to the entire set of standards and procedures so as to give you an idea of the ground that ought to be covered by standards and procedures. The remainder of the appendix contains section 1, which provides a detailed set of standards for naming conventions, and section 10, which describes procedures for specifying system resources and transactions security to IMS/VS.

CBS CORPORATE MIS
DIVISIONAL USERS ORIENTED
IMS STANDARDS AND PROCEDURES

SECTION	DESCRIPTION
1. NAMING CONVENTIONS	Complete naming conventions requirements for all IMS applications.
2. DL/1 PROGRAMMING TECHNIQUES	DL/1 coding standards and guidelines for better performance of programs under IMS.
3. IMS PL/1 PROGRAMMING TECHNIQUES	PL/1 coding standards and guidelines to be used for all IMS PL/1 applications.
4. MFS STANDARDS/GUIDELINES	Message Formatting Services standards and guidelines required to efficiently map IMS messages with devices.
5. LIBRARY ORGANIZATION	Complete list of test and production library names to be used for all IMS applications.
6. USER APPLICATION CODE IN IMS CONTROL REGION	Information about user written routines for data base maintenance and available IMS Data Communications Exits, as well as standards for using each feature.
7. IMS SYSTEM COMMANDS FOR DIVISIONAL USE	List of commands that can be entered from any remote terminal by Divisional users of IMS.
8. DLIERROR	User documentation for the IMS Status Code Analyzer, DLIERROR, which must be included in all IMS programs developed for CBS.
9. SYSTEM TROUBLE SHEETS	CBS Data Center System Trouble Sheet forms and instructions for reporting IMS computer system problems.
10. SYSTEM RESOURCE AND TRANSACTION SECURITY FORMS	CBS Data Center forms and instructions needed to transmit system resources and transaction security requirements to the IMS Software Staff.
11. DATA DICTIONARY/DIRECTORY STANDARDS	Forms and instructions designed for use by the systems/programming user or Division DBA to define data into the DD/D. All IMS related information to be defined must be entered into the DD/D.

CBS CORPORATE MIS (cont.)

SECTION	DESCRIPTION
12. GLOSSARY OF STANDARD ABBREVIATIONS OF BUSINESS KEYWORDS FOR PL/1 DATA NAMES	A glossary of standard abbreviated keywords (commonly used business terms), along with standards and rules for constructing PL/1 data names for use in IMS applications.

SECTION 1. IMS STANDARDS AND PROCEDURES: NAMING CONVENTIONS

IMS NAMING CONVENTIONS

GENERAL STANDARDS

1. The letter D or S cannot be used as the first character of any IMS name.

2. All 8 characters of each specified name must be used, with the exception of DIF and DOF which must be 6 characters.

3. No blanks are allowed and all names used in field definitions of DBD GENs and SSAs must be in Assembler language format.

4. All names will begin with the second two characters of the Group/Division code now presently in use (e.g., CEP would be EP).

5. Wherever possible, use unique and meaningful mnemonic names.

6. Each new real-time and batch application under IMS must receive an application number from the Information Coordinator at the Data Center.

7. Existing JCL job naming conventions will be followed, and each job stream can generate from 01 to 99 reports.

8. NOTE: The segment key/search field name is an 8 character primary name used as the first level identifier for COBOL and PL/1 application names. In fact, the primary name can be created after the COBOL or PL/1 application field/element name is derived (from up to 23 characters).

9. All PSB names must begin with an alphabetic character (A through Z, #, $ and @).

10. Logical terminal names and transaction codes must begin with an alphameric character (A through Z, #, $, @, 0 through 9).

11. IMS/VS null words cannot be used as resource names: FOR, TO, ON, AFTER, SECURITY, and MODE.

12. IMS/VS command keywords and their synonyms cannot be used as resource names. A list of the command keywords and synonyms appears in an appendix in the back of this write-up.

IMS NAMING CONVENTIONS* (cont.)

POSITION

    DBD (Data Base Name—8 Positions)

1–2	2 Alpha Character Group/Division Name
3–4	2 Alpha-numeric Character Data Base Title, First Position Character 'X' for Index Data Base (Secondary or Primary)
5–7	3 Alpha-numeric Character Free Form Unique Data Base Descriptor
8	1 Alpha-numeric Character Data Base Type (P-physical, L-logical, Y-primary index, X-secondary index, F-non-DL/1 file for production status; 1-physical, 2-logical, 3-primary index, 4-secondary index, 5-file for test status)

    SEGM (Segment Name—8 Positions)

1–2	2 Alpha Character Group/Division Name
3–4	2 Alpha-numeric Character Application Name
5–7	3 Alpha-numeric Character Free Form Unique Application Descriptor
8	1 Alpha Character Segment Type (P-physical, L-logical, V-virtual, Y-primary index, X-secondary index)

    FIELD/ELEMENT (Segment Key/Search Field—8 Positions)

1–2	2 Alpha Character Group/Division Name.
3–8	6 Alpha-numeric Character Free Form Unique Element Descriptor; Character 'X' Can Not Be Used In The First Position

    XDFLD (Secondary Index Field Name—8 Positions)

1–2	2 Alpha Character Group/ Division Name
3–8	6 Alpha-numeric Character Free Form Unique Field Descriptor, First Position Character Always 'X'

    PSB (Program Specification Block Name—8 Positions)

    Note: The application program name must be the same as the PSB name.

1–2	2 Alpha Character Group/Division Name
3–7	5 Alpha-numeric Character Free Form Unique PSB Name
8	1 Alpha-numeric Character PSB test version or production type (0 through 9 for test versions; B-batch region execution, P-BMP region execution, M-MP region execution, C-MP region conversation program for production types)

    TRANS (Transaction Name—8 Positions)

    Same as the PSB name (can have only one transaction name per program or PSB)

---

*The conventions below reflect early 1978 standards. Though adequate, significant improvements have been made since that time.

IMS NAMING CONVENTIONS (cont.)

POSITION

LTERM (Logical Terminal Name—8 Positions)

1–2	2 Alpha Character Group/Division Name
3–7	5 Alpha-numeric Character Free Form Unique LTERM name
8	1 Alpha-numeric Character LTERM General Class Type (see Attached Code List)

MID/MOD (Message Input/Output Descriptor—8 Positions)

1–2	2 Alpha Character Group/Division Name
3–7	5 Alpha-numeric Character Free Form Unique Message Descriptor
8	1 Alpha Character Message Descriptor Type (I-MID, O-MOD)

DIF/DOF (Device Input/Output Format—6 Positions)

1–2	2 Alpha Character Group/Division Name
3–6	4 Alpha-numeric Character Free Form Unique Device Format Descriptor

DD Name (As Defined in DBD GEN—8 Positions)

1–2	2 Alpha Character Group/Division Name
3–4	2 Alpha-numeric Character Data Base Title, Same As In DBD Name
5	1 Alpha Character Data Base Type (P-primary index, S-secondary index, I-ISAM, O-OSAM, V-VSAM)
6	1 Numeric Character of Data Base Occurrence Number (Primary and Indexed Data Base = 0, Secondary Index Data Bases = 1–9)
7	1 Numeric Character of Data Set Generation Occurrence (0–9)
8	1 Alpha-numeric Character Test Version or Production Status (0–9 for Test Versions; P for Production Status)

DSN (Data Set Name, Second and Third Level Indexes—8 Positions)

The second level index of the data set name is the same as the DBD name, and the third level index is the same as the DD name.

PGM (Application Program Name—8 Positions)

Same as the PSB name (can have only one program name per PSB).

LTERM GENERAL CLASS TYPES

CODE	GENERAL CLASS TYPE
A	1403-N1 Printer
B	2540 Card Read Punch
C	3210 Printer-Keyboard
D	3270 Terminal
E	3780 Terminal
F	3284 Printer
G	3286 Printer
H	3288 Printer

Note: List will be expanded when other devices will be used by Divisions.

IMS/VS COMMAND KEYWORDS AND SYNONYMS, AND NULL WORDS

The following IMS/VS command keywords and null words cannot be used to name system resources:

KEYWORD	SYNONYM
ABDUMP	
ACTIVE	A
AFTER	
ASSIGNMENT	ASMT
BUILDQ	BLDQS, BLDQ, BUILDQS
CANCEL	
CHECKPOINT	CHKPT, CHECKPT, CHKPOINT
CLASS	CLS
CNS	
COMPONENT	COMPT
CONVERSATION	CONV
CPRI	
DATABASE	DATABASES, DB, DBS
DC	
DONE	

IMS/VS COMMAND KEYWORDS AND SYNONYMS (cont.)

KEYWORD	*SYNONYM*
DUMPQ	DUMPQS
FOR	
FORMAT	FMT
FREEZE	
ICOMPT	
INPUT	
KEY	
LEVEL	
LINE	LINES
LINK	
LMCT	LCT
LPRI	
LTERM	LTERMS
MODE	
MODULE	
MONITOR	MON
MSNAME	
MSPLINK	
NOBMP	
NODE	
NOPASSWORD	NOPSWD
NOTERMINAL	NOTERM, NOTER
NPRI	
ON	
OPTION	
OUTPUT	
PARLIM	
PASSWORD	PASSWORDS, PSWD, PSWDS
PCH	
PI	
PLMCT	PLCT
POOL	

IMS/VS COMMAND KEYWORDS AND SYNONYMS (cont.)

KEYWORD	*SYNONYM*
PRIORITY	PRTY
PROGRAM	PROGRAMS, PROG, PROGS, PGM, PGMS
PRT	
PTERM	PTERMS
PURGE	
QUEUE	QUEUES, Q, QS
QUIESCE	
RDR	
REGION	REGIONS, REG, REGS, MSGREG, MSGREGS, MSGREGION, MSGREGIONS
SECURITY	
SEGNO	
SEGSIZE	
SERIAL	SER, SERS, SERIALS
SET	
SHUTDOWN	
STATUS	
SYSID	
TERMINAL	TERMINALS, TERM, TERMS, TER, TERS
TO	
TRANSACTION	TRANS, TRAN, TRANSACTIONS, TRANCODE, TRANCODES
VID	
XKEY	

SECTION 10. IMS STANDARDS AND PROCEDURES: SYSTEM RESOURCE AND TRANSACTION SECURITY FORMS

IMS DATA BASE FORM EXPLANATION

This form is to be filled out by the Corporate Data Base Administrator (DBA), from information supplied by the Divisional DBA and the data dictionary, to supply information about data bases used under control of IMS.

1. Enter the Division to which the data bases belong. Standard Division abbreviations can be found in the Data Center Standards Manual.

2. Check if the data base is: A. New, B. Modification, or C. Delete. Modify is to be checked if information on the form is being changed from a previous submission.

3. Indicate if the data base is to be used in the online: A. Production or B. Test IMS System.

4. Enter the name of the Data Base Description (DBD). This will be used as the second part of the data set name.

5. Enter the Data Definition (DD) name of the data base. This will be used as the third level of the data set name.

6. Enter a descriptive name of the data base (i.e., deposit entry, customer bill-to secondary index).

7. Check the data base type: A. Data Base, B. Index Data Base, or C. Secondary index. When the data base is HIDAM, a separate Data Base form is required for the HIDAM data portion and the HIDAM index.

8. Enter the type of IMS and OS access methods to be used. Consult the IMS/VS utilities manual for the correct combinations.

9. Enter the name of the randomizing module if the IMS access method is HDAM. Since randomizing modules must reside in the IMS Control Region, when the randomizing module abends the IMS system will be terminated; all randomizing module code *must* be approved by the IMS software staff.

10. Enter the following information about the data base segments: A. The smallest segment size including pointers, B. The largest segment size including pointers, C. The maximum concatenated key length, and D. The number of segments updated or inserted per day.

11. Enter the name of the DASD disk pack which contains the data base.

12. Indication whether the data base will be used Online and/or Offline.

13. If the OS Access Method is VASM, answer the following: A. Does the data base reside in a VSAM data space, B. Enter the number of root Anchor Points if IMS access method HDAM, C. The Control Interval Size (CI), D. The number of cylinders allocated for the data base, and E. The name of the data set and member which contains the VSAM defines JCL for the data base.

IMS DATA BASE FORM

1. DIVISION: _____

2. PLEASE CHECK (✓) ONLY ONE:

   A. NEW DATA BASE:_____
   B. MODIFY DATA BASE:_____
   C. DELETE DATA BASE:_____

3. PLEASE CHECK (✓) ONLY ONE:

   A. PRODUCTION:_____
   B. TEST:_____

4. DATA BASE DESCRIPTION (DBD) NAME:_____

5. DATA DEFININITION (DD) NAME:_____

6. DESCRIPTIVE NAME OF DATA BASE:_____

7. PLEASE CHECK (✓) ONLY ONE. DATA BASE TYPE:

   A. DATA BASE:_____
   B. INDEX DATA BASE:_____
   C. SECONDARY DATA BASE:_____

8. ACCESS METHOD:_____

9. RANDOMIZING MODULE (HDAM ONLY):_____

IMS DATA BASE FORM (cont.)

10. DATA BASE SEGMENT INFORMATION:

    A.   SMALLEST SEGMENT SIZE:_____

    B.   LARGEST SEGMENT SIZE:_____

    C.   MAXIMUM CONCATENATED KEY LENGTH:_____

    D.   NUMBER SEGMENTS UPDATED OR ADDED PER DAY:_____

11. DATA BASE RESIDES ON:_____

12. DATA BASE USED ONLINE:_____OFFLINE_____

13. IF ACCESS METHOD VSAM:

    A.   DATA BASE LOCATED IN VSAM DATA SPACE: YES_____ NO_____

    B.   NUMBER OF ROOT ANCHOR POINTS (RAPs):_____

    C.   CONTROL INTERVAL SIZE:_____ _____

    D.   NUMBER CYLINDERS FOR DATA BASE:_____

    E.   DATA SET AND MEMBER NAME WHICH HAS VSAM DEFINES JCL:_____

DBA:_____ EXT:_____DATE:_____

REVISED 770621

IMS PROGRAM SPECIFICATION FORM EXPLANATION

This form is to be filled out by the Division Data Base Administrator (DBA) to supply the necessary application information used for an IMS system definition.

1. Enter the Division to which the application is to be charged.

2. Check if the application entry is: A. New, B. Modification, or C. Delete. Modify is to be checked if there is a change from a previous submission of the application information.

3. Check if this application is to be entered into the: A. PRODUCTION or B. TEST IMS system.

4. Enter the name of the Program Specification Block (PSB) to be used by the application.

5. Check if the application is to be classified as: A. TP, B. BMP, or C. STAND-ALONE. TP indicates the application will run as a Message Processing Program (MPP). BMP indicates the application will run as a Batch Message Program. STAND-ALONE indicates the application will run without the IMS Control Region.

6. Check if the application can be scheduled in only one region (SERIAL) or whether the application can be scheduled in more than one region (PARALLEL).

7. Enter a descriptive name for the application (i.e., deposit entry, cash inquiry).

8. Enter the name(s) of the Data Base Definitions (DBDs) referenced by the above PSB.

IMS PROGRAM SPECIFICATION FORM

1. DIVISION:_____

2. PLEASE CHECK (√) *ONE* OF THE FOLLOWING:

   A. NEW APPLICATION:_____
   B. MODIFICATION TO OLD APPLICATION:_____
   C. DELETE APPLICATION:_____

3. PLEASE CHECK (√) *ONE* OF THE FOLLOWING:

   A. PRODUCTION IMS SYSTEM:_____
   B. TEST IMS SYSTEM:_____

4. PROGRAM SPECIFICATION BLOCK (PSB) NAME:_____

5. PLEASE CHECK (√) ONE OF THE FOLLOWING PROGRAM TYPES:

   A. TP_____
   B. BMP_____
   C. STAND-ALONE_____

6. PLEASE CHECK (√) ONE OF THE FOLLOWING SCHEDULING TYPES:

   A. SERIAL:_____
   B. PARALLEL:_____

7. DESCRIPTIVE NAME OF THE APPLICATION:_____

8. ASSOCIATED DATA BASE DEFINITIONS (DBDs):

   A._____ G._____
   B._____ H._____
   C._____ I._____
   D._____ J._____
   E._____ K._____
   F._____ L._____

DBA:_____ EXT:_____DATE:_____

REVISED 770621

IMS TRANSACTION FORM EXPLANATION

This form is to be filled out by the Division Data Base Administrator (DBA) to supply information about a transaction necessary for an IMS system definition.

1. Enter the Division to which the transaction applies.

2. Check if the transaction is: A. New, B. Modification to an existing transaction, C. Deletion of a transaction, D. New BMP, E. Modification to existing BMP, or F. Deletion of a BMP.

3. Check if this transaction is to execute in the: A. PRODUCTION or B. TEST IMS system.

4. Enter the eight (8) character transaction code. See the IMS Standards and Procedures for naming conventions.

5. Enter the name of the Program Specification Block (PSB) to be used by this transaction. The PSB name must be the same as the one entered on the IMS Program Specification form.

6. Enter the value to be used to determine the scheduling priority of this transaction. The NORMAL priority is the one assigned to the transaction when the number of transactions awaiting scheduling is less than the limit count. The LIMIT priority is the priority assigned the transaction when the limit count is reached. The LIMIT priority is not reduced to the normal priority until all the transactions awaiting scheduling have been scheduled. The LIMIT COUNT is the maximum number of transactions which can be awaiting scheduling before the LIMIT priority is used. For a BMP the normal and limit priority is to be zero. The *maximum* priority value that can be requested is seven (7).

7. Check the type of transaction; A. INQUIRY, B. UPDATE, or C. CONVERSA-TIONAL. INQUIRY only transactions have less overhead because there is no data base logging done.

8. Specify, for INQUIRY only transactions, whether or not during a warm start of the IMS System this transaction should be rescheduled. System restart/recovery will be faster if INQUIRY only transactions can be entered by the terminal operator.

9. Indicate whether the transaction will be either: A. RESPONSE or B. NON-RESPONSE. RESPONSE means that the keyboard will be locked after either the 'ENTER,' 'PA' or 'PF' key is hit, and the keyboard will not be unlocked until the transaction sends a message to the terminal. NON-RESPONSE means that input can be sent to IMS without a response from a transaction.

10. Enter the message class to be assigned to this transaction. This value can be from 1 to 4.

11. Enter the following about this transaction's processing: A. The number of GET UNIQUE (GU) calls the transaction will be allowed to make to the IOPCB, per transaction scheduling and B. the amount of time (in seconds) allowable for the transaction to process a single message. The limit time is useful in determining if a transaction is in a loop.

12. Specify the threshold value for the number of messages to be queued, at which time an additional message region will be scheduled whenever this number is reached. The Manager, Data Base Management Systems, will have to approve any value above zero.

13. Indicate the largest data base segment this transaction will process. This information will be used to determine if the dynamic log buffer has been allocated correctly.

14. Indicate the maximum number of output messages this transaction will produce. This information will be used to determine the size of the IMS message queues.

14. Indicate the maximum number of data base updates brought about by this transaction. This information will serve two purposes; a determination of the correct size of the dynamic log and an indication of whether the transaction should run as a Batch Message Program (BMP).

16. Enter the following information about transaction input message sizes: A. The smallest message size, B. The largest message, and C. The average message size. The above sizes are to include the MFS control characters. The sizes will be used to determine the correct record and block sizes of the IMS message queues.

17. Enter the following information about transaction output message sizes: A. The smallest message size, B. The largest message size, and C. The average message size. The above sizes will be used to determine the correct record and block sizes of the IMS message queues. The number entered is without MFS control characters.

18. For Conversational Transactions only: A. Enter the size of the Scratch Pad Area (SPA) required and, B. Whether or not the transaction will link to another transaction(s),which will use the same SPA size.

IMS TRANSACTION FORM

1. DIVISION:_____

2. PLEASE CHECK (√) ONLY ONE:

   A. NEW TRANSACTION:_____ D. NEW BMP:_____
   B. MODIFY TRANSACTION:_____ E. MODIFY BMP:_____
   C. DELETE TRANSACTION:_____ F. DELETE BMP:_____

3. PLEASE CHECK (√) ONLY ONE:_____

   A. PRODUCTION IMS SYSTEM:_____
   B. TEST IMS SYSTEM:_____

4. TRANSACTION CODE:_____

5. PROGRAM SPECIFICATION BLOCK (PSB) NAME:_____

6. TRANSACTION PRIORITY:*

   A. NORMAL:_____
   B. LIMIT:_____
   C. LIMIT COUNT:_____

7. TRANSACTION TYPE: INQUIRY_____UPDATE_____CONV._____

8. TRANSACTION RECOVERABLE: YES_____ NO_____
   (FOR INQUIRY TRANSACTIONS ONLY)

9. MESSAGE TYPE. CHECK (√) ONLY ONE:

   A. RESPONSE:_____
   B. NONRESPONSE:_____

10. MESSAGE CLASS:*_____

11. MESSAGE PROCESSING LIMITS:

    A. MESSAGE LIMIT COUNT: _____
    B. MESSAGE LIMIT TIME:_____

12. PARALLEL LIMIT COUNT:_____*
    (IF SCHEDULE TYPE = PARALLEL FOR PROGRAM SPECIFICATION)

IMS TRANSACTION FORM (cont.)

13. LARGEST D/B SEGMENT UPDATED: _____

14. MAXIMUM OUTPUT MESSAGE SEGMENTS BETWEEN GET UNIQUES:_____

15. MAXIMUM # D/B UPDATE BETWEEN GET UNIQUES TO IOPCB:_____
    OR CHECKPOINT CALL BY A BMP

16. INPUT MESSAGE INFORMATION:

    A. SMALLEST SEGMENT SIZE:_____
    B. LARGEST SEGMENT SIZE:_____
    C. AVERAGE SEGMENT SIZE:_____

17. OUTPUT MESSAGE INFORMATION:

    A. SMALLEST SEGMENT SIZE:_____
    B. LARGEST SEGMENT SIZE:_____
    C. AVERAGE SEGMENT SIZE:_____

18. CONVERSATIONAL TRANSACTIONS ONLY:

    A. SCRATCH PAD (SPA) SIZE:_____
    B. FIXED SPA SIZE: YES_____NO _____

DBA:_____ EXT:_____DATE:_____

*CONTACT MANAGER, DATA BASE MANAGEMENT SYSTEMS,
 BEFORE COMPLETING THIS ENTRY.

REVISED 770621

IMS TERMINAL FORM EXPLANATION

This form is to be filled out by the Division Data Base Administrator to supply the necessary terminal information to IMS system definition.

1. Enter the Division which will use this terminal.

2. Check if the terminal entry is: A. New, B. Modification, or C. Delete. Modify is to be checked if there is a change from a previous submission of the terminal information.

3. Check which IMS system the terminal will be used in: A. PRODUCTION or B. TEST.

4. Check the terminal type from those listed on the form.

5. Enter the building location, floor, room number, and the nearest telephone extension number where the terminal will be located.

6. Enter the date the terminal is to be installed in the system.

7. Enter the hardware address of the terminal. This address *must* be assigned by the Manager, Data Base Management Systems.

8. Enter the relative line number onto which this terminal will be placed. This number *must* be verified with the Manager, Data Base Management Systems.

9. Enter the physical terminal number to be assigned this terminal. The number *must* be verified with the Manager, Data Base Management System.

10. Enter up to four (4) logical terminal names to be assigned to this terminal. Logical terminal naming conventions can be found in the IMS Standards.

11. Enter the hardware address of the control unit to which this terminal will be attached. This address *must* be assigned by the Manager, Data Base Management System.

12. Enter the terminal features available if this terminal is a CRT.
    A. does the terminal have Program Function Keys
    B. will the operator ID card be used
    C. is the selector pen feature available
    D. can more than 1 input be entered before a response is sent to the terminal
    E. will hardcopy of screens be needed
    F. deletion of pages created via MFS logical paging

13. If this terminal is a printer:
    A. check the size of the print line
    B. enter the logical terminal names of the CRTs which will send hardcopy (via COPY) to this printer

IMS TERMINAL FORM

1. DIVISION:_____

2. PLEASE CHECK (✓) ONLY ONE:

    A. NEW TERMINAL ENTRY:_____
    B. MODIFY TERMINAL ENTRY:_____
    C. DELETE TERMINAL ENTRY:_____

3. PLEASE CHECK (✓) ONLY ONE:

    A. PRODUCTION IMS SYSTEM:_____
    B. TEST IMS SYSTEM:_____

4. CHECK TYPE OF TERMINAL:

    A. IBM 3277 MOD1_____ D. IBM 3286 _____G. OTHER _____(SPECIFY)
    B. IBM 3277 MOD2_____ E. IBM 3288 _____
    C. IBM 3284_____   F. IBM 3275 _____

5. LOCATION OF TERMINAL:

    A. BUILDING:_____
    B. FLOOR:_____
    C. ROOM:_____
    D. NEAREST TELEPHONE #:_____

6. DATE TO BE INSTALLED:_____

7. HARDWARE ADDRESS:*_____

8. LINE NUMBER:*_____

9. PHYSICAL TERMINAL NUMBER:*_____

IMS TERMINAL FORM (cont.)

10. LOGICAL TERMINAL NAME(S):

    A._____ C._____
    B._____ D._____

11. CONTROL UNIT ADDRESS:*_____

12. FOR CRTs ONLY (CHECK OPTIONS AVAILABLE):

    A. PROGRAM FUNCTION KEYS (PFK):_____
    B. OPERATOR ID CARD:_____
    C. SELECTOR PEN:_____
    D. CAN MORE THAN 1 TRANS BE ENTERED BEFORE ANY OUTPUT:_____
    E. SCREEN HARDCOPY REQUIRED:_____

13. FOR PRINTERS ONLY:

    A. PRINTER SIZE: 120_____126_____
    B. ASSOCIATED LTERMS FOR HARDCOPY (LIST):

       _____ _____
       _____ _____
       _____ _____
       _____

DBA:_____EXT:_____DATE:_____

*CONTACT MANAGER, IMS SOFTWARE DEPT. BEFORE COMPLETING ENTRY.

IMS TRANSACTION SECURITY FORM EXPLANATION

This form is to be filled out by the Division Data Base Administrator (DBA) when a password is required for a transaction or when the use of a transaction is to be limited to specified logical terminals (LTERM).

1. Enter the Division to which the transaction applies.

2. Check if the security is: A. NEW, B. MODIFICATION to existing security, or C. DELETION of security.

3. Enter the transaction code.

4. Enter the password to be used for the transaction. A password can be any combination of one to eight vice alphameric characters.

5. Enter the name of the logical terminal(s) from which the transaction can be entered.

IMS TRANSACTION SECURITY FORM

1. DIVISION:_____

2. PLEASE CHECK (√) ONLY ONE:

    A. NEW SECURITY: _____
    B. MODIFY SECURITY:_____
    C. DELETE SECURITY:_____

3. TRANSACTION CODE:_____

4. TRANSACTION PASSWORD: _____

5. LOGICAL TERMINALS TO USE TRANSACTION

    A. _____   H. _____

    B. _____   I. _____

    C. _____   J. _____

    D. _____   K. _____

    E. _____   L. _____

    F. _____   M. _____

DBA:_____ EXT:_____ DATE:_____

Appendix B
Master Terminal
Operations

This appendix contains a "walk through" of the fundamentals of the Master Terminal Operator (MTO) functions in an IMS/VS environment.

MASTER TERMINAL FUNCTIONS

The IMS/VS online system has two major components:

1. The control region
   An OS/VS JOB STEP or
   An OS/VS SYSTEM TASK

2. The system resources
   Application Programs
   Transactions
   Classes
   Regions
   Data Bases
   Communications Lines
   Physical Terminals
   Logical Terminals

The Master Terminal (Fig. A2–1) acts as a system resource controller.

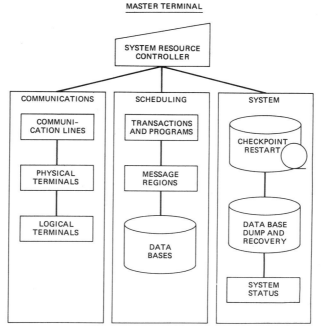

Figure A2–1.

A RUN

These pages contain an overview of the Master Terminal Operations functions and some typical Master Terminal Operator (MTO) responsibilities. The functions are given general treatment within the context of a series of hypothetical actions that might be taken by an MTO.

After IPLing MVS, the operator can start IMS/VS through the system console. As a result of starting IMS/VS, an IMS/VS control region is established, the Master Terminal is unlocked and the IMS/VS Log Writer and Log Buffers are initialized. At this point the log tape should be mounted.

With the Master Terminal now available, the MTO can start the communications lines using an IMS/VS Command. The format for an IMS/VS Command is:

/command (password) text

For example, the start command for the communications lines could look something like:

/START (IAMOK) LINE ALL

TERMINAL USERS CAN ENTER TRANSACTIONS

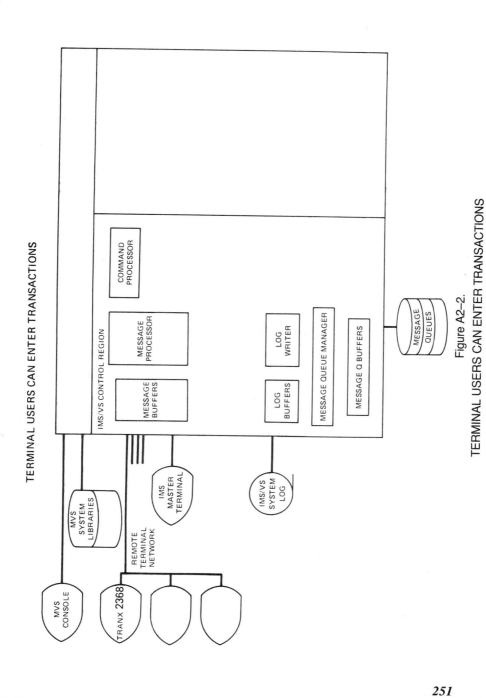

Figure A2-2.
TERMINAL USERS CAN ENTER TRANSACTIONS

251

The command is handled by a module in the control region called the Command Processor. The Command itself initializes a module called the Message Processor and initializes the Message Buffers. The Command itself is written to the Log Buffer and ultimately to the log tape itself.

When the lines have been started, terminal users can begin to enter transactions. Figure A2–2 shows the flow of such a transaction.

What is a transaction? A transaction can be defined as an input message that has been defined to IMS/VS, which when entered from a terminal causes a specific predefined program to be executed. The format for an IMS/VS input transaction message is:

transaction code (password) text

For example the transaction in Fig. A2–2 could be:

TRANX (AX22) 2368

Transactions are queued. Input queues are filled based on transaction codes. The transaction code determines which program is to be invoked. After execution, output transactions are also queued. They are queued based on logical terminals (LTERMS). Each output transaction is given a prefix before it goes on the queue to identify the logical terminal to which it is to be returned.

The logical terminal concept is introduced in order to allow more than one user to use a terminal device (physical terminal) and also to free the application from concern about physical terminal device characteristics. The schematic in Fig. A2–3 shows how physical and logical terminals are correlated.

The logical terminal facility is quite useful in a switched (dial-up) network. In such an environment, a number of different users can interact with a host computer holding a number of different applications. Many users using the same device can dial up, identify themselves and enter into a dialog with the computer. The various applications need not be concerned with a physical device. They respond to a logical device and IMS/VS message processors communicate with the physical device.

There are a couple of rudimentary security procedures that can be implemented at this point. Commands and transactions can be restricted by both logical terminal and by password. The following "mask" type illustration conveys the idea. The "1" indicates that the message in the row can enter the system from the terminal in the column in Fig. A2–4 or when entered by the user with the password in the column in Fig. A2–5. For example the "/START" command, in this case, could only be entered from the Master Terminal with the "IAMOK" password. In this case also, "TRANA" could only come from LTERME, but requires no password.

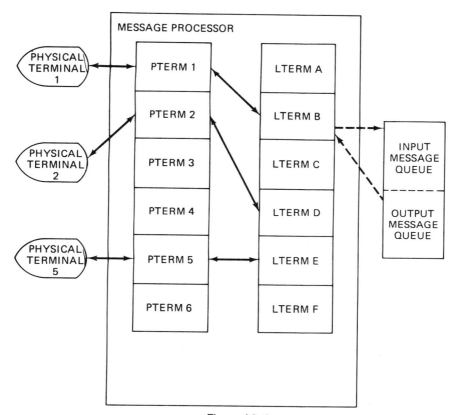

Figure A2–3.

Once the messages have passed the security check, they are entered onto the input queue. They are queued by transaction code. Figure A2–6 shows three messages of transaction x from LTERM B in the queue.

The next step is to start a message processing region (MPR). Upon command from the Master Terminal Operator, a message processing region (MPR) starts; this event is logged. Assume that TRANX has been established as a CLASS 001 job, with a priority of 5 and it causes execution of application program PGMX. The message processing region started is for CLASS 001 transactions. The Message Scheduler scans the queue for CLASS 001 transactions. Control blocks are built and checks are made for conflicts. The Message Scheduler communicates transaction and application program information to the Region Dispatcher which then communicates to the Region Controller. This activity is then written to the log. The Region Controller loads the Message Processing Program (MPP), which in Fig. A2–7 is PGMX.

INPUT MESSAGE

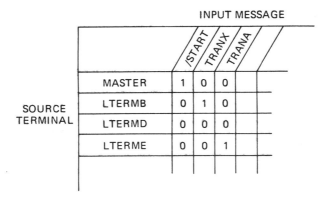

		/START	TRANX	TRANA		
SOURCE TERMINAL	MASTER	1	0	0		
	LTERMB	0	1	0		
	LTERMD	0	0	0		
	LTERME	0	0	1		

A

Figure A2–4.

INPUT MESSAGE

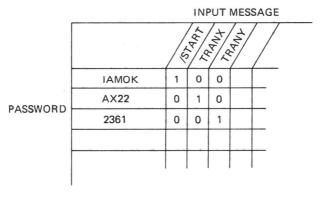

		/START	TRANX	TRANY		
PASSWORD	IAMOK	1	0	0		
	AX22	0	1	0		
	2361	0	0	1		

B

Figure A2–5.

TRANA	TRANX	TRANY	TRANB	TRANC	TRAND
	MSG 1 – (LTERM B)				
	MSG 2 – (LTERM B)				
	MSG 3 – (LTERM B)				

Figure A2–6.

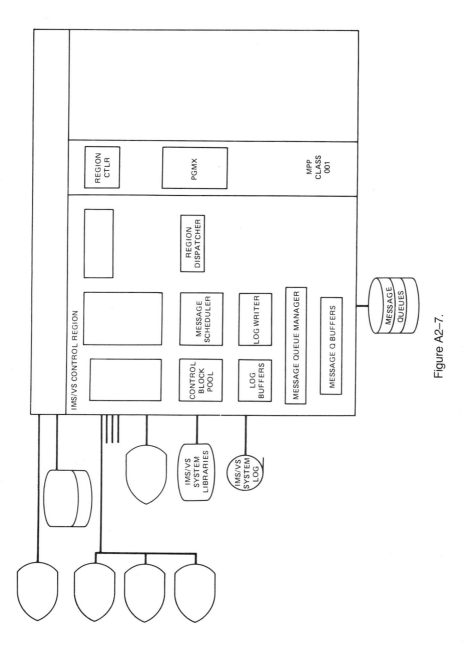

Figure A2–7.

255

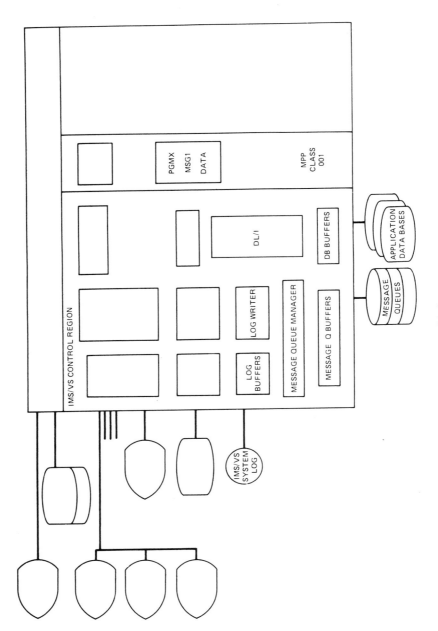

Figure A2–8.

256

Once in place, the message processing program, PGMX retrieves the input message and also retrieves/updates data from the application data bases. Figure A2-8 shows both the message and data in PGMX.

Upon completion of whatever processing is required, the message processing program sends an output message, which is queued on a message queue. The illustration in Fig. A2-9 shows the queue. From the queue, it is transmitted back to the terminal.

All of the activity that has gone on during this time has been logged. The input message is logged; the retrieved and updated data base segments are logged as is the output message.

RECAPPING WHAT HAS BEEN DONE UP TO THIS POINT

1. The Master Terminal Operator has:
    IPLed OS/VS
    Started IMS/VS
    Started the communication lines
    Started a message processing region (MPR)

2. The following events were logged:
    The starting of IMS/VS
    The "START COMMUNICATIONS LINES" command was accepted
    The input message was queued
    The message processing region was started
    A message processing program was scheduled
    The input message was retrieved by the message processing program
    Data bases were opened
    Before and after images of all updated data base segments
    The output message was queued
    The output message was dequeued

3. The following asynchronous activities were taking place within IMS/VS:
    Input messages were received, edited and queued by transaction code
    The message scheduler and region dispatcher scheduled work based on regions available and messages to be processed
    Application programs (MPPs) were retrieving input messages, retrieving/updating data base segments and sending output messages
    Output messages were queued by logical terminal name, edited and dispatched to physical terminals
    The system log recorded all events in chronological order

LTERM A	LTERM B	LTERM C	LTERM D	LTERM E	LTERM F
	MSG 1				

Figure A2–9.

At this juncture, a little more complexity is added to the situation. A "conversational" transaction is entered from logical terminal "D." The function of conversational processing allows a terminal operator to have a continuing dialog with an application program. There are specific commands that a terminal operator has in his repertoire for conversational processing. Establishing a conversational environment is accomplished by defining specific transactions as conversational when defining the IMS/VS system environment. The commands are:

1. /HOLD allows the terminal operator to suspend an active conversation for resumption at a later time.

2. /RELEASE allows the terminal operator to restart a suspended conversation.

3. /EXIT allows the terminal operator to terminate a conversation, whether it be active or suspended.

4. /DISPLAY is used to display the status of conversational processing in the system.

5. /RSTART is used to recover a conversation in the event that the line on which the conversation is is stopped. This command restarts both the line and the conversation.

Both "/DISPLAY" and "/RSTART" are generally restricted to the Master Terminal.

In this case, the conversational transaction is called TRANY. An additional system resource is required. This resource is called the scratch pad area (SPA). This area is used both to hold intermediate information needed in the conversation by both the application program and the terminal. The schematic in Fig. A2–10 shows the required components.

Assuming that the first message (TRANX) has already been processed, and TRANY is awaiting processing, the input transaction queue would look like Fig. A2–11.

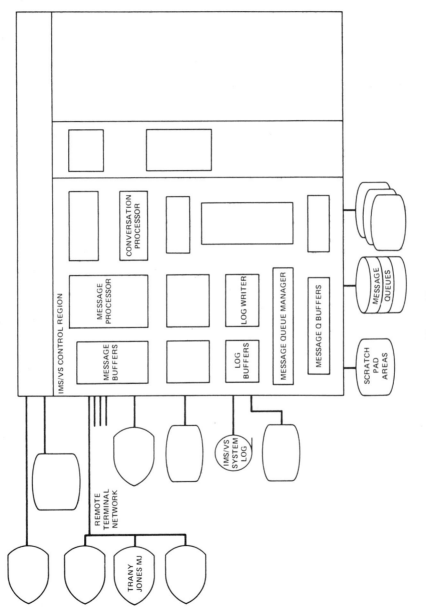

Figure A2–10.

The Master Terminal Operator now starts a CLASS 003 Message Processing Region; assume TRANY has been established as a CLASS 003 job, and causes execution of PGMY. The sequence of operations is the same as those for TRANX, only the names are different. In addition, the conversational process does not terminate when the output message is sent from the queue to the terminal. When the terminal receives the output message, further communication from the terminal is anticipated. This response goes back into the system in the same fashion and the queue then appears as in Fig. A2–12.

This second transaction is then processed and another output message is routed to the terminal. These two transactions just described and their responses constituted a conversation.

CLASS 001		CLASS 003	CLASS 005		CLASS 010
TRANA	TRANX	TRANY	TRANB	TRANC	TRAND
	MSG 2 – (LTERM B)	SPA – (LTERM D) (CONV 1) ↓ MSG 1			
	MSG 3 – (LTERM B)				
	MSG 4 – (LTERM B)				

Figure A2–11.

TRANA	TRANX	TRANY	TRANB	TRANC	TRAND
	MSG 2 – (LTERM B)	SPA – (LTERM D) (CONV 1) ↓ MSG 2			
	MSG 3 – (LTERM B)				
	MMSG 4 – (LTERM B)				

Figure A2–12.

A REVIEW OF THE LOGGED EVENTS DURING THE PRECEDING WILL SERVE AS A RECAP

1. Both input messages (TRANY) were queued
2. The conversation was started and the scratch pad area (SPA) was allocated
3. A CLASS 003 Message Processing Region (MPR) was started
4. Conversational Program (PGMY) was started
5. Input messages were retrieved by PGMY
6. Data bases were opened
7. Before and after images of all updated data base segments were logged
8. Updating of SPA was recorded
9. Both output messages were queued
10. Both output messages were dequeued
11. The conversation was terminated and the scratch pad area (SPA) was deallocated

At this point, it should be pointed out that the data bases used are still open, PGMY is not terminated and the region is still active.

Now suppose that a third terminal has been entering transactions TRANA for some time beginning when TRANX first started. The queue is as shown in Fig. A2–13. The queue is pictured as it looked before TRANY, the conversational transactions, were entered. The TRANA transactions are for a batch program. A batch message processing (BMP) region is set up and a BMP program is set in place. In this case it is PGMA. In Fig. A2–14 the assumption is made that

TRANA	TRANX	TRANY	TRANB	TRANC	TRAND
MSG 1 (LTERM E)	MSG 1 – (LTERM B)				
MSG 2 (LTERM E)	MSG 2 – (LTERM B)				
MSG 3 (LTERM E)	MSG 3 – (LTERM B)				
MSG 4 (LTERM E)					
↓					
MSG N (LTERM E)					

Figure A2–13.

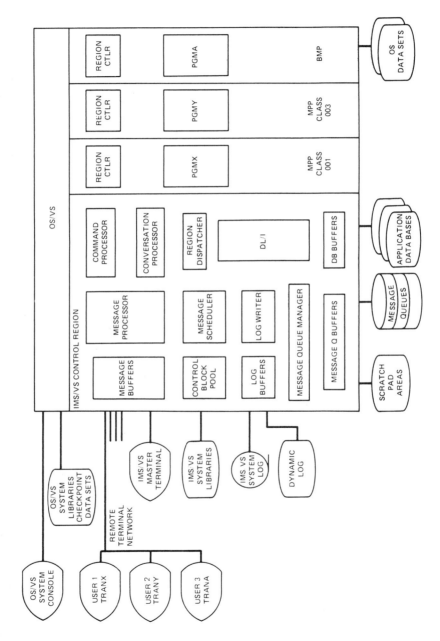

Figure A2–14.

all transactions, TRANX, TRANY and TRANA, are being processed concurrently. All programs, PGMX, PGMY and PGMA, are active and all data bases that were opened are still opened.

ADDITIONAL LOGGING HAS TAKEN PLACE. TO RECAP:

1. Input messages (TRANAs) were queued
2. The batch message processing (BMP) region was started
3. A batch message processing (BMP) program was executed
4. The batch message processing (BMP) program retrieved messages
5. The necessary data bases were opened
6. Data base updates were recorded

Assume that it is now time to shut down the system. The Master Terminal Operator (MTO) checkpoints IMS/VS. The checkpoint stops terminal input, completes terminal output, shuts down message regions, closes data bases, writes necessary queues, control blocks and table to the log file, closes system data sets, closes the log file, notifies the MTO that the checkpoint is complete and terminates IMS/VS. The log then contains the following:

1. Programs X, Y and A have terminated
2. CLASSES 001 and 003 MPRs and the BMP were terminated
3. Data Bases were closed
4. The residual data in the message queues
5. The system status (control blocks)
6. System log termination

The IMS/VS system log is used for

1. Normal Restart
2. Emergency Restart
3. Data Base Recovery
4. Debugging Information
5. Statistical Data
6. Accounting Information

HOW THE MTO WORKS

The preceding has been an overview of the MTO function in a simulated simplistic situation from ''bringing up'' to ''bringing down'' the IMS/VS system. The MTO has command of the IMS/VS system and the following are some of the commands in his repertoire:

MASTER TERMINAL COMMANDS

	COMMAND	*FUNCTION*
Ø	/ASSIGN	RELATE LOGICAL TERMINAL (LTERM) TO PHYSICAL TERMINAL (PTERM)
Ø	/DISPLAY	STATUS, QUEUES, TRAN CODE, ETC.
Ø	/DBRECOVERY ↑ /DBDUMP	RECOVERY OF ONLINE DATA BASE WITHOUT IMS/VS TERMINATION
Ø	/CHECKPOINT /IDLE	TERMINATE IMS/VS
Ø	/NRESTART /ERESTART	INITIATE IMS/VS (IPL)
Ø	/CHANGE /DELETE	ALTER TERMINAL AND PASSWORD SECURITY
Ø	/START /STOP /PSTOP /PURGE /RSTART	AVAILABILITY OF SYSTEM RESOURCES: LINES, PTERM, LTERM, PGM, DB, TRAN, ETC.

A complete list appears at the end of this Appendix.

The Master Terminal Operator usually can work in tandem with the OS/
VS system console operator as follows:

OPERATOR ACTIONS USUALLY PERFORMED IN A
PRODUCTION ENVIRONMENT

OS/VS SYSTEM CONSOLE	IMS/VS MASTER TERMINAL
IPL OS/VS START IMS/VS CONTROL REGION	START IMS/VS (COLD START) START COMMUNICATION LINES START A MESSAGE PROCESSING REGION (CLASS 001) DISPLAY THE MESSAGE QUEUES START ANOTHER MESSAGE PROCESSING REGION (CLASS 003)
START A BATCH MESSAGE PROCESSING REGION SCHEDULE AN OS/VS JOB STREAM TO EXECUTE THE BMP	
	CHECKPOINT IMS/VS AND THEN . . . NORMAL RESTART IMS/VS (WARM START)

Either a typewriter terminal or a CRT can be used as a Master Terminal. Using the Message Format Services option, and the IBM 3275 or 3277 Model II CRT. The Master Terminal screen display looks like Fig. A2–15.

The IBM 3275 or 3277 Model II terminal keyboard comes equipped with twelve program function (PF) keys. These PF keys are defined as follows in the IMS/VS Master Terminal:

PF KEY	*COMMAND/FUNCTION*
1	/DISPLAY
2	/DISPLAY ACTIVE
3	/DISPLAY STATUS
4	/START LINE
5	/STOP LINE
6	/DISPLAY POOL
7	/BROADCAST LTERM ALL
11	NEXT MESSAGE PROTECT
12	COPY FUNCTION

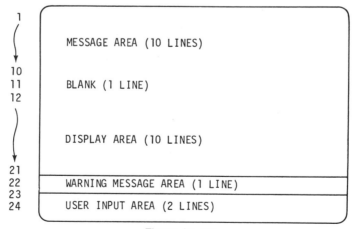

Figure A2–15.

IMS/VS has a number of checkpoint facilities. In order to illustrate these, a reconstruction of "bringing up" IMS/VS into working situation is presented first. The first steps follow:

START IMS/VS

IMS/VS MASTER TERMINAL

STEP 1: DFS810A IMS/VS READ YYYDDD/HHMMSST
JOBNAME, STEPNAME LOG BUFFER=AAAAAA

STEP 2: /NRESTART CHECKPOINT 0, FORMAT ALL

STEP 3: DFS058 NRESTART COMMAND IN PROGRESS
* COLD START—NO PREVIOUS CHECKPOINT
* FORMATS MESSAGE QUEUES
  SCRATCH PAD DATA SET
  DYNAMIC LOG DATA SET
* ALL SYSTEM FUNCTIONS STARTED EXCEPT
  COMMUNICATION LINES
  MESSAGE REGIONS
* SYSTEM LOG IS REQUESTED AND OPENED
* SIMPLE CHECKPOINT WRITTEN TO SYSTEM LOG

STEP 4: DFS9941 *CHKPT 74274/114447**Y4667********
SIMPLE**COLD START COMPLETED.

When these steps are completed, the system stands like this (Fig. A2–16).

START THE IMS CONTROL REGION
ALL SYSTEM FUNCTIONS ARE STARTED EXCEPT LINES AND REGIONS

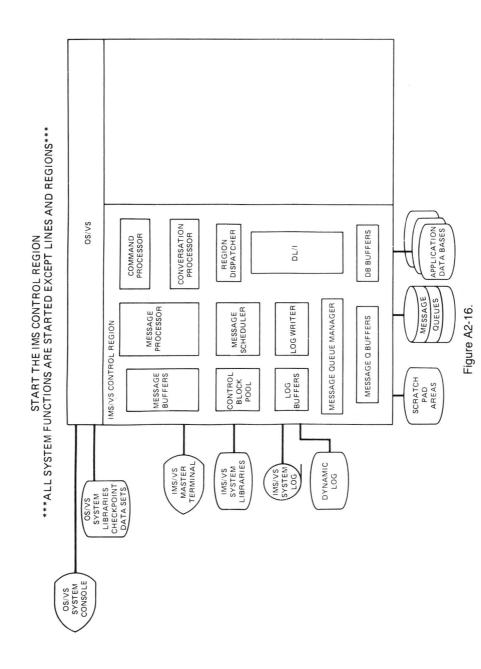

Figure A2-16.

268

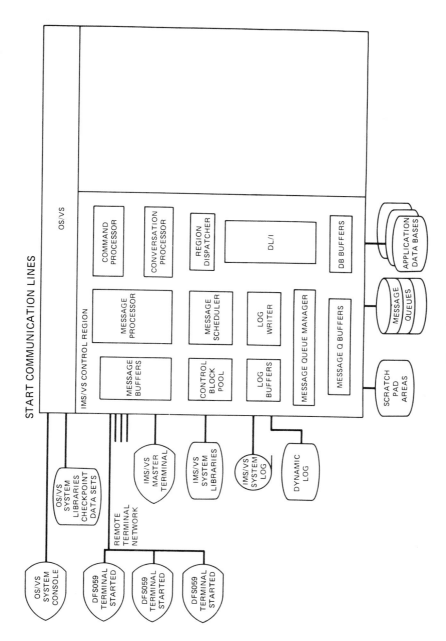

Figure A2-17.

269

The next series of steps are (see also Fig. A2–17):

START COMMUNICATION LINES

IMS/VS MASTER TERMINAL

STEP 1: /START (IAMOK) LINE ALL

STEP 2: DFS058 START COMMAND COMPLETED
* ALL REMOTE TERMINALS RECEIVE
DFS059 TERMINAL STARTED AND ARE UNLOCKED

STEP 3: /BROADCAST TO ACTIVE
GOOD MORNING THE SYSTEM IS READY

STEP 4: DFS058 BROADCAST COMMAND COMPLETE
GOOD MORNING THE SYSTEM IS READY
* ALL ACTIVE REMOTE TERMINALS WILL RECEIVE
GOOD MORNING THE SYSTEM IS READY

After lines are started, start an MPR (Fig. A2–18).

START A CLASS 001 MESSAGE
PROCESSING REGION

IMS/VS MASTER TERMINAL

STEP 1: /START REGION MEMCL1

STEP 2: DFS058 START COMMAND IN PROGRESS
* OS/VS RETRIEVES THE JCL STORED AS MEMBER 'MEMCL1' AND
* STARTS A MESSAGE PROCESSING REGION WITH THE CLASSES
SPECIFIED BY THAT JCL

STEP 3: DFS551 MESSAGE REGION STARTED ID = xx TIME = xxxx
CLASSES = 001

ALL OF THE START FUNCTIONS (IMS, LINES, REGIONS) CAN ALSO BE ACCOMPLISHED BY READING CARDS CONTAINING THE COMMANDS. IF YOUR SYSTEM IS VERY LARGE AND COMPLEX THE CARD DECK WILL SAVE YOU TIME AND MUCH FRUSTRATION.

START A CLASS 001 MESSAGE PROCESSING REGION
WITH PROGRAM

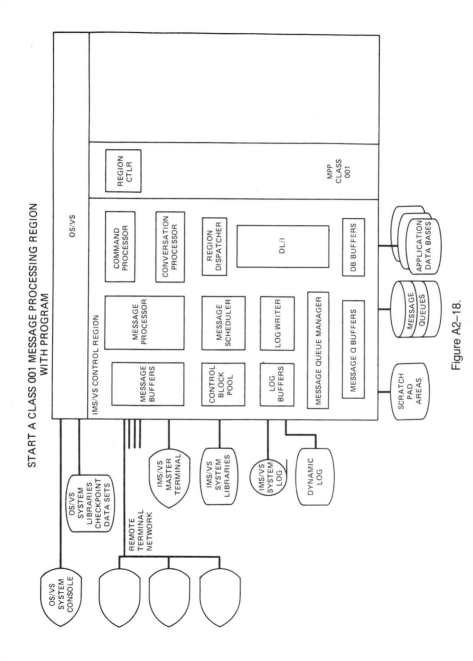

Figure A2–18.

271

Start another MPR (see Fig. A2–19).

START A CLASS 003 MESSAGE
PROCESSING REGION

IMS/VS MASTER TERMINAL

STEP 1:   /START REGION MEMCL3

STEP 2:   DFS058 START COMMAND IN PROGRESS

STEP 3:   DFS551 MESSAGE REGION STARTED ID = xx TIME = xxxx
CLASSES = 003

And then start a BMP (see Fig. A2–19).

START A BATCH MESSAGE PROCESSING
REGION AND SCHEDULE EXECUTION OF BMP

OS/VS SYSTEM CONSOLE

STEP 1:   START AN OS/VS REGION WITH OS/VS START COMMAND

STEP 2:   PROVIDE OS/VS JCL WHICH
* DEFINES THE PROGRAM AS A BMP
* SPECIFIES WHICH TRANSACTION CODE IS TO BE PROCESSED
* DEFINES THE LOGICAL TERMINAL TO WHICH OUTPUT IS TO BE SENT

BATCH MESSAGE PROGRAMS ARE USUALLY SCHEDULED
* ON A TIMELY BASIS (3:00 P.M. EACH AFTERNOON)
* ON A DEMAND BASIS (THE USER DEPT CALLS)

The last schematic (Fig. A2–19) represents the IMS/VS system in a simplistic work situation. While all this is going on, the system log is recording events in chronological order. For example:

1. Command accepted

2. IMS/VS started/stopped

3. Region has been started

4. Message queued/dequeued

5. Application program scheduled/terminated

6. Conversation started/terminated

7. Scratch pad area update

START ANOTHER MPR AND ANOTHER
MESSAGE PROCESSING REGION

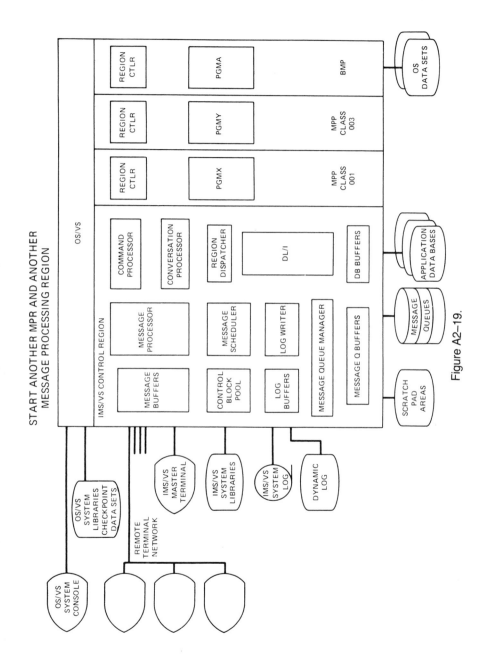

Figure A2–19.

273

8. Data base open/close
9. Data base update before/after
10. Checkpoint taken

There are three checkpoint conditions:

1. The system scheduled checkpoint
2. The Master Terminal request
3. Batch checkpoint

The command to checkpoint is used to record IMS/VS control and status information on the IMS/VS system log. The log is used for restarting either after normal shutdown or after system failure. The checkpoint command is also used to shut down the IMS/VS system.

The command is structured as in Fig. A2–20.

The table below lists the actions taken by the various checkpoints.

	SIMPLE	FREEZE	DUMPQ	PURGE
1. STOP TERMINAL INPUT		X	X	X
2. STOP TERMINAL OUTPUT		X	X	
3. PROCESS QUEUED INPUTS				X
4. FREE MSG REGIONS	X	X	X	X
5. TERMINATE MSG REGIONS		X	X	X
6. SEND QUEUED OUTPUT				X
7. WAIT FOR BMP CHECKPOINT CALL OR TERMINATION		X	X	
8. WAIT FOR BMP TERMINATION				X
9. PURGE IN-CORE MSG-QUEUES TO DISK	X	X	X	X
10. LOG DYNAMIC BLOCKS & TABLES	X	X	X	X
11. DUMP MSG-QUEUES AND DISK-SPAS TO LOG TAPE			X	X
12. CLOSE TO ALL DATA BASES		X	X	X
13. CLOSE QUEUES		X	X	X
14. CLOSE LOG		X	X	X
15. WRITE CHECKPOINT ID TO MASTER & SYSTEM CONSOLE	X	X	X	X
16. TERMINATE CONTROL REGION		X	X	X
17. CONTINUE NORMAL PROCESSING	X			

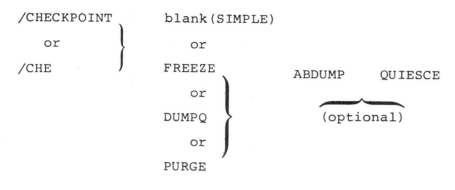

Figure A2–20

The two optional parameters ABDUMP and QUIESCE provide additional enhancements. ABDUMP provides an abnormal termination dump of the IMS/VS control region. QUIESCE allows, through VTAM, the shutdown of programmable terminals to be effected before performing normal checkpoint processing. Some examples:

Simple:

Entry: /CHECKPOINT
Response: DFS058 CHECKPOINT COMMAND IN PROGRESS
Response: DFS9941*CHKPT 74102/110247**A13579********SIMPLE

Freeze:

Entry: /CHECKPOINT FREEZE
Response: DFS058 CHECKPOINT COMMAND IN PROGRESS
Response: DFS9941*74206/120718*A24680********FREEZE

The checkpoint is used to shut down the system. The FREEZE, DUMPQ and PURGE parameters effect a shutting down of the system. When using the checkpoint facility in this way, it is a good idea to use the /BROADCAST facility to communicate that the system is to be suspending operations temporarily. For example

STEP 1:   /BROADCAST TO LINE ALL
            SYSTEM WILL SHUT DOWN IN 15 MINUTES

STEP 2: DFS058 BROADCAST COMMAND COMPLETE
         SYSTEM WILL SHUT DOWN IN 15 MINUTES

STEP 3: /CHECKPOINT PURGE OR /CHECKPOINT DUMPQ

STEP 4: DFS058 CHECKPOINT COMMAND IN PROGRESS
         DFS991 IMS SHUTDOWN (REMOTE TERMINALS)

The following actions take place depending on the parameter (PURGE or DUMPQ) used.

	PURGE	*DUMPQ*
1. STOP TERMINAL INPUT	X	X
2. STOP TERMINAL OUTPUT		X
3. PROCESS QUEUED INPUT	X	
4. FREE MPP REGIONS	X	X
5. TERMINATE MPP REGIONS	X	X
6. SEND QUEUED OUTPUT	X	
7. WAIT FOR BMP CHKP CALL OR TERMINATION		X
8. WAIT FOR BMP TERMINATION	X	
9. PURGE IN-CORE MSG-QUEUES TO DISK	X	X
10. LOG DYNAMIC BLOCKS & TABLES	X	X
11. DUMP MSG-QUEUES AND DISK-SPAS TO LOG TAPE	X	X
12. CLOSE ALL DATA BASES	X	X
13. CLOSE QUEUES	X	X
14. CLOSE LOG	X	X
15. WRITE CHECKPOINT ID TO MASTER TERMINAL	X	X
16. TERMINATE CONTROL REGION	X	X

Further steps that can be taken in the checkpoint process are:

STEP 5: /DISPLAY SHUTDOWN STATUS
STEP 6: SYSTEM PURGING

     LINE/PTERM   STATUS

       5-1   OUTPUT IN PROCESS

       5-2   INPUT IN PROCESS

     MSG-IN 2

     MSG-OUT 5

     MASTER ACTIVE

     74274/171545

STEP 7:   /IDLE LINE ALL

      * ISSUE AFTER SHUTDOWN CHECKPOINT TO IMMEDIATELY STOP INPUT OR OUTPUT

      * INPUT MESSAGE IN PROCESS IS REJECTED

      * OUTPUT MESSAGE IN PROCESS IS REQUEUED

STEP 8:   DFS9941*CHKPT 74274/172010**Y2388********PURGE

      OR

      DFS9941*CHKPT 74274/172010**Y2388********DUMPQ

At the end of all this, IMS/VS is shut down and an OS/VS environment remains as shown in Fig. A2–21.

    The schematic, Fig. A2–22, gives an overview of the various ways of starting (bringing up) the system and terminating (bringing down) the system.

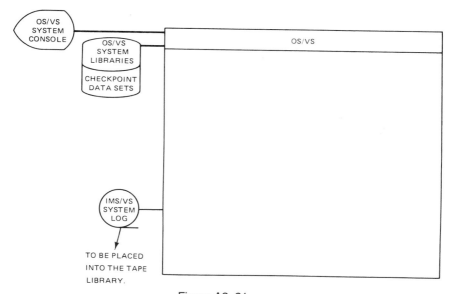

Figure A2–21.

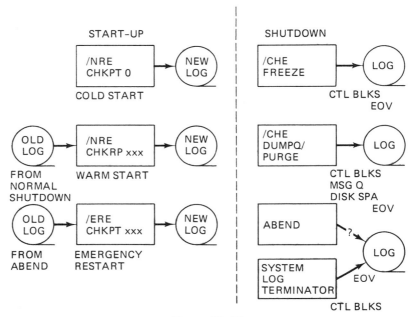

Figure A2–22.

Figure A2–23 pictures an IMS/VS in a simplistic work situation, while Fig. A2–24 shows the scope of the recovery responsibility of IMS/VS. The Master Terminal function should be in a position to recover the following IMS/VS capabilities:

1. Stand alone batch programs/regions
2. Online DB/DC programs/regions
3. Data Bases

The most important element in recovery of IMS/VS is the closed IMS system log data set. In those situations, hardware failure, software (OS/VS) failure, power failure, loops, etc., where the log data set is not closed, a system terminating feature is invoked. There is a utility program, the System Log Termination (DFSFL0TO), that closes the log data set. At the time of the failure, a dump should be taken. Then OS/VS is re-IPLed and the utility is run using the dump as input.

The specific situations to be recovered are treated individually in the following pages.

The first is the standalone DL/1 batch job (Fig. A2–25)

A standalone DL/1 batch program abend is likely to be caused by invalid input data or a program logic error. The abend message comes up on the OS/

IMS ONLINE ENVIRONMENT

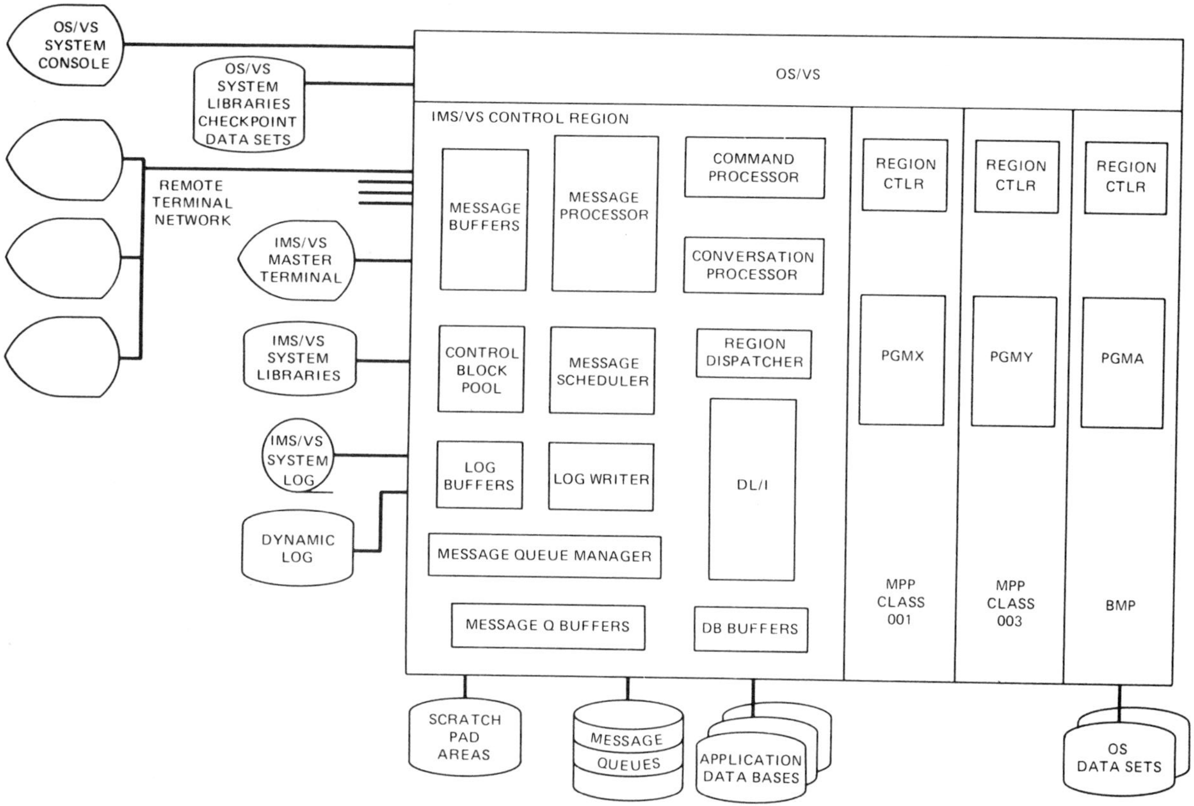

Figure A2-23.

279

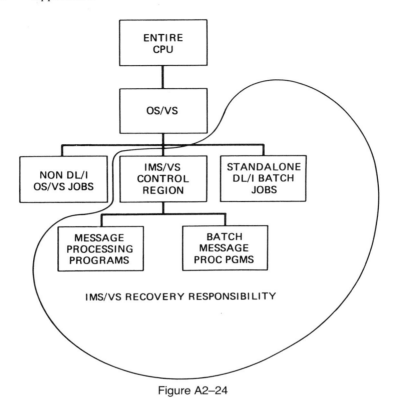

Figure A2–24

VS console. The required action is to back out data base changes, correct the erroneous data or program and rerun the program.

The backout utility (DFSBB0OO) operates as a normal DL/1 batch job. It makes use of the Data Base log records to back out the effects from data bases specified by a PSB. It creates as output a log data set that must be used together with the system log data set for subsequent data base recovery. The schematic (Fig. A2–26) shows requirements of Backout.

The next specific area of concern is recovery (Fig. A2–27) from IMS/VS control region failure. Failure can be caused by a loop, by the region becoming nondispatchable or by an IMS control region abend. If looping or nondispatchable, the symptoms are calls from remote terminal users or IMS/VS commands not being acepted at the Master Terminal. In that case IMS/VS must be ABENDed from the OS/VS system console.

When ABENDing of an IMS/VS Control Region takes place, the effects are partial data base update, the possible loss of some input messages and the STAE routine will flush the log buffers and close the log data set *sometimes*. If the log data set is not closed, then an OS/VS dump should be taken and the

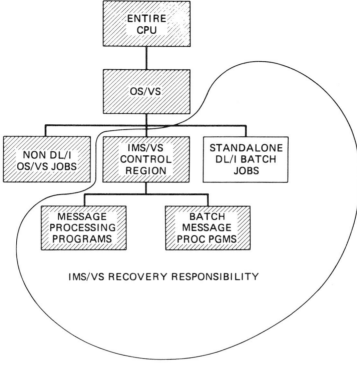

Figure A2–25.

log terminator utility should be run to close it. When the closed system log data set is available, the IMS/VS system can be restarted.

Restarting an IMS/VS Control Region when only main storage was lost is accomplished by starting IMS from the OS/VS console. When the Master Terminal is ready, /ERESTART effects the restarting procedure. In this situation IMS/VS selects the proper checkpoint, initializes the control region control blocks, reinitializes all active programs, backs out data base updates where necessary, requests a new system log tape and creates a simple checkpoint.

Restarting an IMS/VS Control Region when both main storage and message queues have been lost is a little more complicated. The symptoms are messages indicating I/O errors in message queues or message queues reported as filled, followed by another message indicating the necessity of reallocating message queue data sets. The emergency restart (/ERESTART) must be used with a checkpoint that comes from either the most recent cold start or from the most recent CHECKPOINT DUMPQ or CHECKPOINT PURGE. Also a BUILDQ parameter is entered to force loading of message queues and writing disk scratch pad areas. The command would look something like:

/ERESTART CHECKPOINT 74203/203040 BUILDQ

Other parameters that can be included with this command are:

FORMAT
SERIAL
NOBMP

FORMAT specifies which queues and data sets are to be formatted:

SM means short-message queue
LM means long-message queue

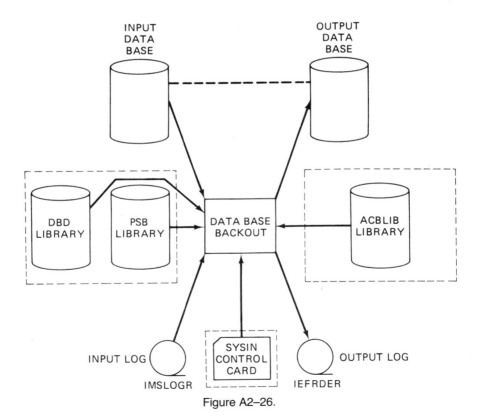

Figure A2–26.

QC means control record data set
SP means scratch pad data set
DL means dynamic log data set
ALL means all message queues and data sets

SERIAL specifies serial numbers of log data sets that are required under most circumstances.

NOBMP specifies whether BMP programs are to be considered as part of the restart.

Schematically: Emergency Restart is shown in Fig. A2–28. If an I/O error occurs while the emergency restart is attempting to back out incomplete transactions for the data bases and programs specified, processing is allowed to continue against the remaining data bases and the emergency restart concludes. At the completion of ERESTART, a DBRECOVERY command is entered. The Data Base Recovery Utility and Data Base Backout Utility are to be executed. After completion of these utilities, the /START command is entered for those data bases that were not restarted by the emergency restart procedure.

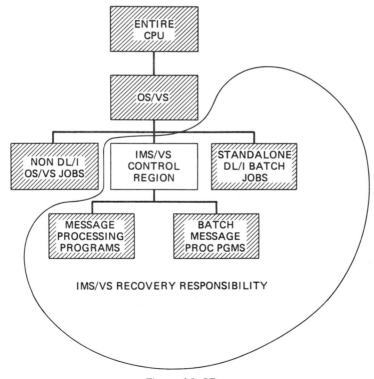

Figure A2–27.

/ERESTART (CHKPT X) (FORMAT Y) (SER Z) (NO BMP)
OR
/ERESTART CHKPT$\left(\begin{smallmatrix}0\\X\end{smallmatrix}\right)$BUILDQ (FORMAT Y) (SER Z) (NO BMP)

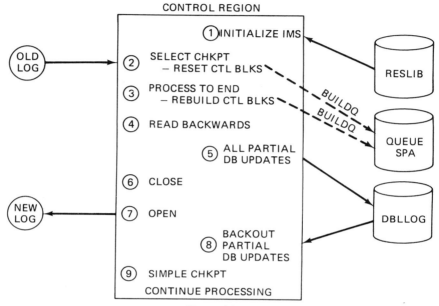

Figure A2–28.

The next specific system recovery situation to be examined is the message processing program malfunction (Fig. A2–29). A malfunction in an MPR or MPP takes the form of either a loop or an abend. After IPLing MVS, the operator can start IMS/VS through the system console. As a result of starting IMS/VS, an IMS/VS control region is established, the Master Terminal is unlocked and the IMS/VS Log Writer and Log Buffers are initialized. At this point the log tapes should be mounted.

With the Master Terminal now available, the MTO can start the communications lines using an IMS/VS command. The format for an IMS/VS command is:

/command (password) text

For example, the start command for the communications lines could look something like:

/START (IAMOK) LINE ALL

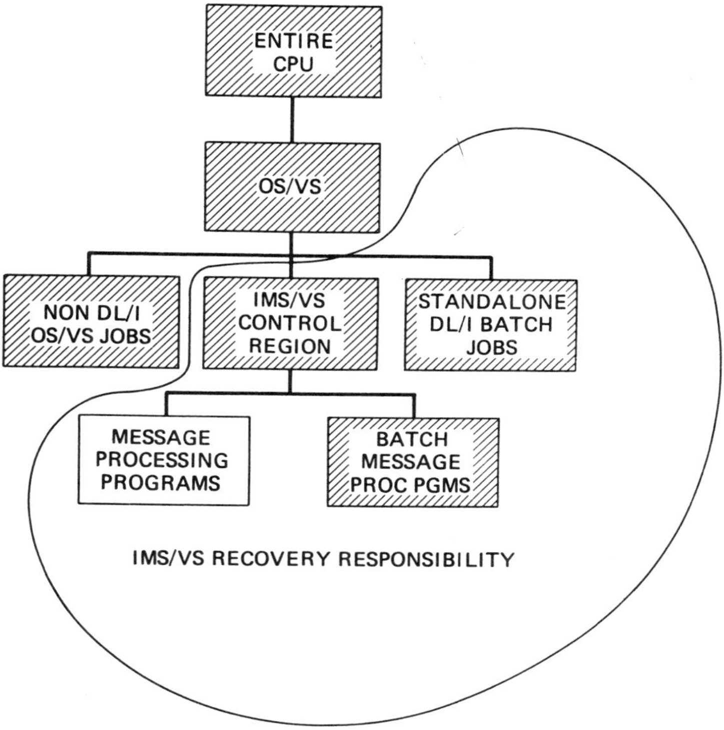

Figure A2–29.

The command is handled by a module in the control region called the Command Processor. The Command itself initializes a module called the Message Processor and initializes the Message Buffers. The Command itself is written to the Log Buffer and ultimately to the log tape itself.

A loop in the system is usually discovered by the /DISPLAY ACTIVE command showing a program active for a long time or when a user terminal operator reports a serious response time delay. To remedy the situation, the OS/VS console operator or the Master Terminal Operator can abend the job. The command may look like:

/STOP REGION 1 ABDUMP TRANX

It is also possible than an MPP can abend because of a bug. Normally, a message processing region abend produces the following messages:

On the OS/VS console: IDF4501
IEF4041

On the IMS/VS Master Terminal: DFS554

The effect of the abend should be termination of both the program and the transaction. Parameters in the DFS554 indicate that both program and transaction are stopped. In an abend case such as this, there is a good possibility that the data bases affected by the stopped program and transaction may have only been partially updated. IMS/VS should automatically back out the data base updates for the offending program and transaction using the dynamic log. When the automatic backout is complete, the region (if necessary), the program and the transaction can be started up, if desired.

In data base backout and other recovery utilities, there is a great deal of dependence on "synch points." What is a "synch point"? A "synch point" is a recovery point, written on a log data set including that all's well up to that point.

Synch points are taken:

1. When data base records are written

2. When the dynamic log chain is purged

3. When output messages are sent

4. Created for each program when

      the program ends

      checkpoint call is issued by the program

      operation does checkpoint

      system checkpoint is taken

      an input message is retrieved

As stated above, when a message processing program (an application program) abends, the operator should follow procedures for that message processing program's abend condition.

If an application program abends and the DFS554 is *not* displayed, the region should be stopped. When the region is stopped, dynamic backout should occur. If it doesn't because of an I/O error in the data base, then that data base must be recovered using the recovery utility, and running the standalone batch backout utility for the abended program. Upon completion of this, the data base, the program and the transaction can be started.

The final system recovery procedure is for the batch message processing (BMP) program or region (Fig. A2–30). The situation is almost identical to that of message processing regions except for recovery duration due to backout volume.

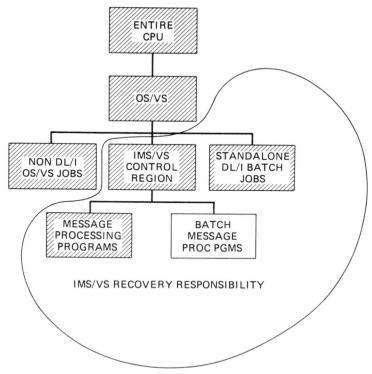

Figure A2–30.

DATA BASE RECOVERY UTILITIES

The next major area to be presented is that of Data Base Recovery Utilities. Some of these have already been mentioned in passing in the preceding material on system recovery. A summary of the topic of DB Recovery Utilities is presented first and is followed by a more detailed study of each. DB Recovery Utilities are the following:

1. Data Base Image Copy—provides a dump format copy at the data set level of a data base

2. Data Base Change Accumulation—accumulates Data Base changes from the log

3. Data Base Backout—removes the changes to a data base made by a program

4. Data Base Recovery—restores a data set of a data base

The following table summarizes the IMS/VS data base recovery commands and their functions.

	/DBRECOVERY /DBR	/DBDUMP /DBD	/STOP***
WRITE DB BUFFERS TO LOG TAPE	X	X	
CLOSE CURRENT LOG TAPE	X	X	
REQUEST, OPEN, & CHECKPOINT NEW LOG TAPE	X	X	
CLOSE REQUIRED DB DATA SETS	X	X	
STOP SCHEDULING UPDATE PROGRAMS	X	X	X
ALLOWS CURRENT PROGRAMS TO TERMINATE	X	X	X
(ALL THREE COMMANDS ARE RESET BY /START DB COMMAND)			

***THE STOP COMMAND CAN BE ISSUED BY IMS/VS

The schematic in Fig. A2–31 illustrates the DB Recovery concept. A couple of considerations that should be kept in mind while using data base recovery utilities are:

1. The frequency of making data base image copies should be determined by the amount of data base activity and the size of the data base.

2. The frequency of running the change accumulation utility is determined by a balancing of two factors. The change accumulation utility produces a file that is in sequence by physical block number within the data base and this allows rapid recovery. Log changes that are not accumulated result in random processing against the data set of the data base being recovered, which is a slow process.

THE IMAGE COPY UTILITY

This utility provides a dump format copy of a data base by data set. It can copy one or more data sets, and multiple copies can be made. The image copy is written in physical sequential fashion. Image copy is used as input to the data set recovery utility. The schematic, Fig. A2–32, illustrates the input and output of this utility.

The following are some operational considerations in using image copy:

1. The size of the data base, the activity against it, its reorganization and recovery requirements should influence the frequency of image copies being made.

2. An image copy should be made immediately after a reorganization.

3. The image copy should be cataloged in the library immediately with a proper retention cycle. Serial numbers, the date, the names of copies, data sets and data base should be recorded.

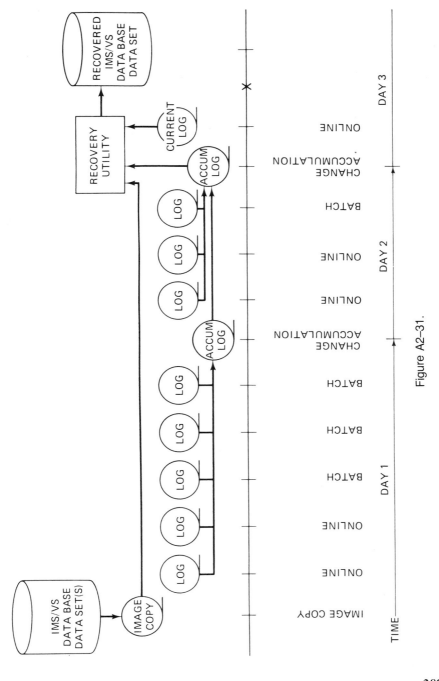

Figure A2-31.

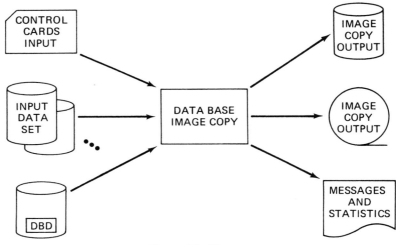

Figure A2–32.

4. All data sets of a data base should be copied at the same time so as to minimize coordination activity.

THE CHANGE ACCUMULATION UTILITY

This utility accumulates change records from the log tapes and from old accumulation tapes. It eliminates log records that did not impact the data base and those records older than a specified purge date. It combines records that update the same data base segment. The output of this utility, which is input to the data base recovery utility, is in sequence by data set within data base. The schematic, Fig. A2–33, illustrates the input and output of the utility.

The following are operational considerations in applying the change accumulation utility:

1. Invalid recovery can come about as a result of specifying a wrong purge date, omission of a log tape input or presenting a log tape to the utility in the wrong chronological sequence.

2. The execution of the utility itself is time consuming, although accumulated changes provide rapid data base recovery.

3. Execution is exclusive of data bases in use but it must be done in a batch region.

4. Caution and control should be exercised so that accumulated tape serial numbers, log tape serial numbers, purge dates, current dates, as well as names of accumulated data sets and data bases are recorded.

5. The accumulated log tape, the new log data set, the old log data sets and the old accumulated log tape should be stored in the tape library, each with a proper retention cycle.

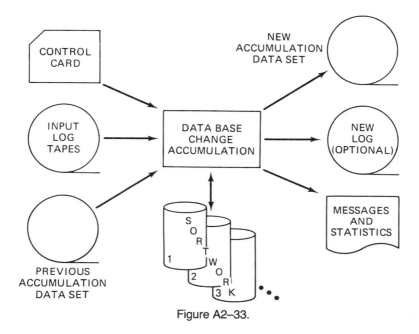

Figure A2–33.

6. The most current accumulated log tape should be related to the proper image copy so that they are readily available for recovery.

DATA BASE BACKOUT UTILITY

The Data Base Backout Utility was viewed in some detail earlier under system recovery. At this point the Data Base Recovery Utility is to be examined in some detail.

DATA BASE RECOVERY UTILITY

The Data Base Recovery Utility assumes that malfunctioning hardware has rendered a data set of a data base unusable. This utility recovers a data set of a data base that has been destroyed. It merges an image copy of the data set with accumulated changes and then completes updating with system log tapes. It is possible to use the output of another utility (HISAM reorganization) as input instead of the image copy. The Recovery Utility operates on a principle of physical replacement in a physical sequence. Figure A2–34 shows the various configurations of input that can go into this utility.

As part of the Recovery Utility, there is an option to recover only those tracks that have been damaged. It is called the Track Recovery Option (TRCV) and works only on VSAM data sets. Since it only replaces damaged tracks rather than entire data sets, it is often faster than recovering the entire data base. The only valid inputs when this option is exercised are the accumulation log and the

DATA BASE RECOVERY UTILITY

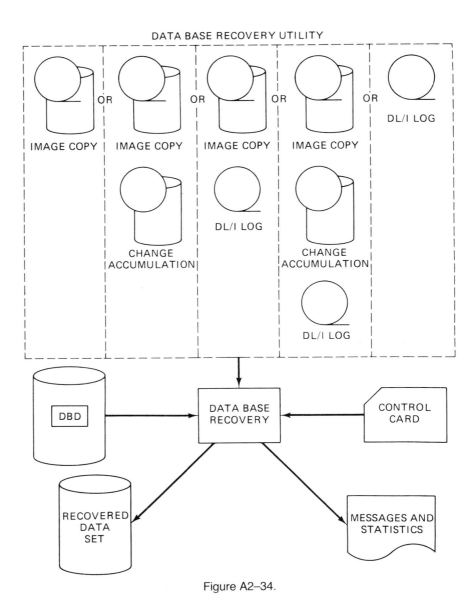

Figure A2–34.

image copy. It operates on the principle of assigning alternate tracks where permanent DASD errors exist and then creates a current version of the track from the accumulated log data and the image copy.

The following operational considerations effect the use of the Recovery Utility:

1. Change accumulation run before the recovery utility might speed up the total recovery. In using the track recovery option, the change accumulation must be done first.

2. Omission of an input log tape will cause an invalid recovery.

3. Certain dates of image copy, accumulated log tapes and log tapes are checked as well as the day/time sequence of log input.

The schematic, Fig. A2–35, shows the information flow of the Data Base Recovery Utility.

There are two basic kinds of error from which recovery is required, a data base read error and a data base write error.

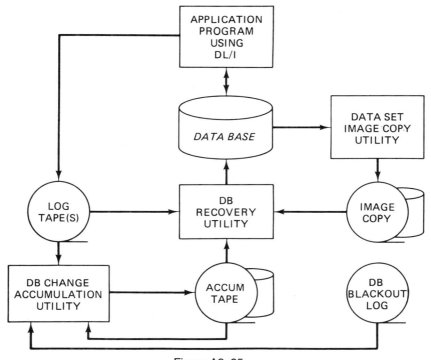

Figure A2–35.

The possible causes of a data base read error include a permanent read error, an invalid data base pointer, an invalid segment code, an error in edit/compression routines or an IMS/VS programming error. In case of a read error IMS/VS will stop the data base and post an appropriate return code (AO) so that programs can terminate their processing normally. An error message is typed on the console. In response, the master terminal operator should record the error, implement data base recovery with image copy, change accumulation and the logs. If the job is a batch job, exclude the last log tape and thereby save backout. Upon completion, the program can be reinitialized.

The possible causes of a data base write failure are permanent hardware failure or a transient write error. In this case IMS/VS will stop the data base, allow current programs to run to completion and keep the error block in buffers in main storage. No status code is returned. An I/O error message is typed on the console. The action taken depends on whether the program abends or not. If the program runs to completion, the master terminal operator should record the error, invoke data base recovery with image copy, change accumulation and logs, including the last one. If the program abends, the master terminal operator should record the error, invoke data base recovery with image copy, change accumulation and logs, exclusive of the last one, if the job abending is a label job. Upon completion of recovery, rerun program.

If there is a failure of either a system log or the dynamic log, other procedures must be invoked.

If there is read error on a log tape, that is, if there is an I/O abend during emergency restart, batch backout, data base recovery, change accumulation, then three courses of action are open. First, try another tape drive. If that fails, try to copy the log tape. If that fails, run the log recovery utility. The purpose of the Log Recovery Utility (DFSULTRO) is to produce a new and usable log from either dual or single log tapes which contain read errors. The schematic, Fig. A2–36, shows the utility.

Write errors on log tape can be remedied by copying the failing tape and then running the log termination utility.

When using the dual logging facility and an uncorrectable write error occurs on one log tape, the option exists to continue processing using a single log or to take a checkpoint freeze and do a normal restart.

If a write error occurs on the dynamic log (IMSVS.DBLLOG), a work data set established for dynamic back and emergency restart, then the data set must be reallocated. The message "SYSTEM WILL BE STOPPED FOR 15 MIN-UTES" should be broadcast to all terminals, a checkpoint freeze should be invoked, the DBLLOG reallocated and then a normal restart with a formatting of the dynamic log should be performed, which includes a simple checkpoint.

If the control region abends, the DBLLOG should be reallocated and an emergency restart with a format option of the dynamic log should be performed including a simple checkpoint.

If the dynamic log data set is determined to be too small, IMS/VS will purge the system and shut down after the current processing is completed. At that point, the dynamic log should be reallocated to a larger size. If the system abends because of this, the data set (DBLLOG) should be reallocated and made larger, and write error procedures should be followed.

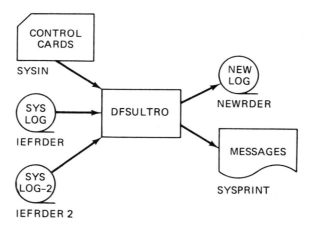

Figure A2–36.

IMS/VS COMMANDS AND KEY WORDS

COMMANDS

The general format of an IMS/VS command is:

/verb (password) KEYWORD PI, KEYWORD P2, P3.   comments

A list of the IMS/VS commands follows. The list is also the terminal security command default, that is, the ''x'' represents the command available to the terminal unless otherwise specified.

COMMAND	Master Terminal	Remote Terminal
/ASSIGN	X	X
/BROADCAST	X	X
/CANCEL	X	
/CHANGE	X	
/CHECKPOINT	X	
/CLSDST	X	
/COMPT	X	
/DBDUMP	X	
/DBRECOVERY	X	
/DELETE	X	
/DEQUEUE	X	
/DISPLAY	X	
/END	X	X
/ERESTART	X	
/EXCLUSIVE	X	X
/EXIT	X	X
/FORMAT	X	X
/HOLD	X	X
/IAM		X
/IDLE	X	
/LOCK	X	X
/LOG	X	X
/LOOPTEST	X	
/MONITOR	X	
/MSASSIGN	X	
/MSVERIFY	X	
/NRESTART	X	
/OPNDST	X	
/PSTOP	X	
/PURGE	X	
/RCLSDST	X	X

COMMAND	Master Terminal	Remote Terminal
/RCOMPT		X
/RDISPLAY	X	X
/RELEASE	X	X
/RESET	X	X
/RSTART	X	
/SET	X	X
/START	X	
/STOP	X	
/TEST	X	X
/TRACE	X	
/UNLOCK	X	X

KEYWORDS

Below is a list of IMS/VS keywords, which are words that can be used as parameters of the various IMS/VS commands. Many of these words have synonyms, which are also listed.

KEYWORD	SYNONYM
ABDUMP	
ACTIVE	A
ASSIGNMENT	ASMT
BUILDQ	BLDQS, BLDQ, BUILDQS
CANCEL	
CHECKPOINT	CHKPT, CHECKPT, CHKPOINT
CLASS	CLS
CNS	
COMPONENT	COMPT
CONVERSATION	CONV
CPRI	
DATABASE	DATABASES, DB, DBS
DC	
DONE	
DUMPQ	DUMPQS
FORMAT	FMT
FREEZE	
ICOMPT	
INPUT	
KEY	
LEVEL	
LINE	LINES

KEYWORD	SYNONYM
LINK	
LMCT	LCT
LPRI	
LTERM	LTERMS
MODE	
MODULE	
MONITOR	MON
MSNAME	
MSPLINK	
NOBMP	
NODE	
NOPASSWORD	NOPSWD
NOTERMINAL	NOTERM, NOTER
NPRI	
OPTION	
OUTPUT	
PARLIM	
PASSWORD	PASSWORDS, PSWD, PSWDS
PCH	
PI	
PLMCT	PLCT
POOL	
PRIORITY	PRTY
PROGRAM	PROGRAMS, PROG, PROGS, PGM, PGMS
PRT	
PTERM	PTERMS
PURGE	
QUEUE	QUEUES, Q, QS
QUIESCE	
RDR	
REGION	REGIONS, REG, REGS, MSGREG, MSGREGS, MSGREGION, MSGREGIONS
SEGNO	
SEGSIZE	SEGSZ
SERIAL	SER, SERS, SERIALS
SET	
SHUTDOWN	
STATUS	
SYSID	
TERMINAL	TERMINALS, TERM, TERMS, TER, TERS

KEYWORD	SYNONYM
TRANSACTION	TRANS, TRAN, TRANSACTIONS, TRANCODE TRANCODES
VID	
XKEY	

MASTER TERMINAL OPERATOR'S REPERTOIRE

Virtually all of these commands and keywords are in the repertoire of the Master Terminal Operator. Each of these commands and keywords receives complete explanation in the Operators Reference Manual (SH20-9028). In addition to that manual, the Master Terminal should also have the Messages and Codes Manual (SH20-9030) and the Utilities Reference Manual (SH20-9029) at his disposal.

The Master Terminal Operator should also possess knowledge of and have reference material from which to get ready access to the following information:

1. LINES AND PHYSICAL TERMINALS
   (ADDRESS, TYPE, LOCATION, TELEPHONE NUMBER)

2. LOGICAL TERMINAL
   (NAMES, RESTRICTIONS)

3. TRANSACTION CODES
   (PROGRAM, DATA BASES)

4. PROGRAMS
   (TRANSACTION CODES, DATA BASES, PROCESSING INTENT)

5. DATA BASES
   (LOGICAL, PHYSICAL, DDNAMES, DSNAMES, EXTENTS, VOLUMES, TRANSACTION CODES, PROGRAMS)

6. SECURITY RESTRICTIONS
   (DATA BASES, PROGRAMS, TRANSACTION CODES, PHYSICAL TERMINALS, LOGICAL TERMINALS, PASSWORDS)

7. MANUAL LOGS
   (SYSTEM LOG TAPE SERIAL NUMBERS, CHECKPOINT NUMBERS, CHECKPOINT TYPE, IRREGULARITIES, RESTART INFORMATION)

8. DESCRIPTION OF RECOVERY PREPARATION
   (FREQUENCY OF DUMPING, LOG ACCUMULATIONS, FREQUENCY OR REORGANIZATIONS)

9. DETAIL OPERATING/RECOVERY PROCEDURES
   (DESCRIPTIONS OF WHO WILL HANDLE WHAT TYPE OF SITUATIONS)

BELOW IS A LIST OF IMS/VS UTILITIES.

1. Generation Utilities

    Data Base Description Generation (DBDGEN)
    Program Specification Block Generation (PSBGEN)
    Application Control Block Maintenance (ACBGEN)

2. Data Base Utilities
    Data Base Reorganization and Load
    HISAM Reorganization Unload (DFSURULO)
    HISAM Reorganization Reload (DFSURRLO)
    HD Reorganization Unload (DFSURGUO)
    HD Reorganization Reload (DFSURGLO)
    Data Base Prereorganization (DFSURPRO)
    Data Base Scan (DFSURGSO)
    Data Base Prefix Resolution (DFSURGIO)
    Data Base Prefix Update (DFSURGPO)
    Data Base Recovery Utilities
    Data Base Image Copy (DFSUDMPO)
    Data Base Change Accumulation (DFSUCUMO)
    Data Base Recovery (DFSURDBO)
    Data Base Backout (DFSBBØOO)
    Utility Control Facility
    Utility Control Facility (DFSUCFOO)

3. System Log Utilities
    System Log Recovery (DFSULTRO)
    System Log Terminator (DFSFLØTO)
    Statistical Analysis
    Sort and Edit Pass 1 (DFSISTSO)
    Edit Pass 2 (DFSIST20)
    Report Writer (DFSIST30)
    Message Select and Copy or List (DFSIST40)
    File Select and Formatting Print (DFSERA10)
    Log Transaction Analysis (DFSILTAO)
    Log Tape Merge (DFSLTMGO)

4. Performance Reporting Utilities
    Data Base (DB) Monitor Report Print (DFSURTR30)
    Data Base (DB) Monitor (DFSMNTBO)
    Data Communications (DC) Monitor Report Print (DFSUTR20)
    Program Isolation Trace Report (DFSPIRPO)
    SPOOL SYSOUT Print (DFSUPRTO)
    Multiple Systems Verification (DFSUMSVO)

5. Message Format Services Utility (MFS)
    MFS Language Utility
    MFS Service Utility

6. Data Language/1 (DL/1) Test Program (DFSDDLTO) DLTO

Index

G

General evaluation of DBMS and Data Dictionary, 205
Generalizations about DBMS, 164
Generalized Sequential Access Method (GSAM), 72
"GEN"ing IMS/VS, 120
GET, 42, 122, 175
GET HOLD NEXT (GHN), 42, 122
GET HOLD NEXT WITHIN PARENT (GHNP), 42, 122
GET HOLD UNIQUE (GHU), 42, 122
GET NEXT (GN), 42, 122
GET NEXT WITH PARENT, (GNP), 42, 122
GET UNIQUE (GU), 42, 122
GHN, (see GET)
GHNP, (see GET)
GHU, (see GET)
Gibson, Cyrus, 216
GNP, (see GET)
GN, (see GET)
GSAM, (see Generalized Sequential Access Method)
GU, (see GET)

H

HDAM, (see Hierearchical Direct Access Method)
HIDAM, (see Hierarchical Indexed Direct Access Method)
Hierarchical data bases,
System 2000, 195
IDMS, 189
Hierarchical Direct Access Method (HDAM), 48, 50–51, 68, 121, 175
Hierarchical Indexed Direct Access Method (HIDAM), 48, 50–51, 71, 121, 175
Hierarchical Indexed Sequential Access Method (HISAM), 48, 50–51, 66, 121, 175
Hierarchical network, 211
Hierarchical Sequential Access Method (HSAM), 48, 50–51, 65, 121, 175
Hierarchical structure, 31, 34, 35 (illustr.), 44
HISAM, (see Hierarchical Indexed Sequential Access Method)
HSAM, (see Hierarchical Sequential Access Method)
Host,
computer, 211, 213
processor, 211, 212

I

IDMS, 1, 165, 183–194
IDMS utilities, 194
IMSMAP, 142
IMS/VS 38–39, 80–81, 119–129, 165, 174–177
design trade offs, 80–81
introduced, 38–39
recap summary, 174–177
using, 119–129, 124 (illustr.)
IMSVS.ACBLIB, 133
IMS/VS batch, 86
IMS/VS Commands and Keywords, 232–234, 296–297
IMS/VS control region, 84–85
IMS/VS data base organization, 48
IMSVS.DBDLIB, 132
IMS/VS master terminal operations, 249–263 (Appendix B)
check point, 263
conversational processing, 258
entering transactions, 251–252
functions overview, 249
logging, 253
message scheduling, 253
program loading, 253
recovery, 286–295
restarting, 274–286
retrieval from data base, 257
start message processing region, 253
start lines, 250–252
start up, 250
transaction queueing, 252
IMS/VS operational recovery, 274–287
BMP, 286–287
control region, 279–283
DL/1 batch, 278–279
message processing region, 284–286
IMS/VS program specification form, 238–239
IMSVS.PSBLIB, 133
IMS/VS terminal form, 244–246
IMS/VS transaction form, 240–243
IMS/VS transaction security form, 247
Index, 66, 71
Indexed processing, 28
Indexed Sequential Access Method (ISAM), 51
Index files (ADABAS), 201
Information retrieval, 6
INSERT (ISRT), 42, 122, 175
Intelligent terminal, 208, 210
I/O PCB, 126
Internal Sequence Number (ISN) ADABAS, 201
Inverted file, 171, 200, 204
ISRT, (see INSERT)